Jewish Secrets hidden in the New Testament

NORTH AMERICA

EUROPE

SOUTH AMERICA

The progressive discovery of these
ancient Jewish principles hidden in
the Christian New Testament is causing
millions of people from all over the
Globe to turn to the Jewish Torah.
This book reveals the current fulfilment of ancient Bible
Prophecies that proclaim a Global Return, to a Divinely
Promised Land with extended borders – to be known as
"The Kingdom of the Creator G-d of Israel."
G-d showed Abraham this Land from the top of the Mt of
Blessing in Shomron, Israel.
Genesis 15:5 "Look up at the sky and count the stars – if
indeed you can count them ... So shall your offspring be."
Genesis 13:16 "I will make your offspring like the dust of
the earth, so that if anyone could count the dust, then your
offspring could be counted."

Source and reference: Yair Davidiy
www.britam.org/Questions/QuesLand.html#Boundaries

Jewish Secrets hidden in the New Testament

THE GLOBAL TORAH REVOLUTION

BY RABBI AVRAHAM FELD   CO-AUTHOR: OVADYAH AVRAHAMI

ISBN-10: 1484113551
EAN-13: 9781484113554

Published by KOL HA'TOR
The Vision for a Reconciled and Re-united 12-Tribed Kingdom of Israel
Web Site: http://www.kolhator.org.il

To order copies of this book or for any other enquiry contact:

Kol Hator Vision
P.O. Box 3174
Karnei Shomron
ISRAEL
44855
e-mail: info@kolhator.org.il

Cover and Graphics: Nicky Dewar, The Service Café,
http://www.theservicecafe.co.za
E-mail: nicky@dewar.co.za

Table of Contents

ACKNOWLEDGEMENTS

This manuscript draws from the accomplishments of generations of people.

We of Kol HaTor have profited from the extraordinary love and dedication of those before us. The sages and rabbis often think of themselves as midgets who stand on the shoulders of the Giants of mind and soul that came before them. All of our nation can be likened to an iceberg, both at the individual and national level. What the world sees of an individual and of our nation is only the small portion that emerges above the ice; the overwhelming greater portion is submerged just below the surface of the ocean's deep waters!

We would like to acknowledge the Goan Eliahu of Vilna (Dr. Kramer) zzal, Rav Dr. Yosef Dov Baer HaLevi Soleiveichik zzal, HaRav Dr. Menachem Mendel Schneerson, HaRav HaGoan Shlomo Zalman Orbach zzal, HaRav Mordecai Sharabi zzal, Rav HaGoan Eliezer Menachem Mon Shach zzal, Rav Moshe Besdin zzal, Rav Dovid Liphschitz zzal, HaRav Avraham Shapira zzal, HaRav Mordecai Eliahu zzal, HaRav Chaim Pinchas Sheinberg zzal, Rabbi Pinchas Pines zzal, a student of the Chofetz Chaim, who I studied with when I was 16 years old, Rabbi Dr. S Rockoff zzal, Prof. Nechama Lebowitz zzal, the pioneer researcher of Orthodox Judaism Yair Davidiy shlita, Rabbi Meir Shuster shlita and many other greats who's teachings have aided us greatly.

Numerous friends have enabled and encouraged us over the years with commitment, joy, wisdom and enthusiasm! Their input, friendship and spiritual team work inspired to reach this stage and complete this book.

We are privileged to be in contact with these covenantal men and women of faith and action, heroes and heroines; each in their own right! They are precious, holy, valuable, brave searchers of truth.

As regards the final editing and compilation of this book, we have been guided and assisted by several dear supporters. This book also would not have seen the light were it not for our faithful band of financial supporters. We are greatly thankful for each and every one's dedicated support.

Author's Message

Most of the contents of this work are taken from our great Jewish teachers throughout the ages, who, to use a Biblical description, are the 'pillars of the earth' (Job 9:6). Our Sages of blessed memory have studied and investigated the deep and 'mighty waters' (Ex. 13:10).

This is in essence an objective commentary on the New Testament from a scholarly Rabbinic perspective of history, based on authentic Jewish Halachic Oral Torah interpretation.

Judaism does not have a "new" testament; neither acknowledges the "Christian New Testament". We believe that we have the whole and only testament, if that word is to be taken as it is understood by the average person. Testament, however, does not mean Torah, but rather covenant. In this case, where one understands testament to mean covenant, then we would say there are many covenants.

The first covenant, which encompasses all of humanity, is the one made with the first conservationist, Noah. We are all, like it or not, sons and daughters of that covenant which is the bedrock of all morality and ethics. It is the ultimate common denominator - a status that unites rather than divides. It is a starting point, a place where Judah can trust, respect and embrace all of humanity. If you research Noahide thought as well as folk, you will only find friends of Judah! There are no anti-Semites, replacement theologists, missionaries or haters of Oral Torah and Rabbis. Biblically speaking, Noahide aware- ness is equal to Righteous Gentile status.

In this review, we will reveal hidden Jewish Halachic elements in the NT. In other words traditional Jewish teaching which have survived the onslaught of all the ages but are unknown to, and rejected by the scholars, promoters and theological inter- preters of the New Testament.

We shall then also reveal and review the modern phenomenon of a masse return globally, to these Halachic Jewish tenets of Faith by serious students of the New Testament throughout the world. Our review will show how this all forms part of G-od's Purpose for mankind.

There are many factions these days that seek accord with Jews and the Jewish Faith (like Christian Zionists, Hebraic Roots Restorers, Ephraimites, re-identifying Lost Ten Tribers, to name but a few). If these people could only understand that they have a Noahide identity (as Righteous Gentiles) in common with Judah, it would effectively put everyone on the same page!

All of the Jewish people (including the seculars) are the proud descendants of Noah and family, who served and walked with G-d (Sotah 14a). We descend through the hereditary line of his son, the great Shem and his descendants. Isaac, and later Jacob, studied in the Torah academy that Shem founded with Eber (Targun Yonatan, Gen. 22:19).

From Shem descended the Hebrews and the Jewish people of today, The loving, concerned G-d of Creation was hardly known and hardly recognized in the world except by a precious few special, solitary righteous ones, like Enoch, Methuselah, Noah, Shem, and Eber.

We learn from the Talmud, Baba Basra 121b, that Methusalah saw (received knowledge from) Adam and passed it on to Shem, son of Noah. Shem thus saw Methusaleh; Jacob saw Shem, Amram (Moses's father) saw Jacob, Ahijah the Shilonite saw Amram, Pinchus (Elijah) saw Ahijah, etc. Thus, with just a handful of people, we have the history of humankind passed on in an 'oral' fashion by word of mouth and personal testimony. There were no radio and television in those days, no printing presses, no Internet. Travel between communities and nations was slow and burdensome. Info and knowledge were transmitted through the covenantal faith communities, with an on-going student/teacher relationship.

In the Hebrew Bible, it speaks of a future redeemed Israel, after the Lost Tribes of Israel will have returned from their world-wide exile, back to the Land of their forefathers, and reconciled and reunited with Judah (the Jews). The third Temple will have been rebuilt and a powerful commonwealth re-established, to rule with justice and love over the entire world in peace. At such a Time a book such as this will be unnecessary, as would be any educational outreach activity, because; "... they shall all know Me" and "...they shall Teach no more each man, proclaiming, 'Know the L-rd'".

In speaking of this future Time with a New Covenant, Jeremiah does not use the term 'a new Torah'! His description is clearly defining a new Covenant with its purpose to strengthen the Torah, e.g. the same 'old' Torah! This is simply because everyone will be extremely close to G-d

The main topic of this book concerns the Christian Writings which have become known as "The New Testament". To Christians, these Writings are the most important, often to the extent of the total exclusion and rejection of the 'Jewish' Bible, which they refer to as the 'Old Testament'. Generally these Writings are regarded and proclaimed by the Church as the 'New Covenant' which they claim the Jewish Prophets referred to.

Even amongst its most ardent readers of these Christian Writings, there rage great controversies, with some insisting on calling it "The Brit Chadasha" (Hebrew translation), "The New Covenant", "The Gospel", or "The Kingdom Message".

For general usage and reference, the main figure of the Gospels who is generally called Jesus or Y'shuah, will be referred to in this publication as 'the Nazarene'. This will hopefully be acceptable to the widely differing categories of readers of this book. The Christian New Testament Writings will be referred to by its abbreviated form, the NT, as opposed to the Jewish Tanach, referred to by Christians as the 'Old Testament' (OT).

Now consider carefully: No one, that is, not a single follower of the early Messianic congregations (followers of the Nazarene) thought for one minute that a new Torah (Bible) was being created in the NT. Over the years that followed their leader's disappearance, a body of teachings began to be compiled. This eventually turned into a 'new testament' - not a new Torah (Bible). Not a single student thought that his/her newly come Messiah was giving over a brand new Bible. What they did all believe, was that this teaching, over a very short period of time, had grown into an additional special agreement - an additional super contract, which entailed a fortifying of relationships.

Simply put, this was all about firming up a pre-existing bond! But not in any shape or form whatsoever did any student, nor the Nazarene himself, think even for one second, that a new Torah had been born. No new Torah had been given, ever! The NT, in their understanding, was simply 'another' covenant to enhance the bond with their Creator and His Messiah. To them it was in a way similar to a Parliament, a Congress or a Senate passing a new law to be attached to their already existing constitution. For instance, the American Bill of Rights is in addition to the Constitution - not instead of it. Except the NT was not legislated or voted in, but moved within the body of Messianic believers. Only in 322 CE, at the Council of Nicea, did the Romans vote in an official NT against loyal opposition. Those who opposed the Roman Canon faced terrible persecution.

The purpose of this book is to reveal the original intentions and understanding of the early Messianic communities, based on the contents of the NT itself, in the context of Jewish Halachic reasoning.

Surprisingly, the NT writing style is much closer to that of the Jewish Mishnah than to the Tanach (Hebrew Bible) which was finalised some 500 years earlier. The Nazarene never visualized that he and his followers were going to make a movement to replace Torah, as most NT followers and interpreters claim. They were only presenting its (Torah) teaching in a slightly different light. They were forming a new group seeking special closeness to G-d and His special teacher, the Nazarene. In other words, a new and special bond was being formed with a new Jewish teacher. This is a common pattern in Judaism itself, as it reflects the special relationship amongst great teachers and their students.

In Judaism we believe that the Torah is the ultimate constitution written by Inspiration of G-d, which has various covenants within it. All followers of Messianic leaders, at that time, believed in the Torah constitution both in its Oral and Written dimensions. They proclaimed a new dimension in relationship, not a new constitution. The early Messianic congregation of the Nazarene did not have a written NT in any form or shape until at least 3 to 4 centuries later. Their guidance was the Torah and their understanding of their new special bond with the Nazarene was defined in a code of oral transmission and statements, similar in some aspects to the Jewish "Rabbinic, Oral Torah" interpretations. It was not a new and radically different Bible, and the early followers of the Nazarene never intended it in any way to replace the Torah or the Tanach (as general Christian understanding of the NT turned out to do).

"Scripture", at that time, referred to the Hebrew Bible (called the 'Old Testament' by Christians today) with its Jewish oral understandings and explanations. It is noteworthy, that every time the NT refers to 'The Scriptures', it refers to this Hebrew Bible – the Tanach. The book of Timothy, in the NT, states that "the Scriptures are divine." At the time of writing, the author was referring to the Hebrew Scriptures which were around. Only the Hebrew Bible (the Tanach) was scripted, written down and organized into a body of Scriptures. NT teachings were still orally conveyed and it was just starting to be written down here and there. It was far from yet being organized into a specific body of writings that could be properly referenced.

The Halachic aspects of the Gospels, as we will soon present in this book, are observed from an advanced Jewish perspective. This should serve as a sobering call especially to those who are so convinced of their Hebraic (Jewish) Roots which they are restoring in their lives these days. Why would a school of thought like Judaism, which in fact rejects the authenticity of the Gospels and their main figure, the Nazarene, recognize and acknowledge the strong Halachic Jewish foundations of the Gospels (as is done in this book) if they did not really occur in these writings? This may be a serious challenge for all who view their traditional concepts as the basis on which ultimate Redemption (Return and Reconciliation) should take place. This Rabbinic perspective is based solely on the contents and the historic context of the Gospels, without any theological acknowledgement of their authenticity. We see it as a collection of Jewish Messianic literature written by hopeful Jews who, to our mind, were mistaken. To the Jews, the long awaited and hoped for Messiah just never showed up to redeem his fellow Jews in Second Temple times.

Islam and Bahai also have strong Hebrew roots. However, this does not mean that we should accept those writings as having any divine stamp on them, even though they can serve to elevate humanity and move it somewhat closer to true concepts. Both claim that their leaders were also our hoped for Messiah. We beg to differ even though, when taken out of context, their 'proofs' sound very convincing.

For the Jews there always were and remain today, the assurance of Redemption. It is just that things failed back then and none of the possibilities worked out, e.g. in the case of the Bar Kochva revolt.

There were over 50 Messiahs that missed the mark after the Second Temple's destruction and many more Messianic sects and groups made their appearance before that time.

It is the onus of each individual to decide to what extent he/she will work for and aid ultimate Reconciliation, thereby establishing peace in Zion. It is in this spirit, that the observations in this book are being published and not to prove or dispute the existence or not of the contentious issue of a specific Messiah or non-Messiah.

The author, with an Orthodox Rabbinic ordination, distances himself firmly from Christian theology and from Christian Messianic positions. The author's commentary in this publication should in no way be interpreted as an acceptance of Christian doctrines or as a personal acknowledgement of Christian Messianic positions.

Jewish scholarship believes that there was no historical Jewish Messiah. They assert that many of the Gospel accounts were simply confirmations of reports of various Messianic leaders of small cults and sects. Historians of that era did not specifically mention the Nazarene. The Catholic Church deliberately inserted events regarding the Nazarene into Josephus's writings (e.g. Wm. LaSor on the Prof. Winston edition of Joesephus, Emil Schurer, "A History of the Jewish people in the Time of Jesus," N.Y.,1961 page 211 – 214). The references in Talmud also do not refer to the exact personage of NT writings. They are over 100 years too early and have such things as the fellow worshiping a Rock with only 5 students. See Shmuel Levine 's "You Take Jesus I'll Take G-d", page 18- 21. Other Rabbinic references are also much later than the Christian time frame, thus do not refer to the specific NT figure but reflex the many influences that were around and contributed to what became Christianity. Please also check out the 'canonization of the NT' in Catholic and Protestant sources to better understand why Jews would view these writings as highly unreliable for themselves.

There is considerable evidence that there were hundreds of Messianic leaders, some contributing to a weakening of respect for Oral Torah, at the end of the second Temple period. The Nazarene is considered by the author and many others as a composite creation of the spiritual and Messianic activity of many groups active at that time.

We could cite an encyclopaedia of sources for the above remarks. We could bring a host of academic books and periodicals and scores of research papers. However we are not here to pick a fight or to destroy other people's faith. Only learning in the loving light of G-d will help the Reconciliation process, not endless disputation or fighting.

The Talmud cries out to foster behaviour and attitudes that pave the way for avoiding enmity, hate and violence on the one hand and for promoting co-existence, peace and friendly relationships on the other hand. Chazal (an acronym which in Hebrew means 'the Sages of blessed memory'), never tired of pointing out the verse in Proverbs 3:18, "The Torah's ways are ways of pleasantness and all its paths are paths of peace". The Mishnah in Avos comes to mind as well, Hillel says: "Be of the students of Aaron (brother of Moses), loving peace, pursuing peace, loving your fellow creatures and drawing them nearer to Torah." As our Midrash Tanchuma , Deut. 3, says; "HaShem gave the Torah to Israel so that all the nations will benefit from it."

The intent of this encounter is one of rather agreeing to disagree and to move on with learning Truth, service (prayer and sacrifice) and the active practice of loving kindness. Through learning Torah with an open and receptive mind, everyone will come to see the light that is appropriate and that will bring healing.

As we pursue this path of reconciliation, we will all gradually come to higher levels of faith, wisdom and understanding. We can all trust in G-d to work it all out for all those who are sincerely searching for His presence, peace and proximity.

The conclusions presented in this publication represent, in a significant manner, orthodox Jewish scholarship. They present an impartial review of the contents of the Christian New Testament (NT), from the historic, theological and religious perspectives of Orthodox Rabbinic Judaism. As such, they will give those who believe in the authenticity of the NT, and the Messiah which it represents, an astonishing and enlightening new perspective in line with the well-established principles of the Creator, G-d of Israel. This new understanding should serve to mould them more firmly into the Divine purpose for mankind, e.g. to become part of the supreme and eternal Kingdom of G-d, which is the reunited Kingdom of Israel on earth, which will rule over the nations in righteousness and loving kindness.

The message of this book should also serve to provide confirmation of the current trend of an amazing phenomenon: the turning towards Judaism and Jewish religious principles by thousands of non-Jews. People from around the world are in search of, and discovering what they regard to be their "Hebrew Roots". This path will lead them to authentic Truth of the ancient Paths that emerge from the Torah.

On the Jewish reader side, this commentary should confirm that the correct interpretation of the Gospels which underlie the Christian faith, as viewed from a Jewish historic and Torah perspective, is not as "non-kosher" as we Jews thought it to be. In fact, this suggests that the Gospels are even more Halachically kosher than what most of the recognized Messianic Hebrew Roots Restoration scholars themselves generally affirm today. In other there is 'kosher' wisdom within what has become a general 'non-kosher' package.

I would like to say a few words directed at some important folk of Judah who may be concerned about the risks involved for them, of such dialogue as is unfolding here through the topic of this book.

Some people cite the Rav z'zal (Rav here means: Rabbi Soloveitchik; z'zal means; 'may the memory of the righteous be a Blessing') to nullify this entire discussion. So please allow me to clarify the issue. Rav Yosef Dov Bare HaLevi Soloveichik (a giant of Torah) most certainly did approve of and bless joint efforts with non-Jews for the good of the general community. He did not approve of ordinary inter-faith conferences which he disdained and viewed with suspicion. He worried that the Jewish representatives would be overwhelmed and be induced in the name of ecumenicalism. He was concerned that Jews may then compromise Torah and offend their hosts with various demands, which even if partially met, might force some kind of reciprocal compromise on the part of the Jewish representatives.

His words were not put into regular terminology of a legal decision but were left somewhat open, thus reflecting the complex nature of the topic. Perhaps to allow those who could properly conduct dialogue, to do so, whilst at the same time leaving the vast majority, who might feel highly uncomfortable, not to have to deal with the confrontation (The Edah Journal, 4;2. Prof. Reuven Kimelman *"Jewish-Christian Relations"*, Kislev 5765, Daniel Rynhold, *"The Philosophical Foundations*

of Rav Soloveitchik's Critique of Interfaith Dialogue", Harvard
Theological Review 96 ,03, pp.100 -20).

However, Rav Soloveichik did indeed bless heartily any efforts
directed at saving lost assimilated Jews within Christian communities. This, by necessity, demands dialogue and debate,
as does knowing what to answer in theological encounters.
In addition, when it comes to informing Gentiles who sincerely have serious questions against Jews and Judaism, it is a
Mitzvah to try and enlighten them. All of the above, he helped
and encouraged.

Certainly, the general movement of Christianity has definitely
moved G-d's agenda forward in educating the world.

The Rambam rules that Jews may teach Torah to Christians,
because they accept the divinity of the Torah in order to correct misunderstandings (Responsa 149). In addition to this,
many thousands are sincerely interested in conversion and/or
the ancient path of the laws of Noah. We need to work hard to
teach and reach out with the basic message of justice, kindness
and knowledge of a G-d who cares and loves all of humanity.
(Sifra Lev. 22:32; Isaiah 2:3; Psalms 96:3 - 10; Mishneh Torah
Laws of Kings 8:10; 1 Kings 8:41-43; Isaiah 56:1-8; Pesachim
87b; Berachot 54b; Yad, Laws of Kings 12:4 - 5 etc.).

May the re-awakening that the message of this book will hopefully kindle in its readers, serve to bring an awareness of the
true requirements of G-d for those who aspire to become prospective citizens for His Kingdom. May it lead its readers to the
true sources of interpretation of these divine requirements in
order to unshackle them from the distortions which have crept
in as a result of Roman pagan control and its impact on Gospel

texts, thereby freeing the sincere searcher to move upwards and onwards.

Recognition of their Hebrew roots will accomplish many good things for those millions of non-Jews who are today drawn to Torah and Jewish Faith principles:

- Firstly, it will neutralize tremendous hatred against Jews and Judaism by NT believers. They will begin to appreciate that we are the authorized custodians and management sitting in the seat of the congregation and the heritage of Jacob (Deut. 33:3-5) and that our sages, mothers and fathers go back to Moses (Deut. 17; Deut. 32:7 -14; Deut. 31:28; etc.).

- It will show that there is no need to missionize the Jewish people – as many of these new non-Jewish Zionists have already come to understand.

- Thirdly, it will prove the existence, vitality and wonderful necessity of Oral Torah. Along with this realization they will comprehend that the leadership, Rabbis and Scribes, have much Biblical authority to protect the Torah with fences of love and care (i.e. Lev.18:30). They do preventive care, saving us from falling or contracting spiritual illness. We learn this right from the Written Torah. For example we are told not only NOT to do deviant immoral things, but to keep far from it (Lev. 18:6). Likewise not only not to lie, but to keep far from falsehood (Ex. 23:7). Keeping far away is the institution of protective fencing and prohibition to avoid the fall into grave transgression! The Nasserite is essentially forbidden from wine, yet the Torah, as a fence, forbids wine products as well. The

Torah forbids false weights in measuring (Lev. 19:35) but goes further, adding protective degrees forbidding even having false liquids or solid weights in pockets (Deut.25).

Hebriac Roots Restorers will discover that the never ending accusations against Rabbis and Oral Torah were all unfounded and simply part of a massive spiritual warfare against the Eternal Truth which had been Divinely entrusted to Judah (refer our Mechoqeck reading in chapter 16). They will come to realize that our sages are the cream of the cream, spiritual giants of mind and soul, products of our eternal heritage and Covenantal action since Sinai and before!

• Fourthly, it will connect people to the authentic mind-set of the apostles of the Nazarene and enhance an understanding of the true Gospel Message which, as we will show in-depth later in this discussion, originally was and now has become again an outreach to the lost sheep of the House of Israel (the Lost Ten Tribes), not Judah. It was an attempt to reconnect lost, turned Gentile Hebrews (Yevamos 17).

• People will realize that Scripture speaks of two Houses of G-d's people (the divided and separated Houses of Judah *and* Israel) and their ultimate reunification - when the long-awaited Redemption of the Kingdom of the G-d of Israel will become established in a world of peace, justice and love.

Religious Jewish people pray many times a day for the Restoration of the twelve Tribes. Christians, even though not fully realizing that the Kingdom refers to the restored

12-Tribed Hebrew nation, are also praying for "the Coming of His Kingdom" in "The Lord's Prayer". May all these prayers be answered in Compassion.

> 1 Chronicles 16:8, "Sing to Him, make music to Him, speak of all His wonders. Glory in His Holy Name, be joyous of heart, you who seek HaShem." May you be blessed in your search for HaShem, His Might and Presence 'inwardness' that it should always be with a glad and joyous heart.

> Psalm 100. "Serve G-d with joy; come before Him with joyous song."

> Psalm 36:8, "May they be sated from the abundance of Your House [also the re-united 2 Houses]; and may You give them to drink from the stream of Your delights. For with You is a Source of Life, by Your Light we shall see Light."

> Psalm 20, "May He grant you your heart's desire and fulfil your every plan. May we sing for joy at your Salvation, and raise our banner in the Name of our G-d. May HaShem fulfil all your requests."

> *B'Ezrat HaShem! (With the Help of G-d!)*
> Avraham Feld
> P O Box 1438
> Jerusalem

About Avraham Feld – the Author

Avraham Feld was born on February 14, 1954, in Manhattan, USA. He graduated from Yeshiva University with studies in Jewish philosophy and psychology, earning his Rabbinic degree in 1983.

Avraham Feld is currently based in Jerusalem. He is involved in educational outreach to the Jewish community. Outreach efforts include finding jobs for young people, directing individuals to various rehab options, supporting unwed mothers in their decision to give birth rather than abort, and programs to assist and visit the elderly and physically challenged. Other activities include researching for politicians and commentators on multiple topics. He is the co-author of several research publications on Biblical and political topics.

Blessed by the Rebbe

Since the young age of 11, Feld has had a consuming passion for the Bible and the Biblical prophetical promise of the Restoration of the House of Israel. He defended the Scriptures in his public school classes against the teachers who were attacking these Writings and their prophetic promises regarding the House of Israel. Feld performed extensive work for physically and mentally challenged young people and adults. He assisted coaching a wheelchair basketball team and was involved in sports, all the while continuing to advance in Biblical polemics.

While studying at Yeshiva University, he acquired a reputation for being able to get youth out of deep troubles, especially in cases where others failed to do so. While a student in a Rabbinical program, he was approached by a leading figure in the Chabad movement who engaged him to handle an especially difficult and dangerous case. Feld agreed and succeeded – and this led to his meeting with the Lubavitch Rebbe Menachem Mendel Schneerson, world leader of the Chassidic movement. He was favored with a blessing from the Rebbe.

From his anti-cult and reachout work as well as from his studies of Torah, Tanach and the Sages, Feld gained the understanding that many Gentiles were of Israelite descent and therefore part of the Lost Ten Tribes of Israel. His experience and studies brought him to the recognition that these "Lost Tribes" would one day be returned to the Land of Israel in fulfillment of the prophecies and the sages' interpretation. His field work revealed the real life people of Israel in their odyssey of Return.

He therefore requested a second blessing from the Lubavitch Rebbe to enable him to be of assistance in furthering the Divine cause of the ingathering of the Lost Ten Tribes from amongst the nations, if the Rebbe agreed that indeed they were to be part of such prophetic promises. *"Avada Gevist*, of course they are," was the Rebbe's reply, upon which he blessed Avraham that he should merit to have a good influence on estranged Jews. In addition, he should have success with Gentiles of Israelite descent. All of this is part of the prophetic process of Geulah (the Restoration and Redemption of Israel).

*Photo of Feld meeting with the Lubavitch
Rebbe Menachem Mendel Schneerson*

Since arriving in Israel '81, Avraham Feld has been the Field
Director of a Public Charity; Maccabee Institute for Family and
Social Aid. Years later, Avraham found the outlet for his vision
and the expression of his passion for the Biblically declared
return of the Lost Ten Tribes of Israel. He became involved
with BRIT AM, which is a research and reach out to Ten Israel
in the West. Brit Am also publishes ground breaking books and
materials. All of Brit Am's activities are under Yair Davidiy, a
Torah Orthodox Jewish researcher who is unquestionably one
of the giants in this field today. Much of our inspiration flows
from Yair Davidiy's definitive and ground-breaking work.

Towards the end of 2005 (beginning of the Jewish year 5766),
he became the founder of *Kol HaTor Vision*. With the amazing phenomenon of the awakening of the Hebraic Restoration
movement amongst Christian Zionists across the world, the
Kol HaTor Vision would now more directly publish and promote its vision on a Rabbinic level, as well as from the Hebraic

Restoration platform amongst Christian Zionists. Basing its vision on Chazal Ezekiel 37:15-28 regarding the restoration of the two houses, Judah (the Jews) and 10-Israel (the House of Yosef and Ephraim or "The Lost Ten Tribes of Israel"), the *Kol HaTor Vision* would spread knowledge from the writings of the Biblical prophets and the great sages of Judaism about the imminent fulfillment of the prophetic vision of the restoration of all Israel. It would also strive to lay the foundations for achieving peaceful Reconciliation between the greatly estranged Houses of Judah and 10-Israel, exiled amongst the nations. The *Kol HaTor Vision* strives to bring awareness on either side of the near 2800 year-long great rift in the House of G-d regarding each side's responsibilities to achieve peace and Reconciliation.

The *Kol HaTor Vision* derived its name from the the vision, inspiration and the writings of the greatest Jewish authority on the subject of the Redemption of the entire House of Israel, the Gaon of Vilna (Rabbi Eliyahu ben Shlomo Zalman – the Genius of Vilna, Lithuania, 1720-1797).

See Kol HaTor Web Site at http://www.kolhator.org.il

**Most of the Articles on
KOL HATOR Web Site**

authored by Rabbi Feld

- "Mohammed Wept" – *the Hebrew Roots of Islam & our present day geo-political situation*

- "Little Sister" – *comprehensive study of the dynamics and interplay of the Oral & Written Torah*

- Numerous Research papers on various topics

    Awaiting sponsorship for publication

About OvadYah Avrahami – co-author

OvadYah Avrahami is an independent Bible researcher. He works tirelessly as an activist promoting Israel and settlement of the Land of Israel, and as Webmaster and co-ordinator of Kol Ha Tor. His publications have been circulated internationally since the early sixties and have affected the thinking and Scriptural interpretation of non-Jewish Bible scholars on all levels - from novice right through to academically qualified teachers worldwide.

OvadYah has been a pioneer since the 60's to enlighten Bible students about the Hebrew Roots of Christianity, long before it became the popular movement that it is today.

The Hebraic Roots Restoration Movement is a non-organizational and highly individualized Movement amongst serious and sincere Bible students of all religious denominations right across the globe. This awakening is also noticeable in the world's largest Christian denominations, where there is growing reference to the 'discovering of the Jewish Roots of Christianity'.

When Rabbi Feld and OvadYah met in Israel in 2005, it did not take them long to discover that they were sharing the same passion and unquenchable zeal for the Reconciliation of the 12-Tribed Kingdom of the G-d of Israel. Shortly after, they founded the Kol HaTor Vision as a publications medium to promote knowledge of this anciently proclaimed prophetic Vision which forms the main theme of the Bible:

viz. The Restoration of the 12-Tribed Kingdom of Israel, i.e.:

- the Redemption or *Geulah,* in Judaism, and

- the 'Gospel of the Kingdom' in Christianity.

It has since transpired that Avraham Feld's knowledge and contact fields in Judaism compliments OvadYah's wide experience and exposure to the Hebraic Restoration awakening across the world. Together they form a powerful representation of both the House of Judah and the re-awakening House of 10-Israel.

The Message of this book emerges from the Heart Land of Israel and the City of Jerusalem.

Articles authored by OvadYah
On KOL HATOR Web Site

- Demographic Solution for Israel.

- Outline for successful Reconciliation.

- Why Jews should NOT be proselytized.

- Historic Evolution of the Redemption of Israel - a Power Point graphic presentation (used in chapter 19).

- Editor of many of the guideline articles on the Kol HaTor Web Site (under the supervision of Rabbi Feld).

- Judah – the Lawgiver (*Mechoqeck*) of G-d – a revelationary expose on Genesis 49:10.

- Jerusalem – Final Countdown to Armageddon – 160 pg. book.

PART I

WHAT'S IN THE BIBLICAL REDEMPTION FOR US?

CHAPTER I

Redemption -
the Main Theme of the Bible

The main theme common to most religions, no doubt, is "Redemption" of one or other nature.

Because this statement will no doubt be challenged, let us confine this conclusion to the area of the two main religions underlying this particular discourse which will receive our main focus. We are referring to Christianity - for which the New Testament forms the foundational Scriptures - and Judaism, which, as the author will point out, is the Faith on the foundations of which the New Testament has built its pillars. For both of these religions, 'Redemption', no doubt, is the main objective.

It is perhaps because of the so common aspect of this concept in each of these two faiths, that 'Redemption' has become an almost vague cliché to most adherents.

Because of the foundational importance of this concept, volumes could be written to properly analyze and define it. For our purposes though, we will contend with a to-the-point basic definition.

In Judaism, 'Redemption' refers to the ultimate establishment of the Kingdom of Israel by the G-d of Israel, the G-d of Creation. This, fundamentally, requires the physical presence of the twelve Tribes of Israel. The problem is that, of these twelve Tribes, only the Tribe of Judah is identifiable today. Jewish tradition and historical data holds that 'The House of Judah' includes the Tribe of Benjamin, Levi as well as some remnants of all the other Tribes. Judah is the banner Tribe, being the majority and having been mandated with leadership as well as judicial guidance of the whole nation (refer ch. 16 – *Divine Mandate for True Interpretation*).

The Northern Ten Tribes of Israel, referred to in the Bible as the 'House of Israel', were exiled two centuries before the destruction of the first Temple in Jerusalem. According to Divine Purpose, they were so effectively mingled with other nations, that they became known as "The Lost Ten Tribes of Israel." Within 10-Israel was Judah 'in captivity' and members of the Tribe of Levi. This lost kingdom has subsequently become totally unidentifiable – but, with the Divine Promise, by Oath, that they would be re-identified in the End Time, reconciled and re-united with the House of Judah, and returned to the Land of their mothers and fathers.

The Divine Promise of Restoration of the 12-tribed Kingdom forms the main theme of Redemption in Judaism. From the beginning of Genesis, with Paradise Lost and exile from the Garden of Eden, everything is about Paradise being regained. Underlying this theme of Redemption and conditional for citizenship of this future New Kingdom, is the requirement of embracing the Torah and repentance.

The global phenomenon of non-Jews turning to the Torah and to Jewish religious customs, which has been observed increasingly over especially the last decade, no doubt confirms the fulfillment of the ancient Biblical Prophecies. These Prophecies foresees the awakening of the 'Lost House of 10-tribed Israel', to be returned to the Biblical Promised Land, the borders of which will be vast and expansive. To settle these innumerable masses (according to the Divine Promise made to Abraham), would require a vast expanse of territory, the borders of which have been specified in the Bible (refer to the front page Map). This does not preclude the fact that re-identified 10-Israel blocs of nations will emerge across the world.

In Christianity, 'Redemption' refers to "the forgiveness of the sins of the individual person upon confession of sins, with the promise of eternal life in angelic surroundings in a heavenly abode, in a heavenly Jerusalem."

Rather than being side-tracked here by the myriads of variations on the main theme as given above, let us concentrate on the common theme inherent in both versions, i.e. "The Kingdom of G-d". It should be apparent, that at the outset, there is a main diversion between Judaism and Christianity as to the abode of the Kingdom.

Our research into the Halachic Jewish foundations of the Christian New Testament, as is the intent of this book, will show how solidly the New Testament's "Gospel of the Kingdom" is founded on the same ancient Jewish teachings about this future Kingdom - though hidden in the New Testament from the faithful

followers of the Christian Faith, because of the traditional interpretations of the Church about this Kingdom. We find confirmation for this Jewish foundation and the reprimand against
straying from it in the following texts of the New Testament:

> Romans 3:2, "... the Jews were entrusted with
> the whole revelation of G-d." (NLT – *New Living
> Translation; other translations: the Oracles, the Word,
> the Teachings of G-d*).

> Acts 7:38, " He (Moses) was in the assembly in
> the wilderness, with the Angel who spoke to him
> on Mount Sinai, and with our ancestors; **and he
> received living words** to pass on to us."

Then, in a warning to Messianic followers against
apostasy already imminent in those days, Hebrews
5:12 "By now you should be teachers, but you need
someone to teach you again the ·first lessons [elemen-
tary truths; basic principles] of G-d's Message [rev-
elation; oracles]." (*Extended Bible Version*).

> 1 Peter 4:11, "If any man speak, let him speak accord-
> ing to the Oracles of G-d." (*King James 21st century
> Version*).

> The Greek words used in the NT for 'teaching' and
> 'instruction' actually mean, in that context, the tra-
> ditional Jewish teachings, i.e. explanations of the
> Mosaic codes.

Entry to any worldly Kingdom is conditional upon compliance with strict requirements. Every country has its own

immigration and naturalization requirements. There are many official requirements to conform with. Failure to comply withholds entry for prospective citizens. Why should this not also apply to entry into the Kingdom of G-d?

It is for this very reason that the contents of this book should come as a serious Call to the millions of sincere souls across the world who, while being so confident that "their papers are all in order," may discover that they are as wrong about this to the same degree that Christianity and Judaism varies from each other.

Not only are there conditions to comply with, but permanent residence in this Kingdom is secured by a Covenant between G-d and prospective citizens. It is the essentials of this Covenant and the hidden and little understood confirmation of these principles by the New Testament, which will be the main topic of our dissertations in the chapters that will follow.

This book will show that it is the very foundations of the Jewish Torah based Covenant, so covertly hidden in the New Testament, which will have the final say about citizenship of G-d's Kingdom.

The latest and current phenomenon of millions of sincere non-Jewish Bible students of the New Testament, across the world, who are turning to these tenets of Judaism without being aware of these hidden and misconstrued guidelines of the New Testament, serves as a grandiose confirmation and holds the strongest evidence of there being universal criteria, for citizenship of G-d's Kingdom.

In this way it confirms the Main Theme of Biblical Prophecy regarding the establishment of the Kingdom of the G-d of Israel.

CHAPTER 2

The Hebraic Roots Restoration Movement - Amazing Modern Phenomenon

The need for an in-depth publication like this would have been superfluous were it not for the recent phenomenon right across the world, of many non-Jews turning to what they themselves define as their Hebraic Roots. This is based on conclusions drawn from their sincere study of the Bible. If Scripture is truly their inspiration for such a controversial decision, then it would validate our search for confirmation of such a collective "turnabout" predicted in the Tanach (Hebrew Bible consisting of the Torah, Prophetic books and other Writings).

The Tanach abounds with prophecies of this "End Time" phenomenon. In fact, it forms the underlying main message of the Bible – because it is so intertwined with the message of the Redemption of Israel and the establishment of the ultimate universal Kingdom of G-d.

We publish in the Addendum to this book, a full list of most of the salient Scriptures regarding this international Event. Refer to Chapter 25, "Scriptures that confirm the Restoration of the House of Israel" in the Addendum.

The most sensational News Event of our Time - Yet, hidden to most people!

It is important to open this book with the topic of the Restoration of all the Tribes to Israel. The Reconciliation and Restoration has not only become a modern happening of great importance, but also an issue that brings great division both in Judaism and in Christianity. A close look will confirm that this issue actually concerns the main Message of the Bible: viz. **the formation of the Kingdom of G-d from the reunited twelve tribes of Israel. This will require the return and peaceful reconciliation of the two greatly divided Houses of Judah and Israel - 'Israel' being referred to in Scripture as the Ten Northern Tribes of Israel lost in exile amongst the nations about 2800 years ago and their settlement in a 'Greater Israel' – far exceeding the boundaries of what is currently known as 'the Land of Israel'**

Our search is rewarded with numerous, detailed prophetic indications for the future of the nation of Israel. Until recently, these prophecies of the re-identification and massive Return of the Lost Ten Tribes of Israel have been greatly overlooked by mainstream Christian scholars and students who focused on the return by Judah (Jews) only to the Land of their forefathers. In Judaism however, the imminent Return of the Lost Ten Tribes is a topic well-known to Rabbis. Though a neglected topic today, Jewish Sages throughout the centuries have written much about it.

It is the hope and intention of the author that this publication will assist in providing better understanding of this event. May the information provided in this publication help to pave the way toward the ultimate Redemption, Reconciliation and establishment of the reunited Kingdom of Israel. Whenever this publication speaks in the above terms, the given understanding is that all of the above be done through the direction of Jewish Halacha as expounded by the giants in Torah at that time. This conclusion should be convincingly confirmed in the coming pages of this book through revealing these Jewish Halachic foundations which underlie the NT.

The Oral Torah also adds its substantial and comprehensive testimony to the topic and the reality of the Lost 10 Tribes and their eventual re-identification and reconciliation with Judah, in the all-embracing Prophetic Promise of Redemption (*Geulah*).

Author and orthodox Jewish commentator, Yair Davidiy, has written numerous books on the topic of the Lost Ten Tribes. He uses evidence from the Oral Torah quite frequently to prove the whereabouts of 10-Israel today and throughout history. Refer http://www.britam.org

With regards to the Tribes of Israel, there are many deep insights into G-d's Written Torah that are readily accessible through the Oral Torah. For example, through Gematriah – numerology – new paths of understanding are explored and additional light is revealed from the Holy Torah. Gematriah is a method used by Rabbis and other Jewish interpreters to attain deeper insight, by computing the numerical values of Torah letters, words, phrases and/or verses for comparing various numerical equivalent Scriptures.

Here is an example: It is a common concept in Judaism, that the Biblical figure Joseph represents the Ten Tribes, as do the Biblical references 'Ephraim and Menasha.' When we compute the numerical value of the Hebrew letters contained in the phrase: 'A fruitful son is Yosef' (Genesis 49:22) we arrive at a total of 732. The Baal HaTurim, great Jewish commentator, points out that this is also the Gematriah (numerical value) of 'Ephraim and Menasha.' Yaakov said that Ephraim and Menashe shall be 'like' Reuven and Shimon (Genesis 48:5). The Gematriah of Reuven and Shimon = 731. This works out perfectly with the Gematriah being one off, which is acceptable in Jewish mysticism for many reasons. This is only one minor example of the application of Gematriah to expound wider on the never-ending number of hidden Biblical gems. All of this is part of the Oral explanations passed on throughout the ages.

Current Developing Phenomenon

For those readers who may have grave doubts about the reality of such a Return, let me share an enlightening fact with you:

Hear the Breaking News concerning Israel!

The big deal is that Returnees from lost Hebrew tribes have over many decades been coming home as regular folk who can enter into the palace of Torah comprehension. Yes, we Jews have thus benefited from the 'well of living waters' (Song of Songs 4:15). These Returnees have revealed to us 'beautiful, fragrant orchards' in droves for some time already, while we have been blissfully unaware of it.

The single, most unreported, undisclosed and fantastic news event of the millennium!

The predicted Return of 10-Israel has quietly, modestly and gently already been happening - and it is gradually picking up pace as the years fly by!

We are speaking of the attractiveness of Judaism for many tens of thousands of converts to the faith who have lost their tribal origins They have proven themselves to make outstanding righteous converts. They arrived on the doorsteps of historic Torah Judaism as pious, G-d loving and respecting citizens, accepting the entire Hebrew Tanach! Most of them had come out of a user-friendly, Hebrew rooted variation of what is commonly called Christianity. Many of them had already forsaken Christianity a long time before starting their conversion process. They were, practically speaking of ancient Hebrew stock, with many of captive Judah mixed in. They have been completely integrated with the rest of the Jewish people. They are loyal to Oral and Written Torah and understand that our Torah Scholars are our spiritual leaders, divinely mandated to guard the Word of G-d. They are quietly living a low profile and Torah life style, without fanfare and publicity.

This means that the Final days before that great happening of the Redemption are upon us! The Return of the Lost Ten Tribes is very much part of that Redemption! This Return has clearly now already started in a process of great humility, without us having recognized it!

Very dear and righteous Gerim (converts) have been and are constantly these days showing up and being absolutely accepted by the larger Jewish community. This is all by the hand of G-d, mysteriously, in a still small voice, with great modesty, working to bring His children Home.

So like it or not, accept it or reject it, the Tribes along with lost Jews, are finally on their way Home. Join them or reject them - this aspect of Redemption will march on till the end of days .

The review of this topic as contained in the pages of this book is for your reading pleasure and will bring you up to date on this great Prophetic phenomenon, the reasons behind it and the Divine Intent as declared in the Tanach to be His ordained Main Purpose. If you already know about this adventure of Return, then this reading will serve you as a review of the dynamics of these great happenings and as confirmation from the book presented by Christians as the 'New Testament'.

CHAPTER 3

Historic progress towards the Redemption of Israel

It is of value to do a short historical review for the benefit of those readers who are not well-acquainted with the main milestones in Israel's colourful and eventful history. Jews the world over are praying for this Universal Redemption daily. Only then can one understand the astonishing implications which the prospects of the fulfilment of Restoration prophecies hold for mankind. And only when we understand that this Redemption also refers to and includes the Ten Lost Tribes and not only the Tribe of Judah (Jews) who have been in a process of Return to the Land of Israel over the last 160 years.

Our quick review of the historic progress of this universal Redemption Process, will take us from ancient Biblical Israel times, right through to today's reawakening amongst non-Jewish Bible searchers to the ancient Hebrew Roots of their Faith. Our journey thereafter into the NT writings, from a Halachich Jewish perspective, will then find, hidden in the foundations of these NT writings, awesome factual similarities with the ancient Jewish perspectives regarding the Jewish background and nature of the Kingdom that the NT proclaims.

The Historic development of the Redemption

NOTE: *These are approximate dates. For the dates before the Common Era we use the Hebraic dating system. There exists no unbroken standard for the non-Jewish calculations. Only in the 1900's did they even agree on a standard Calendar (Gregorian). No one in the ancient non-Jewish world kept any accurate records of long periods of history that were passed on to future generations. Their dating started only in modern times, working backwards, using all kinds of accounts by archaeologists, astronomy, etc. The Hebrews lived their history and recorded it as it transpired from time immemorial using very advanced mathmatical and astronomical computations and traditions. The Jews even have an ancient book dating historical events that has no parallel in the scientific world. There are many ways to interpret secular historic data which leaves much room to argue about dates.*

- 798 BCE - After King Solomon's death, the ancient twelve-tribed Kingdom of Israel split into two opposing sectors:

'Israel' - the Northern Kingdom, Ten Tribes, main city: Sebastia (Shomron, Samaria, Shechem), and

'Judah', Southern Kingdom, two tribes (including small percentages of other Tribes, those of other Tribes who truly wanted to serve G-d and who accepted the spiritual leadership of Judah), main city: Jerusalem.

- 720 BCE: the apostate ten northern tribes were conquered, deported and the land repopulated with foreigners. They gradually lost their identity over the next five centuries. This exile occurred in three stages (1 Chronicles 5:26, 2Kings 15:25, 2 Kings 17). The vengeance of G-d is noted three times corresponding to a three-staged exile.

- In the year of approximately 574 BCE (3187) the expulsion commenced with Zebulon and Naphtali forcibly driven out by Tiglath-Pileser of Assyria (according to Rebbe Shmuel ben Nachman as opposed to Rebbe Elazar). Hosea, son of Elah becomes King of Israel.

- 566 BCE (3195) - Shalmanessar brutally drove the Tribes out from East of the Jordan (the Tribes of Reuben, Gad and half the Tribe of Menashe). As if this was not enough to wake us up, we refused to change for the better.

- So in the year 566 BCE (3205) since the creation of the world, our world completely fell apart. Finally Sennacherib throws out the rest of the Ten Tribes.

This 3-staged exile gave time for some of the ten Northern Tribes to flee South, to find refuge in the Kingdom of Judah, for they wanted to serve G-d uprightly (2 Chron. 11:16-18). Thus, within Judah today, there are representatives of all 12 Tribes. Even at that time, all of the small tribes of Benjamin and Levi were included in Judah, as well as a part of the Tribe of Shimon who bordered Judah geographically.

- Approximately, 555 BCE the Exile in three stages commenced. The Southern Kingdom of Judah was deported to Babylon by Nebuchadnezzar.

With the fall of the commonwealth and the destruction of the first Temple, Judah was now also in exile.

- After about a 70-year prophesied exile, Judah (and Benjamin) returned and rebuilt Jerusalem. The House of the Great Assembly was active, composed of Sages and Prophets. They successfully revived Torah study and observance, and organized the building of the Second Temple. Then follows the eras of Ezra the Scribe, Nehemiah, Chagai, Malachi, Zechariah, Zerubabel, Daniel, Mordechai the Jew of Purim, etc. These were some of the main scholarly Rabbis who played a contributing role in the rebuilding of Judaism, the people and the land, after the exile of Bavel.

- 70 CE (3831) - Jerusalem destroyed by the Romans. Jewish survivors were exiled as slaves. The next 1900 years, until 1948, saw the gradual dispersion of the exiles of Judah across the globe, amidst every country and nation on earth.

- 132 CE (3893) - Hadrianic wars. The Messianic Bar Kokhva revolt against Rome also turns out to be a failure. In addition to these major wars that rocked the oppressive Roman tyranny, there were several minor wars. The war leadership during the Bar Kochva revolution sent messengers to beg people who were still identified at that time as being of ancient Israel Hebrew stock, to aid in the fight against Roman abuse and oppression. They categorically refused to assist in any way whatsoever. This rejection led us to conclude that 10-Israel, who sided with the bitter enemies of Judah, could very well forfeit a righteous portion in the world to come. The reasoning went something like this: "The Ten Tribes shall not return again for it is written: Deuteronomy 29:28, 'In furious anger and in great wrath the L-RD uprooted them from their land and thrust them into another land, as it is now.'" This negative attitude towards 10-Israel was only in the wake of those who refused to help the Jewish people rebel against Rome. This implies that if 10-Israel chose to re-identify with their Hebrew roots, all would be fine. This position is clearly reflected in the sentiments of the Prophetess Devorah. She was accepted on a personal and individual level by the nation as both a Judge and a military leader. In her song (Judges 15) she condemns the Tribes who did not join the fight for G-d and the nation. She even severely curses those Tribes that chose not to identify with the plight of their brethren.

It should be noted here, that the spirit revealed within the current, modern-day, re-identifying 10-Tribers seems to be completely the opposite. Our personal contact and experience with such people is that they are crying out for the opportunity to assist 'their brother' Judah in his plight of a current ever-tightening noose of enforced national suicide by the nations of the world. These nations, almost without exception, are forcing Israel to give their Land to their sworn enemies (the Arabs). We have written testimonies from re-awakening, pro-Israel 10-Tribers who are prepared to die in battle for helping Judah to hold onto the Land - some even in their sixties! Many of these people are virtually 'sitting on their suitcases,' awaiting the opportunity for them to return to the Land of Israel.

The Oral Torah continues to explain: "Like the day grows dark and then grows light, so also after darkness is fallen on the Ten Tribes, shall light hereafter shine upon them once again." (Mishnah Sanhedrin 10:3). This means that we do believe in their Return, "speedily and in our days!" – as reflected in the Daily Prayers of Judah.

Many times various Rabbis made some commotion and published the reality of the Return of 10-Israel. Eldad Hadani (9th century), a Jewish Marco Polo of sorts, came with stories of 10-Israel and caught the ears of everyone in Cordoba, Spain. Even the Torah Giant Casdai ibn Shiprut (900 -970 CE) gave full attention to Eldad's unlikely tales because of the excitement that such a possibility engendered.

- 1380 CE (5141) - John Wycliffe translated the Bible into English.

- 1494 –1536 CE - William Tyndale showed proofs of the essence of Great Britain as a descendant of the Tribes (a Covenant country of sorts).

John Sadler - his supporter Oliver Cromwell and others were inclined to view themselves as a reflection of Biblical Lost Israel. This embryonic Tribal identity made them open to allowing Jews to return to England from which Jews had previously been expelled.

The great Don Yitzchak Abarbanel (1650 CE) explains that faith in the Return of the Tribes is a pivotal, foundational and crucial element of our Torah Judaism. For additional examples, let us cite the following instances:

- Rabbi Manasseh Ben Israel (1604 – 1657 CE) in England, France, Holland, etc.

- The Vilna Gaon and his Perushim circa (1700 CE and later), the Jerusalem Rabbinical public plea, less than 100 years ago, begged the Tribes to return.

- 1611 CE - Henry VIII of England introduces the Bible translated into English. Until then, the Catholic Church had essentially kept it in Latin.

- 1794-1795 CE - the author Richard Brothers, made the notion of the British descent from the Tribes very popular with many well-read publications. Very learned and honored people were involved, i.e. the parliament member and famous Orientals, Nathaniel Halhed and theologian and engraver William Sharp. John Finlayson and separately, Ralph Wedgwood, proclaim the still infantile, but growing Tribal identity. John Wilson founded a society that explained how the British were actually the descendants of 10-Israel and they proved this in a scientific way through studies which embraced migrations of ancient peoples (1870's until today). Colonel George Gawler continued this work of proving Israelite identity.

Since Colonial America, the interest in the Biblical Hebrew language has been a reality. For example, Presidents Adams and Jefferson, despite their many disagreements, found common ground on the issue of the Jews and their part in history. They were intrigued by the role that the Jews played in history. They also felt and placed the fate of the Jews at center stage (*"G-d's Sacred Tongue"*, S. Goldman University of South Carolina Press, 04). They wished to make Hebrew the national language and wanted to identify the lost Tribes. All the best universities taught Hebrew as a Classical language, because it was still a crucial tool for Bible understanding. In Protestant Europe, Hebrew was held in high esteem since the 16th century.

• The 1840's saw a rising interest in a fledgling Hebrew Restoration movement among hundreds of Gentiles, who had a heart for Israel. These groups also called for, and often predicted the imminent return of Jews to Zion. Many Christians, like Prof. George Bush, disagreed with a merely mystical interpretation of the 'End times' and insisted the actual return of the Jewish people to their ancestral Homeland. Yes, the former presidents of the USA are his relatives. These writings and activities served to plant the seeds for more advanced growth in this direction. All of this is leading towards an intellectual infrastructure that would help 10-Israel awaken. Christian Zionism (love for Israel) and Hebrew Roots Restoration had started to take root among Chrisstians and is today rapidly growing to become a serious alternative way to the historic Church's opposing attitudes.

The Restoration of a reunited Israel can also clearly be traced in 'the spiritually evolutionary progress' of Christianity since its inception 2000 years ago. Over the first three centuries, it grew from a Jewish sect in Israel, to the birth of the Catholic Church, formatted on a totally anti-Jewish foundation of theological concepts. In the

Middle Ages, we find the Great Reformation, with reform- ers like Luther and Calvin, starting to question the Papacy. The invention of the printing press helped to spread the Bible among normal congregants of the Church. Soon there was a break away of reformed churches from the Papacy. The western part of New York State in the early 1800s was known as the "Burned Over District." The fer- vor over religion was intense. It was a time and a place of theological turmoil which saw the start of 'a return to orig- inal Bible Truth' among seeking Christian Bible students, to what became known as 'a return to the Hebraic Roots of their Faith'. This period gave birth to several prominent Church leaders who were recognized as 'prophets' by their followers and credited with restoring original Bible-based Truths:

- 1830 – Joseph Smith established the Church of Jesus Christ of Latter Day Saints (Mormons), claiming that he was called on in a vision, to restore the true Church on earth. The Church is philo-Semitic (pro-Semitic) in its doctrines and teaches that its adherents are direct descendants of the House of Israel or can be adopted into it. In another vision Smith claimed to have received from Moses the keys of regathering the Tribes of Israel.

- 1840 - Ellen White restored the Sabbath through the Seventh Day Adventist Movement in the 1840's.

- 1880's - Charles Russell, a Christian restorationist pastor initiated a legacy of tens of rhousands of Bible students. He claimed no special revelation or vision for his teach- ings. He did not seek to found a new denomination, but instead intended merely to gather together 'those who were seeking the truth of G-d's Word.' From 1886 to 1904 he published a six-volume Bible study series which became known as *Studies in the Scriptures*, nearly 20 million copies of which were printed and distributed around the world in several languages during his lifetime. Out of his following, after his death, grew amongst others, the *Jehova's Weitnesses, Watch Tower Society* which mainly was responsible for bringing awareness of the Sacred Name of G-d to the masses. This started an ever-growing great awakening over the last several decades into the true Identity of G-d, called the 'Sacred Name Movement.

- 1930 - William Branham started the *United Pentecostal* charismatic movement through his healing services in the mid-20th century and denounced the popular Christian concept of a Trinity theology, replacing it with 'The Oneness' – viz. 'the Supreme Deity of Jesus' aa manifestation of the Creator G-d.

- 1940-66 - Herbert Armstrong, *'World Wide Church of God'* – pioneer of TV evangelism; using free international mass high quality publications to promote restoration of the Biblical Feasts (Jewish Holy days); promoted *British Israelism* (links to ancient Northerm Ten Tribes of Israel) and required observance of parts of the Jewish Covenant Law including 7th-day Sabbath and dietary (kosher) prohibitions

- From the 90's onwards, out of this Reformation process grew the Hebraic Restoration Movement, which set in amongst the masses of serious Bible students acrtoss the world, rearing individual commentators and teachers all over. The restoration of original Bible Truths which were discovered and proclaimed drew Bible believers away from the regular churches, in a progressive return to Judaism's principles of faith, one after the other. An ever growing interest in conversion to Judaism and physical return to the Land of Israel has been on the roll ever since and to date.

We have many instances where great hope was kindled with mistaken identification of long 'lost' Jewish groups. For example: 1815 - Arabs, who were probably Bedouin nomads, said there was a lost Tribe in Yemen. The poverty stricken yishuv (old Jerusalem Community) sent people to search for them. In 1830 additional attempts were made. Such illustrious names as Rav Yisrael of Shklov, Rav Baruch of Pinsk, Rav Zvi Hirsch Lehren of Amsterdam became involved. They, and many other Rabbis, knew that trying to reach out to the lost tribes, was actually what the Zohar predicted. Namely, that at the beginning of the 'End of Days', the identity of 10-Israel would be revealed and the future people of Judah and Benjamin would go to them and bring them home to Israel (Midrash). This would help wake up Judah and encourage repentance, which is a crucial key to everything (Aliyos Eliyahu, pp. 63-69; *Chazon Tzyon*, pp. 67-69, David Rossoff, *Where Heaven Touches Earth*, 1999, Guardian Press, P O Box 5437, Jerusalem).

What is clear is that in Ashkenazi, Sephardic, Yemenite, Chassidic Judaism, etc., there was always excitement at the prospect of a Tribal return. Jews pray for this return every day, several times a day. We often rise in the middle of the night to cry over the destruction of our Temples, our tribulation in exile and then we switch gears: we cry tears of joy at the prospect of a returning Israel. The symbols of all Twelve Tribes reunited, is a major motif in every Shul from antiquity until this very day. This vision is buried deep in our conscience and has always been expressed in our dreams, our art, music and religious decorations. The famous French master artist, Chagall, had been given a free hand to create a masterpiece for the Shul of Hadassah Medical Center in Jerusalem. He chose to depict the Twelve Tribes in stained glass. This is one of the main tourist attractions in Jerusalem today, at the Hadassah Hospital.

After World War I Jews from around the world returned to Israel, joining their existing brethren. The British Balfour Declaration (1917) and also the San Remo conference recognized 'Palestine' as the ancient Jewish homeland. The Treaty of Versailles in Paris, which ended World War I, called for the establishment of a Jewish National Homeland on one percent of the former Ottoman Turk Empire. That means, my dear friends, that the **entire** British Mandate Palestine was supposed to be, by international agreement and law, a Jewish homeland! Add to this an amazing fact unknown to the overwhelming majority of mankind, that great Arab religious clerics ruled that it was permissible to have a Jewish homeland established on this one percent (British mandate Palestine) of the former Ottoman Turkish empire. The League of Nations voted on this and approved all of the above. They also obligated Great Britain to enable the establishment of such a State.

The world totally ignores these official international declarations today.

The British, instead of turning the entire Mandate Palestine into a Jewish Homeland, gave about 80% to Arab tribes coming from Saudi Arabia. They created a sovereign State that never before existed in history - the Jordanian HaShemite Kingdom of Palestine and another 22 Arab States. Never in history was there an indigenous and autonomous State from the Mediterranean all the way to Saudi Arabia, except for the Hebrew-Jewish Kingdoms. Jordan never existed as a State in history. Jordan was only a river. So with 5000 pounds sterling per month, guns and supplies, the British created an artificial Statem a Moslem Arab State which immediately forbade Jews from living there and from buying land, under penalty of death.

- 1948 - The State of Israel was declared. Millions of Jews returned over the next period of time, many from the death camps of Hitler and the Holocaust. More than 800 000 Jews were thrown out of Muslim countries, often stripped of their wealth and possessions. Thus, an ipso *facto* population exchange occurred.

When it comes to the intrinsic right of possible self–defense, all nations are given the benefit of doubt and are *ipso facto* allowed even preemptive actions, such as the transfer of potential enemy populations! With Israel though, terrible twisted double standards are applied.

- Within two decades of its modern existence, Israel developed one of the strongest armies in the world and a technologically advanced economy with agriculture as predicted in Prophecy. The Jewish population count in Israel, in the year 2009, has reached about 6 million.

Minorities of other nationalities are equally protected under Israeli law in the finest tradition of the best of the Western styled, free Democracies.

This miraculous return of the Jewish nation to the ancient Land of their forefathers, and the resultant struggle between Jews and Arabs (Israel and the Palestinians|) stimulated non-Jews, 10-Israel and the present day Jewish people to think more, relate more and to struggle more with identity issues.

The Jews had already been working and building in the Land for 150 years. Even before that, following each destruction, they were busy rebuilding the Land. But, since the establishment of the State of Israel, all growth and good things would skyrocket in value. Thus Judah, in fulfillment of Tanakh, was the planter, preparing the Land for the even greater Exodus to come, that of the Ingathering of the Lost Ten Tribes from every corner of the globe, when Ephraim would return as Harvester with previously assimilated Jews (captive Jews or 'lost' Jews).

- 1958–60 - a dialogue of sorts began between Judah and Ephraim, which first manifested itself in The Vatican II (ecumenical) Conference. It was to start on the 25th of November. Instead, it was pushed off for one day in order to accommodate some religious Jews to attend. Among these was Rabbi Avraham Yehoshua Hershel (who was personally observant, considering himself as orthodox). He discussed some communal issues, such as the Soviet Jewry struggle under Communism. He also spoke of religious themes, for example, the importance accorded to

Oral Torah, for a Jew to recite the Shemah ("Hear O' Israel" prayer). Though considered to be a liberal, this Rabbi was willing to sacrifice his life, to give it up if necessary, as a martyred one. He maintained that dying in Auschwitz is preferable to conversion to any form of Christianity. On Dec. 8, 1960 Rav Soloveitchik, said that he disapproved of any Jewish participation in the Ecumenical Council (*Archives of the American Jewish Committee*, pp.110-23, Hershel's *Impact on Catholic – Jewish Relations, No Religion Is an Island, The Edah Journal*, vol. 4:2, 5765-2005, Prof. Reuven Kimelman, *Jewish-Christian Relations*).

At approximately this time period, a large collection of anti-Jewish Protestant Churches created the Thailand Convention. They were dedicated to evangelical missions amongst the Jews and hence they scraped together some kind of Christian symbolism which they linked to Jewish traditions - such as the famous line: "The Jewish way to say Jesus is *Yehoshua*". They decided to coat their outreach with Jewish symbols to make it more acceptable to ignorant assimilated Jews. Their goal was to absorb Jews into the greater Protestant world. However, this was to backfire, and instead of Jews flocking to them, Gentiles in their congregations in search of truth, accepted these Jewish tenets of Faith. This became part of the Hebrew Roots awareness phenomenon amongst Christians, as a by-product to the failed Messianic outreach to Jews. The close proximity of the Thailand Conference to Vatican II, prompted Rav Soloveichik to lump them both together, calling all interfaith talks 'Evangelical Deceptions.' In 1964 he labeled all these activities 'Evangelical Propaganda'.

- 1964 saw the Vatican come forth with clear statements that were anti-missionary, concerning the Jewish people.

- 1967 Secretariat for Catholic Bishops agreed to have discourse, devoid of any hope for conversion. In brief: The Jews are so righteous and precious, Church officials maintainedm that the Church would collapse if the Jewish people would cease to exist!

The Six Day War (1967) also served as a wake-up call for Russian Jews, Israelis, the general world Jewish population and pro-Jewish Gentiles.

All the above was important for moving Christianity back to its Hebrew Roots. This in turn is crucial for 10 Tribers to realize their true Hebraic identity.

- 1980's and '90s - Increasing awareness amongst earnest Christian Bible scholars, mainly from the USA and Western Europe, concerning their 'Hebraic Roots'. There is an increasing acceptance and partial symbolic observance of the 'Jewish' Sabbath, festivals, and other customs by non-Jews, recognized under several banners such as: Hebraic Roots, Hebrew Restoration, Sacred Name Movement, Messianic Israel assembly (99% non-Jewish) and Messianic Jewish movements (which are 85% non-Jewish). These seekers of truth within these movements, through progressive return to Jewish tenets of Truth, are increasingly interested in Halachic Jewish conversion. As they progress on this spiritually evolutionary track, they are progressively rejecting replacement theology (where the Church claims to be 'Spiritual Israel') and rejecting the proselytization of Jews in any form whatsoever. They are merely trying to get closer to HaShem and Torah. Many of them are aware of Noahide (righteous Gentile) directives and are enriching their spiritual life. Again, amongst most of these 'returnees' and in an ever-increasing degree, there is not a shred of any desire to challenge, diminish or replace Jews and Judaism – much rather they desire to identify with Jews, Judaism, Torah and Halacha.

- Mid '90's – Millions of pro-Israel Christian Zionists show increasing solidarity with Judah and call for Israel to reject the Oslo 'Peace' Accords which simply empowered Israel's enemies and terrorists. 100,000 pro-Arab terrorist exiles were brought from Tunisia; four to five billion Shekels ($1 billion +) per year were given to them by the State of Israel; $16 billion by the international community; weapons, land and legitimacy were also bestowed upon these potential terrorists through the channel of the Palestinian Authority. The bottom line was an increase in death and destruction for Jews, more so in the last eighteen years than during the forty-four years before Oslo. This increased the appetite and willpower of radical Islam and created a terrorist State in Gaza and a semi-terrorist State in Judea and the Shomron. As the left-wing Jerusalem Post, April 20, 2006 describes things: "... the PA – from whose bailiwick the mass-murderers set out, where they were brainwashed and trained and where the infra-structure for their operations flourished – issued obligatory denunciations of these deeds".

- Year 2000 CE – 5760. Increasing identification by pro-Israel individual members of the above mentioned re-awakening Hebraic movements towards Judah in its 'time of distress', as world pressure and secular, leftist Israeli powers barter Holy Land for 'Peace' with the Arab Jihadist radical Muslims. Remember, that in all Arab Muslim media they proclaim that any negotiations with the Zionist entity is merely to implement the decision of the Cairo Convention (1974) which decided to annihilate the Zionist entity in stages - simply put, to force it to self-amputate and to cut itself up into pieces (peace).

As the battle for Jerusalem intensifies and builds up to an 'Armageddon' scenario, this support for Israel by Hebrew Roots Restorers develops into a search by a 're-awakening 10-Israel' Movement. This entails their searching for definite projects to assist Judah and to realize active immigration of 'non-Jewish' settlers to the land of Israel in a contrite spirit, similar to the British soldier par excellence, Major-General Wingate, who sought to aid Israel and its establishment without any missionary agenda.

- Year 2005 CE - 5765. Increasingly closer identification sought by individuals for conversion to Judaism and a desire to live in the land of Israel. One needs to remember that there was about about a 2800 year break in the relationship between Judah and 10-Israel. Conversion is seen as a terrific means of repairing that relationship. Not to mention the powerful study, experience and spiritual growth that comes along with intensive authentic Torah studies. It all amounts to a validated, objective renewal of the old connection; a renewal of nuptials (marriage), so to speak, for lost or captive Jews and lost 10-Israelites.

- Year 2009 C.E. – 5769. Explosive division, while yet pursuing and treading a united 'way of return', is the order of the day. One of the uniting factors between Judah and 10-Israel seems to be the few who manage to convert to Judaism. Their common beliefs in the Hebrew Bible and prayers for a speedy Redemption and hard work by Judah in their efforts to restore the Land are a few of the factors that unite us and continue to expand.

- Year 2010 C.E. – 5770. As serious searchers of their true Hebraic identity discover more and more tenets of faith which identify them closer and closer with Orthodox Judaism, the ultimate obstructions of Halachic Rabbinism and conversion become more intensive issues in the movement.

Simultaneously, obstructing Jewish elements have become more prominent and intense. Conversion doors close firmer and faster, and anti-Rabbinic Jewish Karaitism (a failed heretical sect that basically was refuted and died 800 years ago) diverts pilgrims from the Jewish Halachic way with their anti-Rabbinic and anti-Halachic teachings. Their heretical teachings present a highly popular alternative for re-identifying and returning 10-Israel. The Karaite anti-Rabbinic and anti-Torah teachings find fertile soil among the good-hearted, returning 10-Tribers whose forefathers succumbed to the same rebellion against Torah authority 2800 years ago. In reality, these Karaites are merely adding to the confusion and erecting a formidable iron curtain between Re-awakening 10-Israel and their eventual Reconciliation with Judah (refer chapter 18).

- Year 2011 CE - 5771 – thousands of 10-Tribers are dumping the last vestiges of former Church affiliation and opting to embrace historic Chazal-guided Judaism. They are quietly, with no fanfare, seeking out authentic websites, Rabbis, and Torah teachers to help guide them forward. There are many forums, commentaries, and discussions to this effect. However, theological differences and various levels of acceptance of the 'restoration process' prevent them from uniting into more formidable and fewer representative bodies.

- Year 2012 - 2013 – Increasing awareness amongst widely spread and disunited 10-Israel of an urge to 'Return to the Land' (of Israel). There is a noticeable gradual weakening of the intense resistance amongst the majority of re-awakening 10-Tribers, against any suggestions of conforming to the normal immigration processes which of course requires formal Jewish identity and hence, conversion. Simultaneously, the process of conversion has become drastically more selective, with the great disqualifying issue being the prospective convert's belief in a 'Christian' Messiah which is unacceptable to Judaism. In addition, it is now well known in the Thrd World, where millions are seeking financial survival in advanced sovieties, that "one merely has to affiliate religiously in order to obtain Israeli citizenship." Thus, to save Israel from a massive flood from the Third World, they are making renewal of the Covenant (Jewish religious conversion) more difficult.

Encouragingly though, many Jewish Orthodox teachers and educators are coming to appreciate the radical difference between true Hebrew rooted, pro-Torah believers and the historic anti-Torah Church. The non-proselytizing spirit and respect for Oral Torah of these deep rooted Hebraic restorers are also doing much to remove the animosity against their Messianic belief. Many orthodox Rabbis have concluded that these seekers of Truth should be reached out to and included into our Covenantal Faith communities, to give them opportunity and time to grow and develop in the Faith of Judaism. These Hebrew Rooted people are user-friendly to Jews and Judaism. When exposed to authentic Jewish Torah teaching and experiences, they rapidly advance in their spiritual quest. Their sincere search for Truth is being recognized and appreciated by more and more educators.

A further notable development is that the 10-Triber camp becomes split between pro-Oral Torah supporters and rejecters. Meanwhile, politically, the Land of Jewish Israel is pushed out of their Biblical Heritage territories while facing a distinct and unsolvable demographical problem. The Jewish nation simply lacks the sufficient numbers to settle the wider expanses of the current Israel Domain. We will discuss the demographic problem in chapter 20 and show how the Return of the Lost House of Israel can provide the multitudes which are required to settle not only the current domain of Israel, but, in fact the far greater expanses of the Biblically defined 'Greater Israel' (Refer to the Map on our front Cover Page).

It is the purpose of this publication to bring a better understanding to all concerned in this Reconciliation process. May we in this way advance the fulfillment of the Prophecy in:

Isaiah 11:12-14, "The envy also of Ephraim shall depart, and the adversaries of Judah shall be cut off:

Ephraim shall not envy Judah, and Judah shall not
vex Ephraim."

More and more groups, at great personal sacrifice, are coming
to learn in the land. Notwithstanding difficult visa restrictions,
they manage to grow and to contribute to the general welfare
of Judah and the Land. If given half a chance, the far greater
majority of them would be willing to place themselves on the
front lines in defense of their brothers of Judah in Israel.

May this revealing review serve to aid them to discover the
hidden Jewish Halachic foundations of the Gospels, which
they claim to regard as their confirming Scriptural guidelines.
May this new realization inspire them to become closer allies
of Judah and Torah – and hopefully in the future, spiritually
secure and physically productive citizens of the Nation and
Land of Israel, as together we strive for the full Redemption of
all of 12-Tribed Israel.

May the many Jewish people who have assimilated with and
welcomed the first Returnees of these pro-Israel folk into the
heart of Jewish Israel, use this publication as a stepping stone to
enlighten their fellow Jewish citizens of their spiritual obligation. According to Torah and Prophecy (Chazal), this obligation rests on Jews to help these re-identifying Returnees back
to our people and into Judaism, the original faith of their ancestors and hopefully their descendants. And may the witness
and the evidence presented in this publication calm the fears
of Judah, their doubts and suspicions and warm their hearts to
receive back their long lost brothers of 10-Israel.

Let us now review the hidden Jewish Halachic principles
underlying the NT writings – treasures of Truth which are

progressively being discovered by those millions of NT readers and students seeking the Original Bible Truth. Thereafter, in the closing sections of this book, we shall further investigate, follow and plan for coping with the trend of this amazing phenomenon of spiritual awakening which is driving millions of sincere seekers across the world to their Hebraic Roots and to the basic and long-standing tenets of the Jewish Faith.

PART 2

THE JEWISH HALACHIC AND ORAL TORAH FOUNDATIONS OF THE NEW TESTAMENT

CHAPTER 4

Hidden and misinterpreted true Jewish foundations in the Gospels

Traditionally, the general understanding among many New Testament readers has been that much of its content rejects Judaism, the Torah and Rabbinic authority. I suggest that much of what is considered by Christians as anti-Rabbinic and anti-Semitic in the NT, is merely a misunderstanding of the Hebraic and historic context in which it was written.

As I will show, irrespective of the great opposing forces that the Gospels unleash between Judaism and Christian Messianism, there is common ground. Notwithstanding that the Gospel writings form the constitution of the new Christian religion, which is partially in contradistinction to Judaism; they also conceal astounding proof that the Orthodox Oral Torah is alive and well and generating life and Truth within the Gospel texts. Jewish scholars can recognize traditional Orthodox Judaism and Oral Torah in many Gospel statements, when taken within the context of their original Hebrew background. These realities, hidden in the Gospel writings, confirm traditional Jewish religious principles which some ardent Christian Messianic followers reject outright.

The Gospels clearly direct its readers to authentic Torah observance as part of the ingathering of the "lost sheep of Israel":

> Luke 6:46, "And why do you call me 'Lord, Lord', and not do what I say?"

> John 14:15, "If you love me you will keep my commandments."

> John 15:10, "If you keep my commandments, you will abide in my love..."

> 1 John 3:4, "Everyone who practices sin also practices lawlessness; and sin is lawlessness."

> 1 John 5:3, "For this is the love of G-d, that we keep His commandments; and His commandments are not burdensome."

> 2 John 6, "And this is love, that we walk according to His commandments."

Some two hundred times the word 'law' is mentioned in the NT. Almost all the time the Greek word *nomo* is used, referring to 'the law of Moses' (as understood by religious Jews).

Obeying His teachings and instructions (laws) will sanctify you. Will we remain 'His own possession' if we disobey and break His Covenant? Here are some benefits for obeying:

> Luke 11:28, "But He said, 'On the contrary, blessed are those who hear the word of G-d and observe it.'"

James 1:22 "But prove yourselves doers of the Word, and not merely hearers who delude themselves..."

v25 "But the one who looks intently at the perfect Law, the Law of Liberty, and abides by it, not having become a forgetful hearer, but an effectual doer, this man shall be blessed in what he does."

2 Cor. 6:17, 'Therefore, come out from their midst and be separate' says the Lord, 'and do not touch what is unclean and I will welcome you. And I will be a father to you, and you shall be sons and daughters to Me.' Says the Lord almighty."

These guidelines merely echo the Tanach, Jewish Halacha and post biblical Jewish writing at that time:

Deu 28:1, "... if you will diligently obey... HaShem your G-d will set you high above all the nations of the earth."

Eze 20:19, "I am HaShem your G-d; walk in My statutes and keep My ordinances and observe them. And sanctify My Sabbaths, and they shall be a sign between Me and you, that you may know that I am Hashem your G-d."

1 Kings 8:57 "...that He may incline our hearts to Himself, to walk in His ways, and to keep His commandments and His statutes and His ordinances, which He commanded our fathers..."

v60 "... so that all the peoples of the earth may know that HaShem is our G-d; there is no one else."

CHAPTER 5

The Christian Messiah was a Jew

The NT proclaims that the way to righteousness is to keep the Torah of the historic Torah Sages. Matthew 23 cries out, "For the Sages (Scribes) sit in the seat of Moses!" Not a dot was to be changed, and the prime directive was to be kind and to love your G-d with all your heart, soul and strength (James 1:22-26, Matt 7:20-24, etc.). Jews are therefore simply doing what these true NT teachings always meant them to. Thus, there never was, neither should there be a justification for Christians to harass or missionize Jews.

When the Jewish NT writings are torn from the Hebrew cultural environment in which they were composed, all that remains is a vile form of anti-Semitism.

Eusebius, under Constantine's directives, had to create one brand of Christianity according to Eusebius's discretion. Constantine needed to create a new brand of religion because the initial followers of the Nazarene were Jewish or had Jewish inclinations. The Roman Catholic Church was anti-Semitic and wanted to minimize any Jewish references and to deny the Jewishness of the Gospels. Therefore, Eusebius chose the texts he felt should be in the Gospels, thus eliminating obvious

Jewishness. Eusebius himself explains this at length in Latin. All good religious libraries contain volumes of all that he did and said to canonise the Gospels. One can look up 'Canonisation of the New Testament' in the Catholic encyclopaedia. Take a look also at the 'Vatican II Conference'. Prepare to be shocked.

Further evidence of Christianity's historic evolution into anti-Judaism and anti-Rabbinism is provided throughout this book. For example, the writings of Paul were donated to the early church in 140 CE by Marcion, a rich Greek fishing merchant, who was excommunicated three years later for heresies. However, it is **his** version of the epistle that made it into Canon. Scholars recognize the anti-Semitic statements contained in the Gospels as being of Marconian origin, and the pro-Jewish statements as being of authentic Paulinian origin. There is no other explanation for this paradoxical canon.

CHAPTER 6

The Jewish Halachic principles underlying the New Testament

The New Testament's position on Circumcision

G-d told Avraham to circumcise himself and all his men (an Oral Torah insight). The term circumcision, for Avraham, was both a covenantal phenomenon and a medical-surgical procedure. Now he was being told to do this thing to himself! But where in the entire Written Torah is it defined?

Remember, whatever it is, it has a covenantal and medical definition and it's not that simple. There are details that, if left out, would not fulfil the Biblical requirement. There were also medical complications which could be life-threatening. Both in ancient and modern societies there are several possible interpretations of the procedure. This is a serious issue - we must have a proper definition and an operating manual.

What does the ancient Hebrew word mean exactly? To me, to you, to all of the Jews and Gentiles, in this modern day, it may be patently clear what it means. But what is the source of the definition that makes it so clear? Where did Avraham get his information in ancient times when there was no written word of G-d? It is not in the simple text of the Bible. Read it and if you are intellectually honest and can detach everything that you've heard, seen, and studied previously from the plain simple text, you will be left with many questions.

So, what was Avraham to do? He did not have access to our 3600+ years of knowledge of those words when they originally rang in his ears. What did he do? Did they have medical practitioners and institutions at the time? Could he pop into the local Jewish hospital? So, where was Avraham to find the exact application and detailed definition of this covenantal term - a term which had medical, anatomical, biological and surgical implications?

The answer my friend, is flowing from the Oral Torah. There was no Written Torah in Avraham's time. The Written Torah (Bible), which came about much later, would completely rely upon the Oral Torah for this complex, technically detailed definition. G-d communicated to Avraham that entirety of what he needed to know. Much later, at the Sinai revelation, the divine stipulations were written down, though only in brief, summarized format. The detailed application of the circumcision process remained in the realm of, and relied completely upon the Oral Torah of the time. In other words, there is no book of the Bible that gives in any revealed way, all the scores of details on how to perform a ritual circumcision.

According to the Gospels of the NT, the Nazarene was circumcised by his parents. John the Baptist was circumcised by his parents. It was such a commonly accepted practice, that certainly all the apostles were circumcised in accordance with Rabbinic Oral directives.

According to the NT record, the Nazarene child not only conformed to the traditional Jewish obligations of circumcision, but all else that goes with it. The following chapter from the book of Luke in the NT carries with it a boatload of evidence of compliance to Oral Torah which is such an intrinsic and inseparable part of Judaism. In scrutinizing this extract, please consider the evidence to Oral Torah inherent in the dedication of the witnesses mentioned in this portion, viz. Jews who were totally dedicated and who spent all their time, 'eating and sleeping,' Oral Torah!

Luke 2:

[22] "When the time came for the purification rites required by the Law of Moses, Joseph and Miriam took him [the Nazarene child] to Jerusalem to present him to the L-rd [23] (as it is written in the Torah of the L-rd: 'Every firstborn male is to **be consecrated** to the L-rd') (Exodus 13:2,12) [24] and to offer a sacrifice in keeping with what is said in the Law of the L-rd: 'a pair of doves or two young pigeons.'

[25] Now there was a man in Jerusalem called Simeon, **who was righteous and devout**. He was waiting for the comforting of Israel, and the Holy Spirit was on him....

[27] Moved by the Spirit, he went into the temple courts. When the parents brought in the child **to do**

for him what the custom of the Law required, ²⁸ Simeon took him in his arms and praised G-d ...

³⁶ There was also a prophet, Anna, the daughter of Penuel, of the tribe of Asher. She was very old; she had lived with her husband seven years after her marriage, ³⁷ and then was a widow until she was eighty-four. **She never left the Temple but worshiped night and day, fasting and praying.** ³⁸ Coming up to them at that very moment, she gave thanks to G-d and spoke about the child to all who were looking forward to the redemption of Jerusalem.

³⁹ When Joseph and Miriam had **done everything required by the Law of the L-rd**, they returned to Galilee to their own town of Nazareth."

All these ceremonies performed on the Nazarene child were more specifically and more broadly defined by the Oral Torah, undoubtedly more so in this case because of the dedication of the role players here!

Paul spoke of circumcision in the NT and debated whether or not it was required for Messianic believers. But never did he question the authority, interpretation and application that the Command entailed for Jews - a Command that begs definition, which is only obtainable in an extensive detailed Oral Jewish tradition, which has been passed on from time immemorial. We are not going to digress here to explain *milah* (circumcision). This would require an entire separate book.

New Testament's position on tzit tzit (fringes) to garments

The Book of Numbers 15:38 tells the Israelites that they should 'put fringes' on their four-cornered garments (Deut. 15:38). The scores of details necessary for the fulfilment of the above, once again, were dependent upon the Oral Torah. Archaeological digs have found fringes of years gone by, identical to the same fringes that Jews wear today. There has never been a debate amongst Jews as to what those fringes are all about, e.g. how to make them, where to put them, what blessings to make, who has to wear them, etc., etc. For all these topics, the Written Torah offers no specifications whatsoever.

We read in Matthew 9:2, "… a woman came from behind him [the Nazarene] and touched his garment," and further on in Matthew 14:35, 36 "… that they might only touch the hem of his garment." The word hem refers to the tzit-tzit, tassels or fringes which Jews are required by Torah to wear on the 'corners of our garments'. The Greek word used in the NT is 'kraspedon', meaning fringes. The Septuagint and Strong's Dictionary interprets 'kraspedon' to refer to the Biblical Command for the fringes on the hem corners of a four-cornered garment.

Speaking of a yet-future time, the prophet defined a time when "…many people and strong nations shall come to seek the G-d of Hosts in Jerusalem and to pray before Him. Thus says HaShem of Hosts: 'In those days it shall come to pass, that ten men out of all the languages of the nations, they shall take hold of the garment (robe) of him that is a Jew, saying, 'We will go with you (*plural*) for we have heard that G-d is with you (*plural*) '" (Zechariah 8:22,23). We see this happening today, as millions of sincere Bible students are leaving their churches in what they themselves refer to as a process of 'discovering and returning to their Hebraic Roots'. It can be no coincidence that the text uses the figure 'ten', no doubt referring to the prophesied return of the Lost Ten Tribes of Israel after their exile of some 2800 years.

New Testament's position on phylacteries

In the Gospels, Matthew 23:5, the Nazarene chastises people who flaunt their religiosity, "by all their works they do to be seen of men. They make broad their phylacteries (tefillin), and enlarge the borders on their garments (fringes)."

First, the Gospels accept the traditional, historic Rabbinic explanation of the commandments as accurate and worthy of fulfilment. The Nazarene did not reject this concept but criticized their **intentions**.

The same applies to phylacteries – the NT simply accepts this physical tradition as applied by the Jews of the time. This assumes and accepts the hundreds of detailed stipulations which are only available through the Oral traditions of Judaism. Just the inscriptions on the parchment, which is contained within the phylacteries in order to be accepted as sacred and acceptable to G-d (kosher), involves hundreds of detailed directives – none of which are specified in the Written Torah (Bible). The same applies to the procurement of the leather used in the manufacture, etc. The Written Torah only gives the instruction to 'lay phylacteries'. The comprehensive and necessary details come from the Oral Torah, throughout Jewish generations right back to Moses.

The word 'phylacteries' comes from the Greek translation that means 'an amulet that protects and brings good fortune'. The original Hebrew word used in the Oral (note, not written) Torah is 'Tefillin', which is the plural form of the word 'tefilah' (prayer). A kind of prayer clothing or boxes. The original written scriptures (Torah) do not answer or define any of the multitudes of questions which arise from the basic statement to: "bind them (the laws) on your foreheads ... place them on your doorposts (the mezuzah)..." etc. These finer details are left for **Oral** interpretation by G-d's mandated Torah interpreters – the spiritual leaders and teachers of Judah (Gen. 49:10). Just the fact that the Gospels accept the Rabbinic understanding of "a sign upon your hand and frontlets between your eyes" proves that the NT Gospels accept Rabbinic Oral Torah.

The Gospels were written by Jews in a Jewish religious environment. It would have been assumed that any Jewish teacher was living a life in harmony with the Rabbis' guidance and the oral tradition. It would be taken for granted, with no need for explanation, that the teacher's general behavior was in conformity with the Oral tradition's requirements. It would be unnecessary to go into the details of all that teacher's actions, for purposes of recording the New Testament. Hence the NT's silence on these issues, which the anti-Jewish influences interpreted and presented as a 'doing away with Torah and law requirements'.

Christian and Messianic interpretation in some groups may hold that the Nazarene, with his statements regarding the length of the fringes on their garments (tzit tzit), actually condemned the wearing thereof. But if we go a step further and deeper into his criticism of the 'length' of the tassels, we will see that he was involved in a famous historic intellectual debate between two schools of legitimate Rabbinic thought and rule about the required length of tassels, i.e. the School of Shammai versus Hillel, which debated a specific variation of 3 vs. 4 threads and their required lengths.

Whose side was the Nazarene on with his criticism of the excessive length of these tassels? Rather than a rejection of the entire tradition, a closer analysis of the Shammai-Hillel dispute will prove that he was in fact siding with Hillel and normative Orthodox position in terms of length and modesty. Shammai would dispute the 'showing off' by claiming that they really try and understand and follow the original intent of the Scriptures. The Gospels, like all religious, *isms* and our own Rabbinic literature, were concerned with the possibility of flaunting religiosity through the ritual "but all their works they do to be seen of men". This was not in the literal sense that everybody was running around showing off their fringes, but as a corrective instruction not to fall into such a trap of exhibitionism. All of our Rabbinical literature preached against religious arrogance and vanity, as Hillel forewarned, "Do not make a worldly use for personal interest or social status of the Crown of the Torah." (*Ethics of our fathers, Mishnah* 1/13; *Talmud Menachot* 41). These values are reflected in all non canonical Jewish liturature.

New Testament's position on Vows

In Mark 7:11 and in Matthew 15:1-9, the Gospels criticize certain members of the Jewish community. What was the problem or activity that drew such censure? It was when a certain fellow vowed everything to the Temple, thereby leaving his parents destitute.

People from time immemorial made vows to their gods and offered sacrifice as a direct result of these vows. The Jewish people, individually and collectively, have always vowed things to their G-d to show their devotion, dedication and thanksgiving. Remember, back in the time of Moses, how the women ran ahead of the men to donate their jewelry for the building of the Tabernacle, the 'Shrine of the Desert' as per Rav Winefsky. In fact, in the 2nd century CE, the famous scholar, Yose ben Yoezer, who was just and kind, actually vowed all his assets to the Temple because he feared his son would do harmful things with the inheritance (Baba bat Basra 133 b). This fellow was the first of the pair of Sages who passed on the Torah from Antigones of Sokho. One of Yose ben Yoezer's famous statements was: "Your home should be open to the scholars. Sit at the dust of their feet and drink their words with thirst."

The Oral Torah recalls another vow where everything was given away. In the Talmud section of Shabbat 122, a follower of Shammai gave everything away, leaving no money to pay an employee. This was frowned upon by the Talmud

There is a remedy for this. The Bible has a process to release people from their vows - Numbers 30. Some of the Shammai School rejected this process of nullifying vows concerning Temple giving. According to the Hillel school, the vowing process may be undone even including vows made to the Temple. Shammai agrees wholeheartedly, that indeed there is a dispensation (remedy) for revoking vows. Nevertheless, in the case of nullifying oaths made to the Temple, the process would not be operative. Shammai takes the Biblical example of the people giving gifts and vows to the Tabernacle in the Wilderness. There was no mention of anyone regretting their generous, spontaneous offers to that Shrine of the Desert. Hence, Shammai concluded that the normative process for releasing one from a vow was incompetent, immaterial and irrelevant, and thus did not apply to Temple vows.

In this context, the meaning of the Gospel now becomes clear, "You reject the Command of G-d (namely the possibility of release from one's vows) and keep your own traditions." This simply corresponds with Shammai's understanding of relevant Biblical directives, that you cannot get released from your Temple vows. However, at this time, the Gospels sided with the School of Hillel, which rejected the Shammai understanding in favor of releasing vows, even if made to the Temple.

The Gospels point out an academic and extremely rare potential problem, namely, the vowing of one's worth to the Temple that would have possible negative results – a problem that was theoretical, at best. The Gospels still, to some degree, would be a reflection of Rabbinic Oral Torah's thinking and practice. The Gospel in this instance merely echoes the lively debate that existed between faithful, loyal Temple-loving good Jews.

The problem that Mark raises in Mark 7:11-13 is one that we have zero historical record for, so we are not sure that it ever existed. The way these lines have been detached from their context makes them come out warped and makes them sound like a vicious anti-Semitic attack on all Jews and Judaism, putting their own traditions ahead of the written Commandments of the Bible. However, when taken within its historical standing, it is really another approach of Jews who love G-d and each other. The lines of Mark, seen in their original frame, will simply show you an insight into the struggle of the individual and his G-d: how much, how fast and how well to express his extreme and overwhelming love of G-d. In his spontaneous ecstatic gesture of vowing to G-d his possessions, does he need to pause and limit it? Does he best inhibit this fiery love with earthly practical considerations? ... The narrowness of the social economic situation he presently is in? His ecstasy is clouding his economic condition, with hopes of G-d showering him with His abundance as a result of his spiritual enthusiasm to donate all his assets. The Gospels merely present one of the attitudes prevalent amongst the religious, good, Temple-tuned-in Jews.

Thus, the criticism should be understood as follows: this case is of an individual, crazy in love with and dedicated to G-d and the Temple, who vows all of his worth to the service of the Temple. So what? - if that is his choice?

The Gospels reflect numerous possible, ascetic expressions of divine service. If you don't give all your possessions away, you cannot be a good follower of the Nazarene. "You must hate your father and mother." (Matt 10:37) "Resist not evil in order to follow Him," - sounds rather extreme, not so? So why can this Jew not serve G-d in the extreme? True Rabbinic Judaism is based solidly on the Bible and prefers the golden mean "moderation, not mediocrity or going to the extreme." Nonetheless, exceptions do exist, e.g. the Nazarite vows of abstinence from wine and haircuts (like Samson, Paul).

The Gospels are addressing here, the very limited question of specific spontaneous generosity. The problem: what if this fellow vows 'all', and his parents are dependent on him? In this fellow's extended family there must be other relatives with the means to support the poor parents? In this solitary exception to the rule, we have a person who vows all, when his parents are just getting by. Their son's generosity to the Temple could very well impinge upon his parents' survival. There are many assumptions being made:

- They were totally dependent on him; without any other relatives to care for them; the son now being as destitute as they were.

- When G-d will decide to reward him for his benevolence to the Temple is anyone's guess.

All this was merely representing the normative, established Judaism of those times. The law on this issue was as Hillel stated, namely, it being wrong to vow everything to the Temple in such a way that the donor may himself become needful of charity to exist.

There are many ways and levels of charity in Judaism, all based squarely on Biblical notions. All authorities agree that a very high form and valuable expression of charity is that which is given to G-d's Temple. The Bible stipulates many tithes that must be given to the Temple. A vow to give more was totally in harmony with numerous verses. For example, even though there is a command to go up to the Temple on the pilgrimage festivals, there was no set limit on it. Or the elevation offering (*olah Reeya*) no specific maximum amount was fixed for it.

Leviticus 8:11 mentions three classes of flexible offerings: the peace, thanksgiving and free-will offerings (Psalms 103:1-5). We have a whole sacrificial system; the hallmark of several sacrifices was their voluntary dimension. Thus, vowing of charity, property and livestock to the Temple was an honourable tradition. But we have very few examples, if any, of people vowing everything they have in their lifetime.

The Talmud applauds charity (over and above tithing). Jacob vowed 10% of his profits to charity (Gen. 28:22). From Jacob's vow we understand that the minimum that must be given of one's profits is ten percent, for the Hebrew, 'tithe' means ten percent. Generous giving is considered twenty percent and above. If one is rich, he/she may give much more. The only stipulation is that one does not give so much as to endanger oneself and so become dependent on charity.

In the Hebrew society of a standing operative Temple service, it is highly unlikely that the over-vowing zealot would be left to starve. On the contrary, in a Jewish society, everyone would be Biblically obligated to assist the extravagant giver and his parents. Free loan societies have been a documented feature of every Jewish community.

Hasty or shallow interpretation of this remark in the book of Mark has provided anti-Jewish opinion-makers with tools to berate the world's documented most charitable people, without rival. That leaves Judaism with the age old cliché, "You're damned if you do, and damned if you don't." Thus, either "those Jews don't give enough," or "they kill their parents financially." The use of this text is a cynical inversion of the love, generosity and Biblically valid vows to the Temple. In reality, Mark was just expressing harmony with normative, Orthodox, Hillel Judaism in contradistinction to Shammai's perfectionism and strictness. The way that Mark's comments were misrepresented and misunderstood, was that this Jew was attempting to comply with the law at the expense of his financial obligation to his parents.

Divorce – incompatibility vs. adultery in the New Testament

According to Matthew Ch. 19, a man may not divorce his wife unless he has found something unseemly in her. Where did this idea come from? It was born out of the orthodox Torah studies on this topic that predated the Gospels by many, many years. Shammai rules that the word in question implies unchaste, lacking in chastity. Apparently, the Gospels now side with the ancient school of Shammai, since in Matthew 5:32 and 19:9 the Nazarene said, "Whosoever shall put away his wife saving for the case of fornication, makes her commit adultery, and whoever marries her, then commits adultery." Here again, the Gospels agree with Shammai when it comes to rules of evidence. Shammai held that a woman cannot remarry without rigorous evidence of the death of her first husband. Hillel was more lenient with these rules of evidence.

In addition, when Hillel looked at the verse in Deut. 24, he did not understand it to mean unchaste, but rather something that was obnoxious in her. As Hillel said, "he may divorce her, even if she spoils a dish for him." Rabbi Akiva emphasizes another phrase in the very same verse, "and she does not find favour in his eyes." This implies that incompatibility is a basis for divorce.

Matt 19:3 criticizes divorce "for every (any) cause", and the Greek translation of the Hebrew verse is 'pornia' (fornication, i.e. adultery). So, the debate was not against good guys and bad guys, nor against conservatives and liberals, but merely how to relate to a verse in G-d's Word and how to interface a legal contingency in real time. Each view merely emphasizes a different part of the verse. The Gospels simply disregarded the segment that read, "She finds no favour in his eyes."

What Hillel and Akiva were saying is that a man's love should be so strong towards his wife that he would find a tasty side to whatever she cooks, and no other woman would be better-looking than she in his subjective eyes. They were setting up a standard that people should strive in their marriage relationship for mutual compatibility, appreciation, passion and love. That should be the hallmark of their relationship. If a couple senses a shortcoming in this respect, it sounds an alarm that the marriage is in trouble, and then immediate steps should be taken to rectify it and rescue the marriage. It seems that the red flag of warning is only raised, and perhaps not raised at all, in Shammai's point of view, until an act of unchastity or immorality has already transpired. If you remember, the students of the Nazarene (Matt 19:10) were upset with the Gospel's ruling along the lines of Shammai. Why? Because the Gospels usually were interpreted according to the positioning and reasoning of Hillel. This entire debate reflects a Jewish in-house, Oral Torah debate.

Sabbath restrictions and allowances in the New Testament

If you read through the entire Sermon on the Mount, you will find that the Gospels did not advocate disobedience to the Jewish law, but in fact confirmed the Rabbinic Oral interpretation of what is often derogatorily referred to as 'the Rabbinic man-made Oral laws.'

Thus, the Nazarene's statements waxed symbolic and philosophical in total agreement with the Oral Torah, e.g. adultery is symbolically committed by simply lusting sexually; murder by simply embarrassing someone. These statements by the Nazarene are virtual quotes from earlier Talmudic discussions.

When the Nazarene was accused of violating the Sabbath, Mark 12:23-27, we read:

> 23 "One Sabbath the Nazarene was going through the grain fields, and as his disciples walked along, they began to pick some heads of grain. 24 The Pharisees said to him, 'Look, why are they doing what is unlawful on the Sabbath?' 25 He answered, 'Have you never read what David did when he and his companions were hungry and in need? 26 In the days of Abiathar the high priest, he entered the house of G-d and ate the consecrated bread, which is lawful only for priests to eat. And he also gave some to his companions.' 27 Then he said to them, 'The Sabbath was made for man, not man for the Sabbath.'"

Christian interpretation joins the Pharisees in accusing the Nazarene and his followers as rejecters of the 'Jewish Sabbath,' or, at best, that he relaxed 'the strict letter of the Law' regarding Sabbath observance. The Nazarene's defensive and corrective response to the accusation of the Pharisees was not a quotation from the Torah or from the Word of G-d, but a direct quotation from the Talmud, which states, "Man was not given to the Sabbath, but the Sabbath was given to man." (*Talmud - Mekilta* 103b, Yoma 85b). The Pharisee School of Hillel was famous for that quote.

The Nazarene did not say that one no longer must keep the Sabbath; he did not propose to relax the Sabbath law as Christians would like to believe. He did not challenge them on the grounds that they were expecting. Instead, by quoting a Talmudic principle, he confirmed that his behaviour was consistent with Rabbinic law interpretation. The famous Talmudic dictum that underlies this statement validates that the possibility of saving of a life pushes aside the Sabbath prohibitions, e.g., not reaping from your fields. In this incident under discussion, his disciples were hungry (as confirmed in Matthew 12:1). To eat raw grain indicates that they must have been truly ravishingly hungry, as was David, who entered the sacred Tabernacle and ate consecrated food.

Even in ultra-Orthodox Jewish hospitals, doctors perform operations on the Sabbath. The saving of life pushes aside the prohibitions of Sabbath. Righteous kings in Israel continued to war on a Sabbath. In 1973, when Israel was attacked on its most sacred holy day, Yom Kippur, the Israeli army was mobilized by calling soldiers out of the synagogues. All of oral tradition confirms these actions.

The proof in this NT-related incident is in the text: his accusers were silent at his response; they understood and accepted his response, namely that his students were extremely hungry and thus within the parameters of Rabbinic Judaism, allowing them to pick the corn on the Sabbath because of the emergency situation.

Another accusation that could be raised against them is that of invading private property and stealing off the lands. The legal response to this comes straight from Biblical and Rabbinic inter-pretation, namely, that in the 7th Sabbatical year anyone is allowed to freely take of the left-over produce on the fields (Exodus 28:10; Lev. 25; Nehemiah 10:32). Furthermore, the Torah makes allow-ance for the poor to take from the corners of the fields and left-overs after reaping. (*Mishnah Seder Zeraim, Tractate Peah*).

Another example would be performing a circumcision on the eighth day even if it falls on a Sabbath. Under norma-tive conditions, certain acts employed in the circumcision would be forbidden on the Sabbath. The power of the positive commandment "thou shalt circumcise on the eighth day", pushes aside the negative commandment, "Thou shalt not ... break the Sabbath", thus allowing its performance on the Sabbath.

We have another Talmudic principle: "if needed, it is better to break one Sabbath in order that you may keep many Sabbaths." The Oral Torah perspective is clear: the Sabbath is subservient to the needs of the Hebrew people; the Jewish people are not subservient to some absolute standard of the Sabbath. In the Temple on Shabbat, certain physically creative acts of work were permitted regarding the sacrificial services, whereas outside the Temple, they would be absolutely forbidden. There are no detailed written Torah directives to rule in these situations. This statement may draw a reprimand from the anti-Rabbinists, "See – they make their own laws in contravention of the Written Law and its spirit." These critics need to be reminded that the Nazarene, by pointing this Oral Talmudic ruling out to the Pharisees, was in fact upholding the Oral Torah and basing his own actions on its prescriptions.

G-d searched His treasure house, and came up with the gift of the Sabbath. The Sabbath was not given to the Jews to be burdened by it, but as a special spiritual gift – as "A Sign between Me and My People".

The NT regarding swearing by His NAME

Deut. 6:13, "You are to fear HaShem your G-d, serve Him and swear by His Name." (Also Deut. 10:20). Then we also have the following prohibition: Lev. 19:12, "Do NOT swear by My Name falsely, which would be profaning the Name of your G-d."

Thus, not the use of the Name, but the swearing falsely is what profanes it. We have a practical example in Scripture in Joshua 9:1-20 of Joshua taking such an oath (verse 19) and refusing to break it for fear of the G-d's anger falling on them.

Some other examples of Scripture are:

G-d personally expresses His Will that other nations should learn from Judah and "swear by His Name" (Jer. 12:14 -16).

Avraham made his servant swear "by HaShem, G-d of Heaven" (Gen. 24:3).

The angel swore by "Him that liveth forever" (Daniel 12:7).

Christians maintain that the Nazarene contradicted this notion by saying that we should not swear an oath at all.

Matthew 5: 33, "Again, you have heard that it was said to the people long ago, 'Do not break your oath, but keep the oaths you have made to HaShem.' 34. But I tell you, 'Do not swear at all: either by heaven, for it is G-d's throne; or by the earth, for it is His footstool; or by Jerusalem, for it is the city of the Great King. 36. And do not swear by your head, for you cannot make even one hair white or black. 37.

> Simply let your 'Yes' be 'Yes,' and your 'No,' 'No';
> anything beyond this comes from the evil one."

The Nazarene though, was not changing Torah. He was simply standing behind the Oral traditions that were also based on Biblical verses. For example, Leviticus 24:10-23 takes a very serious stand on the penalty of death for desecrating G-d's Name. The Talmudic Sages had long discussions about this Mitzvah and determined that we *could* swear by HaShem's Name, but in so doing we might swear falsely, and then we would have misused the Name. Then, we would have broken two Commands - one of which demanded a possible death penalty.

To prevent us from falling to this much greater violation of Torah, it was decided that we should not swear at all using His Name - even though the Torah had given us permission to do so. The level of reverence for all things holy had dropped severely because of the assimilative effects of Greco Roman Hellenization. The Sadducees were an example of this lack of reverence They simply upheld the Rabbinical ruling that served as a protective degree, as a hedge of roses. The Jewish Sages also forbade the taking of oaths in HaShem's Name, lest the entire world be brought to destruction by the sinners who swear falsely. (*Hilchot Shavuot* 11:13).

The Torah calls on us to protect and guard G-d's Name. The Jewish Sages had an obligation to make protective decrees, a hedge to insure that people do not trample on Biblical prohibitions; to help keep them far away from sin. Here however, is a case of applying the original intention of Scripture to protect the Divine Name.

Many times the Bible calls upon us to avoid any desecration of the Divine Name on the one hand and the need for super sanctity on the other hand, when approaching the Name, which is so unusually holy.

In Exodus 3:15 G-d said to Moses, "So shall you say to the Children of Israel. 'HaShem, the G-d of your forefathers, the G-d of Avraham, the G-d of Isaac, the G-d of Jacob, has dispatched me to you…. this is My Name forever (*L'Olam*) and this is My Memorial unto all generations.'"

By the way here the Torah says specifically that G-d is called "I will Be ". In addition, around 300 times the Torah uses *Adonai* as the Name of choice, which means: 'Sir, Master or Lord', Remember the Hebrew text makes a BIG distinction between the Name to be hidden and His Name as a memorial; as a symbol - a remembrance. The Written Torah makes this point. The way it may be written should not be the way it is generally mentioned, but rather a 'memorial remembrance Name', i.e. *Adonai* which must be used instead.

Since the Hebrew word for 'forever' - *L'Olam* - is spelled here without the customary and important 'vav' (which defines the 'O' sound). This sets off alarm bells and flashing lights. The word, as written here, is missing a crucial vowel (the vav). This obviously means that there is a deeper meaning without the vav. The word in question now needs to be pronounced '*L'Alem*', meaning to conceal. You see, the literal text, the simple meaning of the Scripture and the way you would have read the text without an Oral tradition, is *L'Alem*, meaning to conceal. In absence of the Oral tradition, one would thus have had to read it: 'to conceal His Name', implying that the Divine Name should not be pronounced as it is spelled out. Oral Torah says it should here be read with the 'vav' to teach the additional message of saying how indeed it needs to be said.

Christian translators, e.g. St. Jerome and others would have had to translate this text as 'to conceal His real name', not pronounce it as it is written, if they truly just followed the Hebrew written text. It is ironic that people rejecting the Oral tradition have accepted at face value the replacement translation of 'forever' for the word "L'Alem" rather than 'to conceal'. In this, the translators thus chose to follow the Rabbinic Oral tradition!

There is something to be realized and appreciated by today's Hebraic Restorers who discover all these original Bible truths which had been guarded throughout the ages by Judaism. Accordingly, they should realize and admit, that the Sacred Name has been concealed according to Divine ruling and admonition and not, as the accusation from these Restorers often go, that "the Rabbis have changed the Written Word of G-d and hidden the pronunciation of the Sacred Name, thereby causing it to go 'lost'." The Rabbis have simply acted according to their divine mandate to take care of His Oracles (even from the NT perspective in Romans 3:1, 2) and to conceal His Name as a protective measure. Again, the facts on the ground were that criminals and scroffers were on the increase. None of them would hesitate to use a Name for HaShem if it would get him off easy from a suspected felony.

As the Talmud says, recalling ancient Oral Torah (*Eruvin* 13a, also *Mishnah Torah, Book of Love, Laws of Torah Scrolls* 10) warning a Rabbi Scribe, "Be very careful in your work, for it is the work of heaven. One mistake (i.e. omission or subtraction of a word or letter) and you can ruin the world."

This concealing is also the motivation for Judaism's great respect for His Name. For instance if a prayer book is dropped by a Jew by accident, the book is to be kissed – because G-d's Name appears all over in that prayer book and has thus been desecrated. If a Torah Scroll is accidentally dropped in synagogue, the entire congregation has to fast for 40 days and charity, good deeds, and Torah learning have to be increased. The reason why these things are done is out of respect for the Sacred Names of G-d.

The word 'name' in Hebrew ('*shem*'), also means, 'noun' or 'word' in general. This is a further indication that G-d has given Himself to us in every word of the Torah (as explained by Rav Ginsberg, Shlita).

We already pointed out that the 4-letter Name of G-d is written 1820 times in the five books of Moses. 1820 = 70 times 26, 26 is the simple numerical value of the Hebrew letters for his Name. 70 is the value for the Hebrew word 'secret' i.e. hidden and foundation. A foundation is usually hidden and not easily accessible. Amazing, the numerical amount of times that the Name appears, equals 70 times its numerical value, which means hidden or secret. The issue about the unpronounceable Name now all makes much more sense.

Do you know that the Sacred Name appears 725 times in the book of Jeremiah? That is more than in any other prophetic book. The 29th chapter has it written the most times – 18 times, which is the numerical value of the word *chai*, meaning 'life' in Hebrew.

The Command of Torah regarding 'swearing by His Name', should be understood in its correct context, just as the

Nazarene's directives in this connection should be understood in its correct context. Matthew 15 confirms that he, far from annulling the Torah (as modern churches and even most Messianics claim), actually confirmed Torah and even emphasized its implication, e.g. murder entails even being angry with someone (verse 21); and adultery is even looking with lust (verse 28). This likewise, is in line with Rabbinic thinking. We have the Law, and then we have Biblical directives going beyond the letter of the Law to deal with even more abstract ethical, righteous and moral implications of the Law. The Gospels are therefore totally in line with the Pharisaical approach of looking at both the internal and external ramifications of the divine imperatives.

If we apply this same emphasis to the issue of taking an oath, then the Nazarene's directive here is that we should not need to 'swear by His Name', but simply let our 'yes' be yes. This is in harmony with normative Orthodox Judaism as interpreted by the Rabbis. There are numerous actual accounts of righteous Orthodox Jews who, in legal proceedings, preferred to be found guilty, face conviction and public humiliation, rather than swear by His Name (their innocence was later proven anyway). So the Nazarene's position here was totally in line with normative Judaism and Rabbinic Oral Torah interpretation.

Rev. Prof. David Biven has pointed out that the Gospels often use euphemisms for G-d: e.g. a common word for G-d was 'Heaven'. Throughout Matthew the Kingdom of Heaven is used for his group of disciples. In Mark and Luke, the phrase 'Kingdom of G-d' is used, probably, because the Greek readers would not have understood the euphemism for 'G-d'. G-d is called "the Name" (HaShem), the Place, the High, the Tongue,

Heaven and more. He is referred to in many ways e.g. Judge, Reviver, Healer, Divine Presence, which in no way implies that there are many gods.

In summary, all of the words of the Torah combine to become one Name of G-d. First, they are seen to fall into four distinct categories, corresponding to the four letters of the Sacred Name Yud – Hey –Vav - Hey, which join together to become one. Finally, they combine as one long word composed of hundreds of thousands of letters (without spaces between the words, unlike the way they presently appear in the Torah), one essential Name of G-d, with no relation to the individual words at all. This final revelation is the "new Torah" that the Messiah will reveal to the world, the revelation that "G-d is all and all is G-d." (HaRav Itzchak Ginsberg).

The conclusion of all this, is that the Written Word is a lot deeper than any translation or superficial interpretation could ever indicate. It requires a Hebrew mindset, using ancient analytical tools of transmission – the Keys that unlock G-d's Wisdom, in order to draw the correct conclusions. Proper analysis of the NT shows that it was basically in harmony with this traditional Jewish mindset and interpretation.

Love your enemy as yourself

'Love your enemies' is considered the apogee of the Sermon on the Mount. This concept is heralded as an example of the new faith of Christianity's superiority over 'old' Judaism. In fact, when understood within the correct philosophical categories, this line fits in comfortably with Pharisaic Orthodox Judaism. First, in Lev. 19:18 we read: "You shall love your neighbor as yourself," and in Proverbs 25:21 it says: "If your enemy is hungry, give him bread to eat and if he is thirsty, give him water to drink." The Talmud proclaims: "Who is strong? – he who can make an enemy into a friend."

A heathen once came to Hillel and asked to be converted, but only on condition that Hillel could sum up the whole Torah while standing on one leg. To which Hillel responded: "What is hateful to you, do not do to your fellow man. This is the entire Torah. The rest is commentary. Go and study."

Again, we mention Rabbi Akiva who insisted that loving your **neighbor** as yourself is the main principle of the Torah. For as Ben Azzi comments: "The main principle is found in the book of Genesis: 'This is the book of the generations of Adam'", thus stressing our common ancestry.

Some religions go from simplicity to complexity. Everything in Judaism goes from complexity to simplicity, when dealing on adult intellectual scholarly learning levels, as opposed to children's learning levels. 'Love your enemies' is indeed a correct conclusion, but only after one has gone through several stages of intellectual scholarly contemplation. This also applies to all other conclusions of Truth.

In brief, this process would go as follows: "Indeed, we are to hate evil. But as for the evildoer, specifically our fellow Jew and/ or spiritual brother, one would contemplate upon this fellow's divinely given pure soul. Several channels of intellectual analysis open up. We realize that this sinner's soul is comparable to the daughter of the king bound in chains, captured and sitting alone in a dark dungeon. In other words, that fellow's pure soul has been taken over, as a result of a series of wrong choices, by his evil inclination. It is as if his pure soul, the daughter of the king, has been captured by the serpent's skin, meaning the forces of the 'evil inclination', egotism, and heathenism. All of those present obstacles to service of HaShem.

Now, after you've had this insight into the spiritual and metaphysical situation of the sinner, a strange thing starts to occur. From your cold, intellectual, analytical examination of this enemy, an emotive response starts to emerge before you. You now begin to feel a sense of mercy and compassion over the plight of this poor pure soul because of the bad choices of that individual - and the sense of mercy and compassion grows within you, fanned by the intellectual understanding of the plight of the soul: alone and tortured in the dungeon created by the wrong exercise of the freedom of choice. Now this flaming feeling of pity, compassion and mercy grows and turns into love for that respective enemy. But it is a love that came from complexity to simplicity. It is not a compromise with evil, nor is it surrender to your enemy. By merely understanding the nature of this cosmic war between good and bad, and a human role and trauma, pity was aroused over the poor soul, which turned to love. But it is, indeed, a highly qualified love.

Thus the Gospels' statement of 'love your enemies' is far from being superior to Pharisaic Judaism, as well as not being a naive and unrealistic request to make of real human beings. It can be seen as a result of deep, structured, Orthodox Pharisaic philosophy (32nd chapter of The Tanya).

Also in this context, the word 'enemy' does not mean Amalek or Hitler, Arafat or Ahmadinejad. In the context of the Hebrew mind, and the lecture being given to an audience of Jewish people, the word 'enemy' would be synonymous with your fellow Jew with whom you are at your wits' end. And that is precisely the message of the book of Proverbs: feed your enemy. And in the book of Leviticus, this includes even your enemy's animal. This is not about the Philistine that is attacking you, nor the Egyptian warrior on horseback who has stumbled on his way to plunder the fleeing Hebrews. These many laws contained in the Oral Torah concerning your enemy, refer to your pain-in-the-neck neighboring Jewish or brotherly enemy. Lev. 19:17: "You shall not hate your brother in your heart, but should surely rebuke him." Rebuke means to lovingly reach out, touch and teach him and guide him back to the proper path. You should not avenge or bare a grudge against one of your own people.

We have the famous command of loving your neighbor as yourself. Torah Law forbids taking vengeance or holding a grudge against one of your own. It is absolutely clear here that we are talking about a co-religionist, or at least someone within the greater community.

Within Orthodox Judaism, there has always been tension between the universal and sectarian aspects of the faith. In fact, the Commandments, in general, vary between these two dimensions like a pendulum. For example, at the festive meal on Shabbat, the first part of the service starts out with a universal declaration that 'He is the G-d of Avraham, Isaac and Jacob!' G-d is not Aristotle's 'Unmoved Mover', who created a world and walked away, but a G-d who relates to a specific, particular people within the fabric of history.

The second half of the sanctification service speaks of G-d taking the Israelites out of Egypt. Rabbi Dr. Shlomo Riskin who teaches the above, never tires of saying that it is through recognizing the fatherhood or "creator-hood" of G-d, we will come to recognize the brotherhood of humankind.

Shammai and Hillel reflected this dilemma in coming to terms with the nitty-gritty of Jewish-Gentile relationships. Shammai took a more rigorous and protective approach and favored law and customs that would seek to stop assimilation and acculturation, whereas Hillel, while sharing Shammai's concerns over heathen assimilation, generally presented a more open attitude. His was a less-fearing and a more-encompassing attitude of interaction with the Gentile, who also could be a future righteous convert.

The Gospels likewise reflect these trends in openness or closedness as regarding the Gentiles who lived within the greater Jewish community. An appreciation of this division will also bring a better understanding of the background underlying the NT recorded statements of the Nazarene to the Samaritan woman in John 4, and his reference to 'dogs' in Matthew 15, when talking with a Canaanite woman. These comments are normally contorted by NT interpreters to indicate Jewish exclusiveness. What sounds to the non-Jewish outsider as an almost racist remark should be understood as concern for Jewish survival. In its correct historic and Jewish Halachic contexts this understanding serves to further confirm the Halachic influence of the New Testament.

The Gospel literature presenting the writings of a Jewish Messianic sect contains that same cultural Hebrew mindset: the community at large. Hence, 'love your enemies' sounds far less radical and much more sane and culturally acceptable with this new information presented above, rather than endeavoring to buy peace from your international enemies by kindness and giving in to their irrational demands.

Yud or Tittle

> Matthew 5:17: "Think not that I have come to abolish the Law and the Prophets. I have come not to abolish but to fulfill them."

Christian theology generally interprets this as meaning that, "because he fulfilled the Law, therefore the Law has been done away with". This conclusion is formed despite the fact that a double statement of non-abolishment of the Law precedes the statement of 'fulfillment'.

In Hebrew, the word 'fulfill' (Greek: *plerosai,* as used in the Gospels) does **not** mean: "… now you have complied with the Law, you don't have to do it any further." It means that you complied with and satisfied the legal requirements of Torah for that specific requirement, at that specific time, in that specific circumstance and that you are entitled to the eternal reward associated with that Commandment. That means you bring down G-dly light into this lower world, thereby elevating it to a higher plane. It means you did an act or had a thought that allows you to participate with the covenantal faith community's destiny. It does not mean that you are exempted from fulfilling that commandment again - such as observing the Passover Commandments, the Festivals, Tithing, agricultural laws, civil, criminal, etc. The very sentence in that Gospel statement says that the Commandments are NOT to be abolished or destroyed.

So whatever interpretation you want to give for the word 'fulfill', it cannot have as its bottom line the nullification of those said laws. Many times in the Gospel text it speaks about preserving, protecting, sustaining and living up to the righteousness of the law-abiding community (Matthew 23:3).

Further proof is in the very next sentence, where the Gospels say: "Not a dot or a tittle will ever pass away." This refers to the 'yud' which is the smallest letter in the Hebrew alphabet. It looks like the shape of a single inverted comma. (Prof. David Biven). Do you know what the 'tittle' represents? Well, first of all, in Greek it was called the 'keraia' meaning 'horn', based on the Hebrew '*kots*', meaning 'thorn'. It was translated into English as 'tittle'. In brief, it was a decorative barb or spur (*Ittur Sofrim*) added to various letters in the original Torah scrolls by the traditions received through the generations of Rabbinic Sages. These little decorative attachments were laden with secret, mystical, and legal vitality or meaning. For example, Rabbi Akiva drew out nuances of the Law from these signs on the holy letters of the Torah. This entire department as well as the shapes and sizes of the regular letters in the written texts, are under the exclusive authority of the Sages of the Oral tradition.

This is an amazing confirmation of the Nazarene's qualifications. Anyone using this insight would necessarily have in-depth knowledge and recognition of Oral Torah and tradition. Here we have an example par excellence, a confirmation of faith by the Gospels in the authority of the Oral Torah's transmission of the true form of the Written Torah.

Fulfilling the Law

The Nazarene claims in:

Matthew 5:20, "For I say unto you, that unless your righteousness exceeds the righteousness of the Pharisees,
you shall in no way enter the Kingdom of Heaven."

The sentence did **not** say the Pharisees **won't "get to heaven"**,
but rather, in the tradition of the Mishnah, (a moralistic style
presenting high goals), the Nazarene asks from his students
that they strive for **even higher righteousness than that of
the Pharisees.**

This is in step with many Jewish teachers who hope and pray that
their students will be shining examples for the rest of the righteous
Scribes and Pharisees, just as parents demand a higher standard
from their children than from other people in the play yard. G-d
says that He judges His beloved righteous ones strictly, down to
a hair's breadth. And He chastises those whom He loves.

The Nazarene simply stresses and demands more from His
followers, as any coach would expect more from his star ath-
letes. He thus confirms that the Scribes and Pharisees are
indeed righteous. He reminds his followers in Matthew 23:2-
3, that the Scribes and the Pharisees sit in Moses' seat (as the
Lawgivers – ref. ch. 16) and admonishes them to "listen and do
what they tell you".

It is incorrect to think that the directives set by the Nazarene in
his Sermon on the Mount (Matthew 5:20-48), are giving a newer
and higher righteousness than what was previously required.
He is merely using a Hebraic method of teaching, which keeps

the student interested and contrasts different important ideals. "Ye have heard that it was said to them of old: 'You shall not murder', but I say unto you, anyone who is angry with his brother shall be in danger …" (verse 20-22). According to Prof. Freedlander, the Nazarene as a teacher of inwardness, wanted to show that the true fulfilment of the Law implied an enlarged interpretation of leading moral enactments. (Montefiore, *The Synoptic Gospels* and *Benjamin Jowett lectures*).

This was the work of the Scribes, Pharisees and Sages who, although they were not called by Montefiore "prophetic teachers of inwardness", would agree with the sentiments of the Gospel's interpretation of the 6th Commandment. The Rabbinic Jew has nothing new to learn from the sermon but would agree with it.

The Gospels, in imitation of the Rabbis, made 'a fence' to protect the essential Law, viz. they broadened the stipulations of the Law in order to protect the outer parameters between breaking and observing the Law, even before actual transgression occurred, e.g. controlling your anger will keep you from murdering someone. The Torah says in many places you should protect and guard the Torah. Thus, you need to make protective decrees, erect fences around the Biblical prohibition, to keep people from violating the Biblical injunction. As Rabbi N. Lamb, president of the Yeshiva University says, "we are making a hedge of roses to protect the Torah injunctions."

Observance of Chanukah

It is the Nazarene's observance of the Jewish festival of Chanukah which presents probably the strongest confirmation of his sanctioning of Jewish Oral Torah. Nowhere in the Written Torah is Chanukah referred to as a mandated observance. It is a purely Rabbinical enactment. Yet, the NT relates the Nazarene's observance of this festival as a major metaphoric indicator of his purported mission.

The Jewish Chanukah feast is often hidden in various versions of the NT under its alternative titles as the Festival of Lights, the Feast of Dedication, or the Feast of Maccabees.

A search of the Tanach for the term *Chanukah* (Hanukah, Festival of Lights, Feast of Dedication), the popular Jewish Rabbinical mandated festival which often coincides with Christian Xmas!) will yield no results at all! The Tanach has scant Biblical references for the observance of Chanukah. Yet, the NT, the followers of which reject Rabbinic 'man-made' rules and festivals, has the most explicit reference to it! It is a profound fact that the observance of Chanukah appears only in three sources, viz. the NT, the book of Maccabees and the Talmud!

Many Jewish scholars see a deeper spiritual meaning to Hanukkah, as the editors of the popular Jewish *Artscroll Mesorah Series* states: "Then, the light is kindled to give inspiration, for the light of Messiah must burn brightly in our hearts." (*Chanukah*, Mesorah Publications, Brooklyn, 1981, p. 104). Hanukkah is a celebration of deliverance, of re-dedication of the Temple, of a Return to Torah. Thus, it has become a time to express Messianic hope, just as the Maccabees were used by G-d to redeem Israel,

This underscores the Nazarene's celebration of the feast 2000 years ago and his subsequent statements to the enquiring Jews (after his true identity) as presented by the NT in John 10:22 onwards. His answer to this very appropriate question is contained in the Nazarene's Hanukkah message as recorded in this chapter. He uses this occasion to metaphorically reiterate his claims to Messiahship (John 10:25–39).

This is a firm recognition by the Nazarene of the Rabbinic authority to institute times, dates and festivals.

CHAPTER 7

Hidden Message in the Gospels about "The Kingdom"

Undoubtedly, the greatest confirmation of the Jewish Halachic foundations which underlie the NT must be found in its Message regarding the Restoration of the Kingdom of G-d. Commonly well-known and accepted topic in Judaism, this is also the most hidden Message of the NT, notwithstanding the fact that it is the Main Theme of the entire Bible and of the Purpose of G-d for mankind, viz. the 'Good News of the Kingdom'. As such, it also is the very reason for the timely publication of this book.

Though the true Restoration Message of the Kingdom of Israel has laid hidden and undiscovered for Christians in the NT right until this Time, it seems that the Roman Church was well informed of the matter. Consider what Pope Benedict XVI stated about this great insight into the Hidden mysteries of the NT. The Pope wrote regarding The Eucharist and Eschatology – and for those who are not conversant with these Church terms, let us provide the definitions first:

> *Eucharist - the Christian ceremony in which people eat bread and drink wine as a way of remembering Jesus*

*Christ's last meal at The Last Supper, before his cru-
cifixion. In some Christian churches, this ceremony is
called Communion or Holy Communion.*

*Eschatology - the body of religious doctrines concern-
ing the human soul in its relation to death, judgment,
heaven, and hell*

"31. Reflecting on this mystery [of the Eucharist], we
can say that Jesus' coming responded to an expecta-
tion present in the people of Israel, in the whole of
humanity and ultimately in creation itself. By his
self-gift, he objectively inaugurated the eschatological age. Christ came *to gather together the scattered
People of God* (cf. Jn 11:52) and clearly manifested
his intention *to gather together the community of
the covenant,* in order to bring to fulfillment the
promises made by G-d to the fathers of old (cf. Jer.
23:3; Luke 1:55, 70). In the calling of the Twelve
{Apostles}, which is to be understood *in relation to
the twelve tribes of Israel,* and in the command he
gave them at the Last Supper, before his redemptive
passion, to celebrate his memorial, Jesus showed
that he wished to transfer to the entire community
which he had founded the task of being, within history, the sign and instrument of the eschatological
gathering that had its origin in him. Consequently,
every Eucharistic celebration sacramentally accomplishes the eschatological *gathering of the People of
G-d.* For us, the Eucharistic banquet is a real fore-
taste of the final banquet foretold by the prophets
(cf. Isa. 25:6-9) and described in the New Testament
as "the marriage-feast of the Lamb" (Rev 19:7-9),

to be celebrated in the joy of the communion of saints (100). (*Post-Synodal Apostolic Exhortation, Sacrament of Charity*, 30-31)."

We have tried to show through the use of italics in this statement, that the Church has been well aware of the 'hidden' Promise of the Ingathering of the Tribes of Israel. Whether they deliberately hid this message from the masses, or whether it was due to their own lack of insight – fact is, that it took all these centuries (2000 years) for the Ten Tribes exiled within Christianity, to wake up to their Hebraic Roots. The evidence of this spiritual transformation, which forms the Main Theme of Biblical Prophecy, i.e. the re-identification and return of the Lost Ten Tribes of Israel to their Hebrew Roots and even to the physical Land of Israel, abounds across the entire earth today. Millions of sincere and seriously searching non-Jewish Bible students are reverting to what they regard as their "Hebraic Roots" and in the process 'coming out' of the Churches.

As emphasised in our overview of the phenomenon of the Hebraic Restoration Movement across the world, a publication like this would not have been called for without the real prevalence of such a Movement.

This Restoration Movement is the very foundation of the Kingdom Message:

- Without a physical Return of the Lost House of 10-Israel, there can be no Kingdom.

- Without a spiritual Return (by repentance) to the original Hebraic Roots and Torah principles of this re-identifying House, there can be no physical Return.

We will now investigate why it is such a hidden topic for NT students and readers and what the NT records reveal about the approach of the Nazarene towards this well documented Jewish Halachic topic.

The Nazarene's revelations about the Kingdom to Come.

It is significant that all four Gospels disagree about what was written above the Nazarene on his cross. Yet, all four recorded the phrase 'King of the Jews', thus identifying his Jewishness. In Revelations 15:3, he is called 'King of the nations.' Despite the numerous variances in the resurrection accounts in the Gospels, we find that when the disciples met him, their first question was, "Master, will you restore again at this time, the Kingdom to Israel?" (Acts 1:6).

As the Hebraic Restoration movement today becomes more and more aware of the longstanding belief of Judaism in the return of the Lost Ten Tribes of Israel and their reconciliation with Judah into one nation (Ezekiel 37:18 etc.), they also start realizing the deeper meaning of Gospel texts like these. They are beginning to understand that the 'Messianic Kingdom' refers to a re-united 12-Tribed Kingdom of Israel which has to be restored according to the main theme of the Jewish Bible (derogatorily claimed to be the 'Old' Testament by Christianity). Thus, this question posed to the Nazarene was the focal point of their clear understanding of the prophecies - the ingathering and reuniting with Judah of the Ten Lost Tribes who were exiled among the nations.

As a youngster, who was pushed by non-Jewish friends to read the NT, I automatically understood the gist of the writings about the prophesied Redemption. In other words, even as a kid, to my Jewish mind, the Good News of the NT meant the overthrow of Rome and the reunification of the Kingdom of real Israel. Not hocus pocus, up in the air, pie in the sky, spiritual stuff. That's why Jews of the time were disappointed and surprised that an immediate restoration of the Jewish Kingdom did not occur.

Restoration of the Fallen Tabernacle of David

Before we embark on a review of this revealing phrase, it is important that the non-Jewish reader becomes aware of the awe and love that Jews hold for the historic King David. This awe compares with that which the Messianic believer holds for the Nazarene – and perhaps even for Paul.

> Amos 9:11. "May the compassionate One reestablish for David his fallen *Succah* (Tabernacle, booth)."

Allow me to share the following song of my own heart in the spirit of the above text:

> "This verse is a heartfelt prayer and a song to always be with David and never to be apart. King David lives and exists for us in our every part. He is thought of, spoken of, sung about and very much a part of everything we do and everywhere we go. We dream of his re-established Kingdom and the defeat of the foe. King David, King David lives and exists!"

> "He prepared the construction materials, the plans, the musical instruments, wood, stone, fabric and

gold. For HaShem's House that he was prevented from building; the work fell upon his wise son. King David removed the shame being dumped on our G-d and nation; when he removed Goliath's head and defeated the Philistine time after time. Oh, King David lives and exists for us in so many ways!"

"He is a source of inspiration that pushes and pulls us onwards and upwards!"

"He helps us through his life and Psalms to try to fulfill the Commands of HaShem, that we may say:

'Every day and in every way, we're getting better and better'".

"He is the Rebbe and teacher for all repentant sinners. He is our guide in the day of battle and shows us a light in the night, his words both comfort and inspire. They are a delight."

King David is synonymous with the Kingdom of G-d. With the Kingdom of Israel having split 2800 years ago, and the resultant exile of the nation (both Houses), the 'Tabernacle of David' had fallen, tumbled, was demolished. The Hope of Judah is in a Restored future Kingdom.

Amos 9:11, "In that day will I raise up the Tabernacle of David that is fallen, and close up the breaches thereof; and I will raise up his ruins, and I will build it as in the days of old."

The NT affirms this return of the Lost House of Israel from amongst the Gentiles when, in a meeting of the Apostles, James said in:

> Acts 15:14, "Simon has described to us how G-d first intervened to choose a people for His Name from the Gentiles. [15] The words of the prophets are in agreement with this, as it is written:
>
> [16] 'After this I will return and rebuild David's fallen Tabernacle. Its ruins I will rebuild and I will restore it,
>
> [17] that the rest of mankind may seek the L-rd, even all the Gentiles who bear My Name, says the L-rd Who does these things'-
>
> [18] things known from long ago."

With this statement, the NT underwrites the entire Message of the Bible as it was Halachically understood by the Sages and teachers of Judah: viz. the Return, Restoration and establishment of the re-united 12-Tribed Kingdom of Israel, based on Covenantal compliance with the Law of G-d. Numerous verses of the Prophets foretell this Return and how the whole World will fall under the Reign of the G-d of Israel.

This World Vision is also recited in the concluding prayer of every Jewish worship Service daily, three times a day and at other ceremonies in addition, throughout the year – the Aleinu Prayer:

This Prayer concludes with the universal Kingdom Message:

"Therefore we put our hope in You, HaShem our G-d, to soon see the glory of Your strength, to remove all idols from the Earth, and to completely cut off all false gods; to repair the world, Your holy Empire. And for all living flesh to call Your Name, and for all the wicked of the Earth to turn to You.

May all the world's inhabitants recognize and know that to You every knee must bend and every tongue must swear loyalty.

Before You, HaShem, our G-d, may all bow down, and give honor to Your precious Name, and may all take upon themselves the yoke of Your rule.

And may You reign over them soon and forever and always.

Because all rule is Yours alone, and You will rule in honor forever and ever.

As it is written in Your Torah: 'HaShem will reign forever and ever.'

And it is said: 'HaShem will be Ruler over the whole Earth, and on that day, G-d will be One, and His name will be One.'"

David was promised that his Kingdom and Davidic dynasty would one day be restored. The *Succah* of David - the very word comes from a root meaning safety and protection. Here it likewise means the Holy Temple, a source of blessing and protection. The very same Temple that David worked to make the preparations for, that which he dreamed of, desired and helped so much to plan. The Temple to be made out of cement and star dust, so to speak, the same spiritual building materials used to re-establish settlement in Israel today; cement and star dust.

This inspires the powerful emotional attachment that Jews have with our teacher and King David Ben Yishai. His father, Yishai, was counted as one of the few people who never sinned.

The image of his reunited Kingdom is deeply ingrained upon us. In fact, this passion is expressed in all our religious art work from time immemorial. All our Synagogues, Study houses, Yeshivas and a host of Judaica are decorated with the motif of the re-established Kingdom of David, in other words the re-established and re-erected fallen Succah.

Let us cite a few verses that indicate this return:

Isaiah 11:11,

"It shall come to pass that HaShem will set His hand again the second time [the first time was the Exodus from Egypt] to recover the remnant of His people who shall be left…"

After the time of 'Jacob's trouble' Isaiah 10:20 says,

"In that day the remnant of Israel, the survivors of Jacob … will rely on   the Holy One of Israel."

The prophet Hosea likewise points out that after educational punishments and exile they will return, at least a remnant.

> Jeremiah chapter 30 clearly shows, "that I will bring back from captivity My people Israel and Judah!"

> Then the Prophet goes on to ch. 46:27 to say "Do not fear, O my servant Jacob, and do not be dismayed, O Israel! For behold, I will save you from afar, and your offspring from the land of their captivity. Jacob shall return, be at rest and no one will make him afraid. Do not fear O Jacob My servant...."

According to Jer. 23 G-d will gather His flock and will set shepherds who will feed them.

Again, in Ezekiel 20:33, it is clear that He will bring the Tribes of Israel back from the countries where they have been scattered.

> Ezekiel 39:25, "Now I will bring back the captives of Jacob, and have mercy on the whole house of Israel; and I will be jealous for My Holy Name, ... When I have brought them back from the nations and have gathered them from the countries of their enemies,"

In the Addendum to this book (Chapter 25), we feature a comprehensive compilation of the multitude of Prophetic Scriptures of the Tanach which deal with this Return and Reconciliation.

Getting back to the verse in Amos, we need to understand that he was a prophet of great importance to the Northern Kingdom of Israel (i.e. the 'House of Israel'). As Dr.Hertz says in the *Soncino Pentateuch and Haftorahs*: "After pronouncing judgment on the surrounding peoples for their violation of the dictates of universal morality and their participation in barbarous practices, Amos turns to the Northern Kingdom of Israel, judging its inhabitants with the same standard and in the very same words as the heathens".

Now let us ask, what is so special about using the imagery of the Succah (Booth) for the restored Kingdom of David? What is so special about the Festival of Succot? The four species which we are commanded to take on this Festival, symbolize all the different types within the nation. The Theme and main Goal of the Succot Celebration is to establish **unity** amongst these various factions within the nation of G-d. It symbolizes the Unity which is so dearly required between the two estranged Houses of Israel today. Without the unity depicted by these species, the commands of the Festival cannot be fulfilled.

> The etrog (one of the four species) is a fertility symbol.

> The willow show our dependence on water (Torah).

> The myrtle is a symbol of success and immortality.

> The Lulav is symbolic of victory.

Also, the same four species represent the body of the individual and the nation of Israel. These species represent our patriarchs and subsumed within, also the matriarchs - our covenantal men and women!

Remember, way back in the beginning, G-d promised Abraham that his descendants would become a multitude of nations with numbers as countless as the sand of the sea, the dust of the earth and the stars of the universe. Our Fathers and Mothers, our Mammas and Pappas treasured this Promise and carried it forward in faith.

Now we can better understand the intent of the original Jewish writers of the NT. The book of Acts is speaking of the Restoration of the Kingdom of all 12 Tribes.

> Matthew10:5-7,
>
> "Do not go among the Gentiles or enter any town of the Samaritans. Go rather **to the lost sheep of the House of Israel.** As you go, proclaim this message: 'The Kingdom of Heaven has come near'" - meaning the gathering of the lost Tribes, helping them come back Home to Judah.

The Gospel of love and of the Kingdom now makes sense. When will love guide the planet? When the Kingdom of G-d rules the earth in a manifest open way through the re-united Tribes of Israel.

The Parables – Key to revealing the Hidden Message of the Kingdom

The Gospel of the Kingdom regarding the re-uniting of the House of Judah with 10-Israel (the House of Israel), underlies several Parables of the NT.

- The Prodigal Son – portraying the remaining "faithful son" who has faithfully been safeguarding his father's

Faith (which represents Judah), and the returning prodigal (which represents the House of 10-Israel).

- The Ten Bridesmaids and Oil for their lamps – representing the Ten Lost Tribes awaiting their Bridegroom. Oil = used in the Temple's Menorah = light = Torah wisdom, Kingship (1 Sam. 10), Priesthood (Lev. 8:30), anointing of the Prophet (Isa. 61), closeness and care under G-d's protection (Ps. 23, Ps. 45, Ps. 92), healing (Psalms 23), prosperity (Job 29:6, Joel 2:24). Oil is also connected to those coming back to the land for pilgrimage (Ps. 133) and in general, there is a strong Land of Israel symbolism (2 Kings 18:32, Jer. 40, 1 Kings 17:12, Deut. 11). Thus, they were found wanting, not involved in a dynamic relationship with G-d and a return to country and hence they will not be ready to greet the Bridegroom when he comes. Many of them will not be up to the tough tests, John 15, Matthew 6, John 14:13-22.

Matthew 5 speaks of obeying Commandments, light which equals Torah, treasures which equal Torah and a personal relationship with G-d who is very close. All of this reflects the language and spiritual requirements needed to help 10-Israel come Home.

Francisco Mateo Gago of the Catholic Church insisted that Jews are cursed and in exile according to the Gospels because of their failure to embrace the Church. However, the Jews were already in exile in Babylon for 70 years, more than 500 years before there was any kind of Church. Their exile therefore can have no bearing on whether they rejected the Church and its Message or not. This claim is also disqualified by the fact that the Ten Lost Tribes, who formed a great proportion of those

who accepted the Church and its Message, were also exiled –
as far back as 900 years, almost a millennium before there was
any Church!

In the words of Rabbi Avraham Joshua Heschel, "...there is
nothing in the words of Jesus that leads us to believe he envi-
sioned desolation that would endure to the end of days..." He
also states, "According to the book of Acts, the disciples ...
asked him: '...is it at this time that thou restorest the Kingdom
to Israel?' And he answered, 'No one can know the times and
seasons which the Father fixed.'" (Acts 1:6-7).

At that time, Rome ruled the Holy Land. But there was a hope,
a hope of deliverance from the pagans. There was the promise offered by the prophets, of returning to Jerusalem, to the
Kingdom of Israel. It was the most urgent question. So when
they saw the Nazarene for the first time in these extraordinary
circumstances, it is understandable that this was the first question they would ask. Their supreme concern: "Is it at this time
that thou restorest the Kingdom?" In other words, they asked
the question about the Restoration of the Kingdom of Israel
(*Israel, An Echo of Eternity*, A.J. Heschel, Farrar, Straus and
Giroux New York copyright 1967 p. 163-164).

"To 'restore' in this passage, means to set up again that which
was broken down and disfigured by many ruins ... for out of the
dry stock of Jesse should spring a branch, and the tabernacle of
David which was miserably laid waste should rise again." (*Calvin's
Commentaries, The Acts of the Apostles*, (Edinburgh, 1965), p. 29).

Returning to the words of Rabbi Doctor Heschel, "But of that
day or the hour (of the parousia) no one knows, not even the
angels in heaven, nor the Son, but only the Father" (Mark

13:32). A similar awareness is common in Rabbinic literature. "Nobody knows when the house of David will be restored." According to Rabbi Shimeon ben Lakish (ca. 250), "I have revealed it to my heart, but not to the angels." (Ibid, Heschel, p.164). The Nazarene with these statements regarding the unknowable quality of the exact times for Redemption, is once again echoing Oral Torah.

According to the Torah and the Gospels, the twelve tribes have a unique calling and a special connection to HaShem.

> Malcolm Hedding, Director of the International Christian Embassy in Jerusalem, in *The Basis of Christian Support for Israel* states:
>
> "...the Avrahamic Covenant is a one-sided covenant. (There is an irrevocable nature of the Avrahamic Covenant, Jer. 31:35-37). There were no conditions attached. Nowhere in the cutting of the Covenant with Abram, and through him the nation of Israel, is there a condition attached – "if you do this, then..." Instead, we read that G-d undertook to do everything required to enact this Covenant. All the promises begin with "I will ...I will ... I will..." Four times in Gen. 12:1-3 G-d engages Abram and tells him what He will do as the Covenant Maker. Avraham is merely the Covenant acceptor...."

The apostle Paul, himself a Jew from the tribe of Benjamin, has this to say about Israel's unique calling in his letter to the Gentile Church in Rome: "What advantage then has a Jew? Much in every way because to him were committed the Oracles of G-d" (Rom. 3:1-2).

Malcolm Hedding, has this to say about the reason for Israel's existence: "So herein lies the chief reason why the nation of Israel came into existence. They came into existence to be the custodians of world Redemption, the vehicle by which G-d would bring His message of eternal salvation to the world." (Hedding, M., *The Basis of Christian Support for Israel*, Pg 9). (Examination of the Biblical Texts that Form the Basis of Evangelical Christian Support for Israel, with Special Reference to the Response of the International Christian Embassy Jerusalem, as yet unpublished, by J.E. Carstens, July 2008, Pg. 29, 30).

According to the *Dictionary of Biblical Imagery,*

"...the image of Israel is of a people who enjoys the status of a uniquely advantaged minority under G-d: 'Their's is the adoption as sons; their's the divine glory, the covenants, the receiving of the Law, the Temple worship and the promises. Their's are the patriarchs, and from them is traced the human ancestry of Christ, who is G-d over all, forever praised!'" (Rom. 9:3-5 NIV).

Paul reminds Gentile Christians of G-d's Promises and long-term relationship with Israel. In the extended image of the Olive Tree (Rom. 11:16-21), Israel makes up the root, trunk and branches of G-d's cultivated olive tree, and Gentiles are only wild branches grafted in. If G-d prunes some Israelite branches from this tree to make room for wild branches, the Creator G-d can just as well graft in the pruned branches at a later time." (*Dictionary of Biblical Imagery...*).

CHAPTER 8

Examples of Judaism and Oral Torah in the Gospels

Let's give examples of Judaism and Oral Torah within the Gospels that demonstrate the true intention and underlying meaning of the written text. From these examples, the Gospel texts can be seen in a new light, which is really the ancient light, and the way it was experienced by the Nazarene and his original apostles.

A Sanhedrin court of 23 to 71 judges which condemns one person to death in a seventy-year period, is considered to be a murderous court (as they would say in the western U.S.A., "a hanging judge"). Rabbi Eleazar, the son of Azaryah, said, "Even one person in seventy years." Rabbi Tarfon and Rabbi Akiva said, "If we had been sitting on the court, no one would ever be put to death." (*Mishnah Makkot* Chapter1, Halacha10).

With the above in mind, let's discuss the court system during the time period of the Nazarene.

We had courts of 3, 23 and 71. During the Nazi-like Roman occupation, the Romans decided to interfere with their workings. The Torah court (Sanhedrin) went into self-imposed exile 40 years before the destruction of the second Temple. Rome ruled with an iron fist and wanted a Jewish court to rubber stamp their unpopular verdicts. There was no Torah Sanhedrin in Jerusalem at the time of the Gospels, because of this Roman interference. The word 'Sanhedrin' in Greek is 'Synedrion' which is the word for "council, committee, or court". Israel was divided into at least four such council/court zones for the administration of Roman civil and criminal law.

There also were the Sadducees, who held to heretical views, e.g. they did not believe in the resurrection of the dead, in the Messianic age, angels, or Oral Torah. Whereas a large majority of the people did believe in the above and were loyal to the Oral and Written Torah, the Sadducees were loyal only to the Romans.

In general, the Sadducees were assimilated Hellenists: in other words, secular. They did not meet the standards of the rigorous Rabbinic order of the time, simply because they were partially Hellenized and were not interested in such intensive and advanced Torah study. They were not interested in upholding the many Commandments.

The Sadducees owed their positions in various courtroom settings to the interference of imperial Rome. On the Temple Mount there was a Sadducee priestly court which was completely dominated by Roman dictatorial rule. The Romans always wanted representatives of various conquered people to make nasty legal decisions which only Rome could carry out. This was to create the illusion of some kind of autonomy among their oppressed, conquered peoples. The Sadducee priestly court was a puppet of and a rubber stamp for Roman imperial rule.

This Sadducee puppet court met at night to rule on the capital case of the Nazarene. For the court to meet at night was illegal, according to Torah Law. They met on the eve of Pesach, a major Jewish Sacred holiday, which would not have been the case for a Torah court. And they found a Jewish man, the Nazarene, guilty of sedition: political activity against the tyranny of Rome. From a Torah Orthodox Pharisaic view, Rome was like a pagan Nazi death machine. Again, from a Pharisaic Orthodox Jewish perspective, any activity against Rome would constitute heroism, righteousness, and goodness.

Messiah means 'anointed king'. In the mind of the Romans, a messiah king was a political reality. Thus, if someone thought he was king, or even if other people looked toward him as some sort of king, then in the eyes of Rome, it equaled treason and deserved immediate execution. The job of the collaborating, heretical sect of Sadducees was to immediately and swiftly approve of Roman State executions. The Romans executed hundreds of thousands of Jews. The Sadducees justified their collaboration with Nazi-like Rome by saying, "it is better that one man should die than a whole nation" (John 11:51). Similarly, the Vichy French collaborated with the Nazis and sentenced French freedom fighters (e.g. Charles De Gaulle) to death.

These Sadducee puppets met at a place called Gabbatha (John 19:13), which was a small court next to Roman high command (Antonia Fortress). Probably not more than a hundred Jews could have crowded into that spot. And who would have been allowed there by the Romans? Only members of the heretical, collaborating Sadducee sect would have had access. By the way, many of these priests were not Halachic priests; they were simply put there by Rome. In addition, the high priesthood was often purchased at that time. In the eyes of the entire Orthodox Jewish nation, the Sadducee priesthood was entirely corrupt. To a great extent, they were traitors to the Jewish people as collaborators with the Roman oppressors, and as a result they were almost all killed by the Jewish Orthodox community during the revolt against Rome. After the destruction of the second Temple the Sadducees no longer held political and organizational power, and soon became extinct.

Pontius Pilate was an arrogant, murderous monster. However, the Roman Church put such a spin on the Gospel text, that people to this day are fooled into a completely erroneous interpretation of the text surrounding Pilate's participation. Luke 13:1 testifies that "he mixed the blood of the Galileans with their sacrifices". Roman Emperor, Vitellius, ultimately sent Pilate back to Rome for fear that his indiscriminate murdering would incite full rebellion. Why would they let Barabbas, who allegedly murdered members of their own Sadducee sect, go free? Obviously, so as to prove their abject loyalty to Rome. Caiaphas (a Sadducee) and the other Sadducees served Rome and were held responsible for any rebellions that might break out. It was the kingship issue for which the Nazarene was finally convicted by the Roman puppet collaborating Kangaroo court, comprised completely of Sadducees. So again, better that one fellow die (who is accused of being king, meaning a spiritual, political rival to Roman power) than an entire nation be destroyed (threatening their own position of political and economic control and leadership).

From a Jewish perspective, it does not need prophetic insight to know that anyone making claims on 'kingship' (messiahship), would be marked for death under Roman rule. From a 10-Israel 'return' point of view, here we have an absolute proof text that the NT is serving the function of a reach-out to the Lost Tribes of Israel, NOT to Judah (who were not lost or dispersed at that time).

> John 11:52, "He did not say this on his own, but as high priest that year he prophesied that the Nazarene would die for the Jewish nation, [52] and not only for that nation **but also for the scattered children of G-d, to bring them together and make them one.** [53] So from that day on they plotted to take his life."

The NT confirms this 'crime of rebellion against Rome' by stating on the inscription above the convicted Nazarene: **"this is the king of the Jews"**, Luke 23:38.

You, my dear readers, must understand that Pilate was mocking and humiliating the Sadducee pseudo-court. He was taunting them. For example, Pilate said, "He is your king?" (John 19:14) - which made them grovel at his feet and beg him to believe them, that they had no king, except the king in Rome. We are dealing here with a very high stake encounter. If the Sadducees failed to prove their absolute loyalty to Rome, the outcome would have been disastrous for them. Their possessions, wealth, homes, animals, positions and honor would have been immediately lost! All of their material comforts would have gone down the drain, after which the Roman death machine would have torturously, methodically, and efficiently murdered them and their families.

To digress momentarily, I have often wondered at, and been amazed by the success of the Roman spin on the Gospel text. Here were the Hellenized, relatively secular Sadducee Jews trying to survive against the brutal, crushing iron boot of the

Roman Empire. However, the Church dumped all the blame on one of Rome's victims, the Sadducee court. They victimized the victim. The whole point of the passion play should have been against Rome, who was the true pagan bad guy. They made Pontius Pilate look as if he was a good Christian churchgoer.

If Rome thought you were a bad guy, that meant you were a good guy in the eyes of the Pharisaic people of Israel. According to all Torah sources, someone killed by a Gentile *pagan* military because of being a Jew, or because of their Jewishness, dies a heroic death and is called 'holy, a saint, and a martyr.' Torah sources agree that the death of the righteous brings atonement (*Moed Katan* 28A). Rabbi Ami says, "Why was the death of Miriam juxtaposed with the section of the red heifer? To teach us that just as the red heifer atones, the death of the righteous atones". Rabbi Elazar says, "Why was the death of Aaron juxtaposed with the section of the priestly garments? To teach that just as the priestly garments atone, the death of the righteous atones." *Bava Batra 10B, Pesachim 50A, Taanit 18B* are a few sources in the Talmud that explain, that Jews who were murdered (by Gentile forces) in Lod, those who die in Israel's wars, and under occupation of foreign invaders, are like the Holy of Holies. They shall experience the most honored place in the world to come.

So, the Sadducees knew in their hearts that it wasn't right for Nazi-like Rome to rule in Israel, just as the Vichy French knew in their hearts that Nazi rule of France was unnatural. The Roman rule was ruthless, cruel and totalitarian to the extreme. The Sadducees needed to act as a cheering section for imperial Roman decrees and actions for what, in their minds, equaled their own prosperity and survival. The Sadducees, which were less than 3% of the population, had a huge number of relatives who were good, religious, Pharisaic Jews. They knew someone executed for being Jewish (or a possible king-like savior) was really a righteous and saintly being. Such a person would have the status of a heroic, righteous individual and his death would bring atonement.

Again, the Sadducees were cheering Rome and proclaiming their absolute loyalty to Roman rule, motivated by fear for their own safety and the prosperity of themselves and their families Both Paul (1 Cor. 2:8) and Luke (18:31-33) put the responsibility on the Romans (rulers/Gentiles) and not the Jews. The Greek word used for Gentile in Luke 18:32, is *"ethnos"*, which means, according to Strong's #1484, "a *race* (as of the same *habit*), that is, a *tribe*; specifically a *foreign* (*non-Jewish*) one (usually by implication *pagan*): - Gentile, heathen, nation, people".

Because some Jews, according to NT, were looking at the Nazarene as a kingly figure, the Roman rulers felt threatened and had the puppet Sadducee court condemn the Nazarene to death. When in Luke 23:34 the Nazarene said, "they know not what they do," he was referring to this situation. If the Sadducees had been properly versed in Torah, they would have known they were wrongly ruling against the Nazarene. At an earlier time, when the Sadducees tried to trick the Nazarene with their questions, the Gospel records that they were very ignorant of the Torah. As it says in Matthew 22:29, "You are mistaken, not knowing the Scriptures nor the power of G-d."

For example, here is a way in which the Sadducees were mistaken because of their lack of Torah expertise: the Sadducees, being secularized, Hellenized, and ignorant of Written and Oral

Torah set Rome rules. "Rome is our government." Therefore, someone who may be heralded as a possible rival to Rome e.g. a Messiah figure, is guilty of treason and of betraying the law of the land. However, in Jeremiah it says the law of the land is your law. So what is the problem that they didn't care for the Written and Oral Torah? They were lacking in Rabbinic ordination. They were put there by Rome living the life of Riley, enjoying living high on the ham, and worried only about losing their position of relative power. Had they been good Yeshiva students, Jeremiah's directives would have been very clear. The Written and Oral Torah never advocate accepting immoral, criminal, or pagan laws of 'the powers that be'. The Torah advocates the respect of neutral laws needed to run a quiet, stable society, nothing more. The secular forces have no right to tell us how to serve or not serve G-d. And there is nothing wrong with heroic Jews in each generation struggling against despotic rule over our exiles wherever we find ourselves.

According to Oral Torah, if someone is under great duress, it changes an intentional sin to an unintentional sin. If a person or group feels they are under tremendous pressure and are coerced, that reduces significantly the measure of guilt of their actions. See Acts 3:17, which states that the Jews who were involved, were ignorant and thus a lot less guilty.

Finally, now we can understand what it meant in Matthew 27:25, when the Sadducees said, "his blood be on us and on our children." In Greek the word, *epi*, (on) in Hebrew is *"al"*, which means 'over us' or 'upon us', or a covering on us. What that would mean to a Hebrew mind is: "his blood be atonement upon us". Atonement is the whole idea of something covering or being upon the sinner. Since the Nazarene was being killed because he was Jewish, he died a righteous death; as such, it served as atonement for sins. Thus, Matthew 26:28, "For this is my blood of the new testament, which is shed for many for the remission of sins," should be understood in the spirit of the above-mentioned sources of the Oral Torah.

Just to remind our dear readers, the death of the righteous brings atonement. For example, Rabbi Aryeh Levine, a student of Rabbi Avraham Yitzhak HaCohen Kook, says of the death of the tzaddikim, "They ascend upward to the root of life and the essence of their lives brings an encompassing value of goodness and blessing to the overall structure of the world, in all of its values and nuances." (*A Tzaddik in Our Time*, by Simcha Raz, Pg 108).

Remember in Biblical times, the death of the high priest achieved atonement and freed the people who had killed accidently, from the cities of refuge. In the Talmud, in *Tractate Moed* Katan 28, it says that anyone who cries over the death of the righteous person, achieves a measure of atonement, meaning a degree of forgiveness of their sins.

What the Sadducees were really saying, which the ignorant Romans missed, was a coded praise, an acknowledgement of the supreme sacrifice that this young Jewish hero was making, in defiance of the tyranny that was pagan Rome. The Romans murdered many hundreds of thousands of Jewish people. The worst crime a Jew could possibly commit, in Roman eyes, was not paganism (they were pagans themselves), nor adultery, nor robbery, nor even murder of their fellow countrymen, but rather laying claim to or being considered a possible Messianic leader. The mere possibility that a want-to-be-Messianic fellow was around, would get instant attention from Rome. In the case of the Nazarene, the claims involved being possibly

Messiah, which to Rome was a threat of anointed king. This was a geopolitical position in addition to any spiritual implications it may have.

Remember, the Romans had on their books for over 400 years a law which demanded the death penalty for any Jew who might be considered as being of the seed of David. This law stood even after Rome became Christian, simply because in their minds, any Messianic aspirations were equivalent to rebelling against Roman authority. Even if the potential leader clearly did not consider himself a candidate for such a role, as long as other people did, he would become an immediate target for elimination by the Romans who had zero tolerance for potential political rivals.

This kangaroo court could make up false rulings. The Nazis imitated Rome with a Vichy French rubber-stamp of false approval. The French who collaborated with Nazi tyranny, used a fake court system to justify Nazi rule. The Third Reich did, with a tiny portion of Vichy French, exactly as Rome did to the Jews by way of the tiny (less than 3% of the population), heretical Sadducee cult. All this was to create an illusion of autonomy, thus neutralizing the spirit of revolution.

Another example of Judaism and Oral Torah in the Gospels, is found in Acts 8:2 where G-d-fearing men buried Stephen and "made great lamentation over him", a phrase used often in connection with funerals, where it is a mitzvah (a very good and truly kind deed) to honor the deceased. However, the Mishnah in Sanhedrin 6/5 forbids eulogies and public lamentations for people legally executed! Therefore, the people surrounding this riotous crowd were not Pharisees, but Sadducees, because if a person was really guilty of heresy, he was not mourned publicly. This proves that Stephen was unjustly condemned to death by a Sadducee puppet court. First, it was very hard to receive a death penalty from a Torah court. Second, there were no such functioning courts of at least 23 saintly judges in that area and time. Remember, the Torah 71 Sanhedrin members had already gone into self-imposed exile and again, it was never the habit of legitimate Jewish courts to kill Jews over ideology.

Third, nothing Stephen did or said would have so upset a Torah (pro-Pharisee party) crowd. They would have simply brushed him off, or ignored him, or have taken some words of correction, but not condemned him. Keep in mind also that according to the NT, Gamaliel was to make clear that Paul was OK and these folks were not to be annoyed. Any regular Jew, i.e. affiliated with the Pharisee party, would have had Gamaliel's attitude, as they do today. Stephen did not say anything that would warrant his death. What warranted Stephan's death was the public allegiance to another king, namely a Messiah, which again means anointed king! This was a serious crime against imperial Rome. The job of the Sadducees was to maintain order and if they failed, they very well may have paid for it with their lives and the lives of their families!

The only thing Stephen did wrong was to not pay attention in Bible class. Perhaps whenever his teacher was speaking, he took a snooze or he forgot some information. However, this was not illegal, or criminal, or immoral or unethical! He confused a few verses. He said that Jacob was buried in Shechem, but any Israeli child in cheder (religious school) could tell you that Joseph was buried in Shechem and Jacob was buried in Hebron. Stephen confused the people from whom Avraham purchased the burial plot for Sarah, with a different bunch of Canaanites from the Shechem area. He also said that Avraham came to Israel after his father died, but any rendition of the math in that section would show you that his dad lived for many years after his son Avraham had made aliyah. And, Stephen said the Torah was given by angels, but Exodus 19 states the Torah was given straight from G-d to Moses on Mt. Sinai.

Again, nothing in these mistakes was illegal or criminal or would get anyone upset or arouse anger. It was the king issue that got him in trouble. Stephen was only guilty of confusing texts, which is not a crime in law! At worst, he could have looked silly, which is how the Hebrew mind views most off-beat polemics. When our father Avraham, after having given a lovely meal to an elderly pagan, told him to praise G-d for the food, the pagan insisted on thanking the sun god! Whereupon Avraham corrected and chastised him, which the old pagan rebuffed. Avraham abruptly asked him to leave. In a later dialogue with HaShem, G-d chastises Avraham saying, "I put up with this fool for 70 years and you could not put up with him for one meal." The emphasis is on the fact that Avraham had to be less zealous for the honor of HaShem and more concerned for the dignity of his fellow man!

As a side point, for an example of another riotous crowd, I would like to share with you the following. Daniel Gruber, in his book *Copernicus and the Jews*, remarks, "the Greek word used to describe this riotous mob in the city theater is *ekklesia*. 'The ekklesia was in confusion. Some were shouting one thing, some another. Most of the people did not even know why they were there.' (Acts 19:32). Whether or not that accurately describes some Church to which you have been, Luke simply used '*ekklesia*' to refer to an assembly of people." This assembly was not a Jewish house of prayer, meeting, or study. When the Pharisaic-oriented

Jewish people refer to the theaters of the Greek and Roman oppression they are quite negative! Torah Jews would not be found at the Roman theater, for they were places of assimilation of Hellenistic Roman pagan immorality (as many are today)! Who would hang out there? First of all, pagans, and if there were any Jews they would be of the Sadducee sect, because they were relatively secular and pro-Hellenization and enjoyed Roman everything, or at least had to pretend they did

At the crucifixion, the Nazarene indorses forgiveness for the Sadducees, "for they are ignorant and do not know what they do!" As explained earlier, people acting under terrible duress (fear of Roman retribution) have a much lower level of spiritual guiltiness.

Oral Torah inherent in the New Testament refutes anti-Rabbinic interpretation of the Gospels

Under Roman influence, every single passage in the Gospels was read and twisted to remove or excise the Jews out of the Bible – to reduce the influence of Judaism – to disengage the Gospel from its Hebraic roots – simply put, to discredit Jews and Judaism. The divine intent underlying the return to Torah of the re-identifying Ten Lost Tribes in 'the End Time' and their peaceful Reconciliation with the House of Judah will therefore entail the reversal of this process of demonizing Judaism, Jews and the Torah.

Again, the purpose of this book is to reveal the Oral Torah which lies inherent and concealed in the New Testament, in order to bless and encourage this process of Reconciliation. Consequently, it could serve as a reminder to the Hebraic

Restorer in this wonderful re-enlightening age, of the importance and necessity of sober minded Rabbinic Oral interpretation of the Torah and of G-d's requirements for would-be citizens of His Eternal Kingdom.

The 'Jewish' Sabbath

Nowhere is there a clearer sign that the 'End Time' restoration of all things entails a reversal of the process of anti-Judaism and anti-Rabbinism, than in the acceptance by millions of modern-day non-Jewish Hebraic Restorers of the 'Jewish' Sabbath as the True Biblical Sabbath. This commonly is one of the first main issues of Restoration that these sincere Bible students apply on their progressive Way of Return.

A church official in Jerusalem said to me in a personal discussion: "What have the Jews to do with the Bible?" While infiltrating neo-Nazi groups in the USA for a research project, I was often confronted with the statement that "The Nazarene was not a Jew. It's merely Zionistic propaganda."

Clifford Goldstein, editor of a Christian magazine, criticizes Adventists who reject a Jewish connection to the Sabbath. They say they received it from a spiritual remnant (for which there is no historical proof) or, they are the heirs to the spiritual remnant and do not owe the Sabbath to the rejected Jews. The problem here is that every circumstance where Christians have adopted the Jewish 7th Day Sabbath has been done by virtue of 'the Jewish Bible' (the Tanakh or 'Old Testament'). Throughout the centuries the Jews have been a living testimony and witness to observance of the Sabbath. Others would say that the Sabbath has nothing to do with Jews but it comes straight from

G-d. Apart from thereby confessing the 'righteousness' of Jews in sticking to Torah, this is merely a subtle way to disguise the anti-Semitic repulsion to the idea that they could possibly be seen as reverting to Jewish customs.

Goldstein uses the term: 'Supersessionism' (from Latin 'supersede' – sitting in the place of). The generally accepted term is 'Replacement Theology'. (Tertullian, in his book, *Against Marcion* 4.12.7, Note *10).

Marcion reasons that the Church replaced the Jews – Tertullian does not. This idea was first in ecclesiastical terms in the 4th century Catholic Church, i.e. that the Church, being the 'New Israel', has replaced the synagogue of the 'old Israel'. Five hundred years ago the Protestant Reformation claimed that it was the new spiritual Israel, with the grace of the Gospel, and had replaced the Israel of the flesh bound to the Law of Moses.

Franklin H. Little in *The Crucifixion of the Nazarene* speaks of the red thread that ties Justin Martyr to Auschwitz and describes Hitler's Final Solution as a logical extension of the theology of supersessionism. In other words: "I am the true Israel, and you are not, and you do not deserve to live as Israel."

Replacement theology ignores the statement by Paul that "to the Jews pertain the adoption, the glory, the covenants, the giving of the Law, the service of G-d and the promises" (Romans 9:4). To paraphrase Goldstein: In the beginning of the Christian era, the Church separated itself from its Jewish roots in order to gain the world. Could it be that, at the end of its course, the Church will gain the 'World to Come' by 'returning' (teshuvah) to the Jewish face of its identity?

In the *Jerusalem Talmud Nedarim*, Rabbi Aha in the name of Rabbi Huna said: "Asaf (Esau) the wicked will put on his tallith with the tassels and sit with the righteous in Paradise in the time to come, and the Holy One, Blessed be He, will drag him and cast him forth from there." What is the meaning? "Though thou mount on high as an eagle, and though thy nest be set amongst the stars, I will bring thee down from there, says the Lord" (Obadiah 1:4). The 'stars' mean the righteous. Daniel 12:3, "They that turn many to righteousness (shall shine) as the stars forever and ever."

The above passage contains an unmistakable allusion to Christianity becoming the official religion of the Roman Empire. 'Asaf' is a stock phrase in the Scriptures to denote the Roman Empire. That Asaf should wrap himself in this prayer shawl, worn by Jews when praying, means that the Roman Empire which had now become Christian, pretended to be the true Israel (Galatians 3:7). The claim of the Christian Church was very exasperating to the Jews. Asaf, in a certain way, was related to the Jewish people. We see that from our own distant relatives comes forth much hatred against us. As Amnon Goldberg, a wise man of Tzfat explains of the verse in Leviticus 26:17, "Those that hate you shall rule over you." And our Oral Torah explains, "I will set up enemies only from your own ranks." And Isaiah 49:17: "Those who destroy you and waste you will emerge from you."

The *Zohar* 1-25 says that there are five categories amongst the Erev Rav (the mixed multitude of Egyptian proselytes who were incorporated into the Hebrew nation at the time of the Exodus). In the generation before the Redemption, the Jews will be ruled by this tiny minority of corrupt officials (the Erev Rav), and some will ally themselves with the Edomites and

Ishmaelites and even with Gog and Magog (*Zohar* 4-246). The Zohar even talks of this minority (a mixed multitude) of Jews who appear to be religious but act contrary to G-d's Will.

This disturbing phenomenon is clearly evident today in the way that the government of Israel reacts to world pressure against Jews 'occupying' the Promised Land. Their actions, under the banner of 'Peace', favour and benefit their declared enemies and restrict and persecute the righteous, loving and loyal in Israel today who believe in the Promises of Torah and the Prophets.

Perhaps the same must of necessity be true of the re-awakening and re-identifying 10-Israel. Their greatest opposition will come from within their own ranks: those who profess to be returning to Torah and Hebraic Israel identity but who oppose the spiritual leaders of the Torah, the divinely mandated guardians of His Torah, the Rabbonim. Those who want to physically live in the Land of Israel but who oppose complete physical identity with Judah; those who want to change Judah to their own brand of anti-Halachic Judaism are the accusers of the nation who, throughout the ages, clung to their Hebraic heritage.

Only by recognizing these two striving spirits in each other, and striving for the prophesied goal of peaceful Reconciliation between the two divided Houses of Israel, can peace be attained in Zion. The uncovering of the original Oral Torah foundation of the New Testament, which for 2000 years has been wrapped in anti-Jewish disguise, will go a long way amongst both sides to promote this Reconciliation.

In brief, the Gospels are confirming the authenticity, sanctity and obligations of both the Written and Oral Torah.

The scholar, Mordechai Alfrandry uses more or less the following metaphor to explain the above: imagine that, through G-d's Wisdom, the traffic laws were imparted to the minds of men. G-d then sees that His various laws, meant to preserve life and safety, were being trampled on by the children of man when those lousy human beings were not coming to a full stop at stop signs; and they were not yielding at yield signs. They were running red lights. They were exceeding maximum speed limits – making a total mess of the way He had planned and had wanted the world to be: an orderly, safe place for humans. So G-d decided to send His only begotten son John to live amongst men, to grow up, pass his theory and driving test, get a license, and show how the highways and by-ways of the world should really be traveled. John would simply fulfill all of those traffic laws – and then dies in a fatal crash while keeping those selfsame traffic laws. Now all of those lousy drivers are living in grace by virtue of John's proper fulfillment of those traffic safety laws – and the huge debt which has accumulated over the years of unpaid traffic tickets, fines and penalties, will now be paid retroactively and into the future by virtue of John's proper driving habits, e.g. never forgetting to signal that right turn, or come to a full stop.

Foolish – you say? I agree. But yet, this is the stuff that the whole Christian Grace theology is based upon. It wouldn't help the world to have one good driver and say that everyone is now living in the grace of his good driving. Traffic laws of safety apply to all drivers at all times, as long as there will be cars. Similarly the Creator's laws cannot be abrogated while the heavens as we know them exist. The Nazarene in Mathew 5:18 (in the very verse about the 'yud and tittle' discussed above, confirms: "I tell you the truth, until heaven and earth disappear," the Law will stand. As the Rabbis comment on the book of Leviticus, "Even if all the nations of the world would come together to uproot or cancel one word of the Torah, they would not be able to accomplish it." Again we are not picking a fight here merely giving an insight of how the Hebrew mind set would look at things in the Gospels and come up with an entirely different spin than that given it by the Greco Roman controlled Church.

PART 3

THE NEW TESTAMENT AND ANTI-JUDAISM

CHAPTER 9

Does the New Testament proclaim anti-Rabbinism and anti-Torahism or does it confirm Rabbinic Oral Torah based statements?

First of all: We find the following statement by the Nazarene in the Gospels, in which he refers to Deut. 6:4 and Lev. 19:18 as confirmation of the principal tenets of the Torah.

> Mark 12:28-31 "One of the teachers of the Law came and heard them debating. Noticing that the Nazarene had given them a good answer, he asked him, 'Of all the Commandments, which is the most important?' [29] 'The most important one,' he answered, 'is this: 'Hear, O Israel, the L-rd our G-d, the L-rd is one. [30]Love the L-rd your G-d with all your heart and with all your soul and with all your mind and with all your strength.' [31]The second is this: 'Love your neighbor as yourself.' There is no Commandment greater than these."

The Nazarene's response proves his belief in Judaism's foundational religious principle of One and only One G-d, and love of His fellow Jew. Here, in one text, is the refutation of all the anti-Semitic statements in the name of the Gospels.

According to the Gospel, the Nazarene was really distressed with the activities at the Temple. Certainly, in today's most volatile political atmosphere surrounding the Temple Mount in Jerusalem, no seriously-believing Christian should be contemplating surrendering Jewish sovereignty over the Temple area! What would the Nazarene say? He most certainly would participate in the protests against surrendering the Temple Mount property to a new non-Jewish religious entity, or to succumb to fanatic, pan-national Arabism. Yet, how many Churches and Christians choose the fanatic Arab/Muslim narrative over the righteous Jewish/Biblical narrative?

It is quite clear from the NT records that the Nazarene's followers expected him to bring a national Jewish salvation and to rescue them from the oppression of the Romans. As demonstrated in the previous section, the Nazarene's teachings as proclaimed by the NT are in agreement with the Oral Torah, the Written Torah, and Judaism.

So how did the NT become known as supporting anti-Torahism and anti-Judaism?

The source of anti Judaism and anti-Rabbinism has historical roots.

- Firstly, Roman influence and political strategies during Roman rule over the 'modern' world of their time.

- Failure of the Christian Church to distinguish between historic Judaism's Pharisees and Sadducees as representatives of the Original True Biblical Religion of Judaism.

- The perceived Message of the NT itself by the masses.

- The Apostle Paul's anti-Rabbinic teachings in the NT

CHAPTER 10

ROMAN INFLUENCE – breeding ground of Christianity's anti-Judaism

The Roman Empire's war on Jewish culture

The Jew-hatred which is commonly imputed to the NT by its interpreters was attached to it by the Roman authorities, who fought bloody wars to suppress Jewish independence. The Roman Empire for many years fought ghastly wars against the Jews in their efforts to suppress the belief in One true G-d and His Torah.

In fact, Eusebius *Op.cit.III.20 1-6* recounts Roman attempts to hunt down anyone suspected of having come from the House of King David. Under Vespasian, and later under the Emperor Domitian (81-96 CE) special forces were enlisted to search out anyone suspected of being of David's seed. Before the destruction of the Temple (70 CE) under the supervision of Vespasian, there is much reason to believe that the Romans despised and were highly suspicious of anyone who could be of the line of David, simply because that individual represented a possible future political rival who could wield authority over Jews.

Rome occupied the land of Israel at the time and was struggling to maintain its control over it.

The Roman Church chose to remove many NT passages from their cultural context, and reinterpreted those sentences to reinforce their politically-motivated hatred of Jewish people and Torah.

Dr. Dwight Baker, in *Reconstructing Some Faulty Christian Theology in the Light of Biblical Truth* and A. Roy Eckhardt in *The Anguish of the Jews* both express the idea that the secular Gentiles projected upon the Jews their own hatred of what the Nazarene stood for. To quote Morris Samuel's 'Indictment': Christian anti-Semites "must spit on the Jews as the Christ-killers because they actually long to spit on the Jews as the 'Christ-givers'". Dr. H. D. Leuner charges, "Instead of confronting the world with a 'Jewish Servant of G-d dying for the world's sin', the Church presents the nations with a picture of the Jews betraying and killing their Messiah."

A. Roy Eckhardt writes, "In Christian Europe there have been three established policies regarding the Jews: Conversion, Expulsion and Annihilation."

- Conversion: The missionizing 2nd century Christians said, in effect, "You have no right to live among us as Jews."

- Expulsion: The secular rulers who followed, said, "You have no right to live among us."

- Annihilation: Lastly, the Nazis decreed: "You have no right to live."

- The categories are: first theological, then cultural and finally political anti-Semitism.

The world at this time (2013) seems to be heading down this destructive path once again in history – this time, not constrained to national borders surrounding Israel (as in Biblical times), or world areas (like Europe in the 30's) – but internationally.

CHAPTER 11

Failure to distinguish between historic Judaism's Pharisees and Sadducees

Josephus and other historians say that 50,000 Jews died in a mini-war against Herod. The Pharisees, Scribes, Sages and a considerable number of common people supported Aristobulus. They even tried to enlist the help of Greek warriors in a desperate effort to topple the evil pagan Roman regime that was supported and funded by the Sadducees. Aristobulus supported historic Judaism and the belief in one G-d, and shared with the broad populace a deep animosity to Roman rule and the Sadducee sect that sided with the Roman oppressors.

The Sadducees only kicked off under Greek influence. Tzadok and Boethos rejected belief in reward and punishment and future revival of the dead and formed the Tzedokim and Boethusian sects which turned into the Sadducees. There existed a "subtle but overwhelming allure of the surrounding Greek culture ... acting upon their new theology. These ... apostates gave themselves over to a life of pleasure and luxury, and ate from 'dishes of gold and silver all of the days of their lives' (*Avos D'Rabbi Nosson*, 5:2, Rabbi Dr. Berel Wein,

The Oral Law of Sinai, Pub. Jossey-Bass, San Francisco, Ca. 08, I Maccabees 1:44-50).

Many of my Christian friends see no difference between these various Jewish sects. They consider them as much the same. It reminds me of the humorous story of a Jewish fellow who told a Chinese man that he was angry at the Chinese for bombing Pearl Harbor, to which the Chinese fellow indignantly exclaimed, "It was not the Chinese but the **Japanese** who did it and whom we also hate." The Jew responded: "What's the difference ... Chinese, Japanese", to which the Chinese man responded, "I hate the Jews for killing all those innocent people on the Titanic, when that Jew sank the ship." The Jew protested that it wasn't a Jew, it was an **iceberg!** To which the Chinese exclaimed: "So, Iceberg, Goldberg, Hillberg ... what's the difference?" The moral of the story is that there was a big difference in the details.

Perhaps this will help many readers understand why the Pharisees frowned on capital punishment. The Roman authorities forced Jewish courts to allow Sadducees to be judges. These generally lacked genuine legal credentials. They didn't practice normative Torah observance or the Jewish belief system. They had no interest in the courts serving a divine will or serving Jewish nationalism – just the opposite. Their job was to force artificial rulings, appealing to and appeasing Roman authority. The Sadducees were the ones to fear a spiritual revolution instigated by a spiritual man – not the Pharisees, who every day and in every way advocated a sincere, immediate spiritual revolution on a national level. Even if you want to say that, as individuals, many were not up to it. However, on a nationalistic level everyone was willing to eventually fight and die for a Torah Revolution!

In contradistinction to much misinterpretation and slander against the Pharisees, the only true way that they would have had power, would have been with the fall of the Roman Empire. Only when G-d rules and Torah is supreme will their words be taken seriously and backed up by government authority. They had no stake in continuing the oppressive Roman rule. The entire spiritual and legal life of Jews and Judaism is dysfunctional when it suffers under foreign domination.

Much the same applies today to the Israeli ruling government which bows to international anti-Jewish pressure. The current Prime Minister, Benjamin Netanyahu, has gone beyond even the most leftist Prime Ministers of the last few governments in curbing further building of Jewish homes in the settlement areas. Their anti-religious attitudes are also clear from their treatment of righteous Jews in Israel. It is not uncommon for Torah-faithful Jews to be harassed and arrested. They are backed by a biased press and media. These Jews, who believe in the Torah and fulfill the Torah Command to 'settle the Land,' are our in the front line of defense. They are made out to be the prime political danger to peace with the Arabs who reject the ancient birthright of the Jews to the Land.

There is virtually an internal 'warfare' against these Jews who confirm their faith by settling the Land. With the majority approval of the Jewish government, these righteous settler families are physically carried and banned out of their homes in the midnight hours, even in winter. Their belongings are removed from their homes and piled on a heap, after which their homes are bull-dozed. The occupants are then left to find their own way!

An additional misunderstanding of the Pharisees is the accusation that they enjoyed some kind of illegitimate dynastic control of the people. Nothing could be further from the truth. The only people who would listen to them, were seeking to follow and understand Biblical directives. There was never a community more democratic and open in the ancient history of the world than the Jewish one. Pharisees were merely a political party set up to represent the historic nation to the evil Roman oppressors. As political representatives, some failed, while others were sometimes not up to par. Just about anyone could join and become a member of the Torah community. Remember, the Torah cries out that the entire Hebrew people are to be a Kingdom of priests and a holy nation. Inclusion into this faith community was achieved by acquiring scholarship in Torah texts along with a righteous, ethical lifestyle. The Pharisees imperfectly represented us to the Romans, just as today's politicians often fail to properly represent the general population.

We have three crowns in Judaism: the Crown of Kingship and Priesthood are circumscribed by pedigree and heredity, but the Crown of Torah is available to anyone who would devote his or her life to its study and observance.

Why was Joshua chosen to replace Moses? After all, there existed the 70 elders who were more advanced in Torah than he was. It was because Joshua never left Moses' tent. He learned and loved Torah so much, that he 'ran away' with it, meaning that he successfully absorbed the most Torah and hence was G-d's and Moses' natural choice to be the next leader.

Jethro, father-in-law of Moses and priest of Midian was a Gentile who afterwards became a Hebrew. He was able to give advice to Moses on how the judicial system of G-d should operate. We have many examples of Gentiles who learned Torah and were able to contribute to the wisdom practiced and to be held up as examples by the Rabbis. The crown of Torah sat nicely upon the head of many women as well, e.g. Bruria, the wife of Rabbi Meyer Baal HaNes, was such an outstanding scholar that 300 laws were decided according to her knowledge, rather than that of the Sages. Many children of converts e.g. (Rabbi Akiva) and converts themselves comprised the leadership of the Rabbinic covenantal faith community.

There were two converts, Aftalom and Shamaryah, who, as leaders of the Sanhedrin, confronted Herod and handed down the ruling that he was guilty of murdering Jews. In response to this, Herod ordered his soldiers to slaughter the Sanhedrin. These brave converts, who had become Sages in the Pharisee Sanhedrin, were not afraid to insist on the true interpretation of Torah Law, even in the face of brutal death staring them in the eye. Such was the character, honesty and sincerity of the Pharisees towards the G-d, Land and people of Israel.

The Sadducees - forerunners of today's secular leftist factions

Part of the reason for growing anti-Semitism during the first century also lies at the feet of Jews who could not withstand the temptation of choosing an easier life, rather than facing torture and a horrendous death. They opted for joining the Church. These Jews, in their zeal to be accepted by their newfound community, set out on their own personal crusades to blacken everything about Jews and Judaism. They searched through Rabbinic literature for anything that could be perverted to demonize Judaism. To prove their loyalty to their Church masters, these turncoats encouraged the Church to use a heavy hand towards the Jews. They inspired public debates and instigated many pogroms throughout history, so it wasn't always the fault of Gentile anti-Semitism - Jews also stoked the fires of hatred against their own people.

They also sided with our enemies during the Greek Syrian Hellenistic oppression and occupation even though they were less than one percent of the populace. Their power with the rulers was enormous, since they were loyal collaborators. They even succeeded in convincing the pagan Greeks to decree severe bans against the foundations of Judaism (Max Radin, *The Jewish Community under the Greeks and Romans*, Philadelphia, Jewish Publication Society, 1916, pages 124 – 138. Paul Johnson, *History of the Jews*, Harper and Row, '87, pages 99-103).

Prof. Gerald Freelander in *The Jewish Sources of the Sermon on the Mount*, (Katav Publishers) presents scholarly arguments, bringing proof of the Judaic nature of numerous discussions in the Gospels. He is upset with what Christians have done to highjack Jewish themes and philosophies, repackaging them with unacceptable theories.

In NT times, the Sadducees sided with the Greek Hellenists against mainline Jews. They are still alive and well today as secularists who side with the world against their fellow Jews. They were heretics as far as Torah Judaism is concerned, since they denied many cardinal Jewish beliefs, e.g. the Messianic Kingdom, Resurrection and Rabbinic Oral Torah interpretation.

The Herodians, a radical Jewish, pro-Roman group, were a branch of the Sadducees. They took over the Sanhedrin and used this body of judicial power for their own purposes to support Roman edicts and punish possible adversaries. This actually fulfilled some predictions in Leviticus 26:17 which warned: "Those that hate you will rule over you," and Isaiah 49:17..."those who destroy and waste you, will emerge from you."

In Matthew 27, we see that it was the Sadducees who encouraged Judas to facilitate the arrest of the Nazarene. They held a court session at night (John 18:13, 24) which is strictly forbidden by normative Pharisaic Law - John 18:28. After his death, they requested the Roman authorities to put a guard on the tomb (Matthew 27). Also, they are the ones who, in Acts 5, had the students of the Nazarene arrested. (For an excellent source, see Vince Garcia, *What you never knew about the Pharisees*).

The Sadducees are comparable to the extreme leftist secular Israeli government authorities who control Israel today and who serve foreign investment powers and special interest groups. They quite gleefully destroy homes, farms and gardens of their fellow citizens while turning over parts of the country to terrorist entities and enemies of the land. All this is quite legalized when they use the secular court system to ratify their actions. They do this even in the face of all of Torah giants who pointed out why the giving away of the Holy Land would only further endanger human life and create a new terrorist entity. In this way they throw gas on already enflamed radicals and thus inspire them to create new terrorist bases (like 'Hamastan') on the Land. They wake up such previous sleeping monsters as the President of Iran.

After Israel's declaration of intent to destroy the Israeli presence in Gaza (Herzliyah Conference, eight months before the actual destruction) Ahmadinejad, president of Iran, realized that it is indeed possible to turn back the clock. Before that, he said that the Muslim world, despite the rhetoric, did not think that they could turn back the clock. However, now with the Zionist plan of self-expulsion of its most loyal citizens, to occur in a matter of months with Israeli Army and Police assault on their own citizens, the termination of 34 years of growth and control will come to pass. Well, this proves that if the clock can be turned back 34 years, then why not, reasoned the President, then why not 57 years? And if you can destroy the little Satan (Israel), it gave him hope that he could also destroy the big Satan (America)!

In addition, the Shi'ite Muslims would also believe that the time has arrived for the coming of their Mahdi (Messiah), the Hidden 12th Imam, which he imagined himself to possibly be!

For when the enemy (Israel) retreats without (and not because of) a military defeat, then this is a sign that the Mahdi is finally on his way, after 1000 years of being hidden.

All of the above – amount to the price that Israel has to pay for the leftist Sadducee spirit.

The Sadducees of the Gospels who acted with the most venom against the Nazarene, were likewise hated by the vast majority of the Jewish Pharisaic population. They were viewed as traitors and heretics.

It was the Nazarene's rejection of this faction of Judaism which is so often used by critics as having been addressed at Judaism in general. Prof. H.A. Hart protests this confusion in *The Journal of Theological Studies* vol.11 p. 58, as do many other great scholars, like William Dankenbring in *Prophecy Flash*!

The truth about the Pharisees and the Sadducees

It is simply amazing - and should serve as a sobering indictment against Christian critics of Judaism - to see how wrongly they have condemned the Pharisaic order of NT times. Simultaneously there is great ignorance about what the Sadducees really stood for.

During the Greek occupation of Israel, the heretical Sadducee cult sided with the Greek authorities against normative Rabbinic Jews. The Hasmonean king, Alexander Jannaeus, originally followed pro-Torah Judaism. Eventually, for issues of personal vanity, he sided with the Sadducees which led him to hunt down and murder important Rabbinic leaders. Josephus (Antiq. XII.13, 13, 5) records how the Sadducee-influenced king illegally took the role of high priest. At the famous Water Libation Ceremony during Sukkot, he arrogantly poured the water upon the floor, which resulted in a riot. The people were angry about his flagrant violations of Orthodox Pharisaic Judaism, and some people even threw etrog fruits and palms at him. His soldiers ruthlessly slaughtered 6000 Jews to quell the incident. This is yet another example of how the Sadducees did not represent the general public and it was their court that handed out death penalties on feast days and at night. Because of their infiltration into the court systems by authority of the Roman government, normative Jewish courts for capital punishment were suspended over forty years before the destruction of the Temple. A Jewish court, even theoretically, could not give out capital punishment with fewer than twenty-three righteous judges.

Dr. Gerald Friedlander quotes Dr. James Hastings *Dictionary of Christ and the Gospels* pg. 467, which says: "The Pharisees are not characterized by luxurious living, however; the Sadducees were in comfortable circumstances." (Vol. 2, pg. 549). It will not be disputed by any impartial student that the Pharisees preached keeping of the Law with the coming world of bliss as a reward for obedience. Dr. Hastings Dictionary admits that "the Rabbis taught their disciples to seek first after Heaven and its righteousness, to look past the present legal life to a future world of grace and bliss" (Vol. 2, pg. 552). They did not believe whatever wealth they might have was a reward for keeping the Law. As a class, they were mostly poor.

The wealth of the nation was in the hands of the aristocracy - that meant the Sadducees. (Dr. Buchler). In *Antiquities XVI*, ii.3 Josephus writes: "If anyone asks the Pharisees which of two things they wish to part with, their lives or their religious observances, they would readily prefer to suffer anything whatsoever, rather than dissolution of any of their sacred customs". The Pharisees lived modestly, and despised delicacies, and followed the government of reason. They believed that souls had an immortal vigor and that in the hereafter there would be rewards or punishments. Accordingly, they lived virtuously and they were able to excellently articulate these Torah doctrines.

Dr. Sandey, in *Sacred Sites of the Gospel* and Friedlander, in his writings, point out how the mass of the people were Pharisees, and suffered terribly at the hands of the cruel tax collectors who represented Roman imperial occupation. Friedlander continues, "Herod helped impoverish the people, so we can then better appreciate the early sayings in the Mishnah, 'Let the poor be as the children of Thy House.'"

The poverty and misery of the Pharisees are also referred to in the *Psalms of Solomon* IV.V in the *Assumption of Moses*

C.VII and also in the *Talmud* (*'Kleiternot'* by Dr. Krauss in his *'Talmudische archaologie I'*, pp 134, 135). The Rabbis gave their services as teachers and advisers freely and were then forced to engage in some profession or trade to earn their living.

This should enable the reader to correctly reinterpret Luke's accusation that they were lovers of money. The Nazarene seems to have wished his followers to renounce all their wealth. Only in such a context of extreme piety could Luke be understood as being upset with those righteous Pharisees who would not take that radical leap – but not that they were objectively lovers of money. Luke himself had to forsake his family and friends, as it says, "hate your father and mother" (Luke 14;26, Matthew 10:34) and embrace a life of charity for his daily living and following his teacher.

No objective evaluation would claim that a poor Pharisee should have to rely on other people's charity and be a burden to the community. Judaism teaches that to receive your daily bread free is shameful. One should work for a living, as the Pharisees did. The situation was turned on its head by the Church, pointing judgmental fingers at the Pharisees to make them out as gross materialists.

The poverty of Hillel and Nachum of Gimzo were not the exception but rather the general rule (*Taanith* 21a). Rabbi Chanina ben Dosa was so poor that he and his family had to survive a week at a time on a small measure of carobs (*Brachot* 17b). His rejection of the title 'prophet', despite miracles performed by him, is characteristic of Pharisaic teachers. Josephus says, "The Sadducees are able to persuade none but the rich, but the Pharisees have the multitude on their side. The poor cry for relief (*Ps. of Solomon* IV) and the Rabbis try to help them in their distress."

Dr. Hoennicke, in *Das Juden Christentum*, pg 50, mentions special laws for the relief of the poor which Rabbi Gamaliel intro-
duced. Dr. Charles points out that '*The Assumption of Moses*',
written between 4 BCE and 30 CE, which was a contemporary
document, vividly describes the injustice and avarice of the
Sadducees. They had no patriotic sentiment, they were indif-
ferent to the religious ideals of the Torah, and believed that the
Roman regime was better than a Jewish government.

In 1862, Geiger pointed out that the Nazarene stood on
Pharisaic grounds and followed generally the lines of Hillel
(*Jud, zeitschrift fur weissenschaft und Lieben II* pg 37). It would
be well for modern Christian theologians to bear these facts in
mind when criticizing the Pharisees. It is a sign of better times
in store to find that J.H.A. Hart protests against the wholesale
condemnation of all the Scribes and Pharisees in "*The Journal
of Theological Studies*", vol. XI pg. 40. All of the above is clearly
the standpoint of G. Friedlander in his classic work *Jewish
Sources of the Sermon on the Mount*, KTAV Publishing House,
New York, New York, p. 196.

Again, to sum up the situation: The Sadducees were the bad
guys who pushed the Syrian Greeks to attack Torah Judaism.
Antiochus IV Epiphanes, King of the Seleucid dynasty (175
B.C.E.) agreed with Sadducee sedition and instituted a series
of horrible decrees (I Maccabees 1:44-50).

G-d forbid that we should forsake the Law and Ordinances! We
will not hearken to the king's words, to go from our religion,
either on the right hand or the left (I Maccabees 2:21-22).

Judah the Maccabee's name says it all: for it means: "Judah the
hammer", and it is the acronym for "Who is like You among the

powers, O G-d" (Exodus 15:11). As Josephus says in *Antiquities* 12:255-6, "And indeed, many Jews complied with the king's decrees, either voluntarily, or out of fear of the penalty. But the best and noblest men did not pay him attention … Every day they underwent great miseries with rods, and their bodies were torn to pieces and were crucified. And if there were found any sacred book of the Law, it was destroyed and those with whom they were found sorrowfully perished as well." (See article by Rav Naphtali Hoff, *Heroism Personified,* Hamodia, 2 Teves, 5771).

CHAPTER 12

The perceived Message of the NT

Analysing the New Testament as a Source of Christian Rejection of Jews and Judaism

We have outlined above how the political interests of Rome used religion and the newly established Christian Church to further their anti-Jewish agenda. The effect this agenda had on what is regarded as the anti-Jewish and anti-Rabbinic directives of the NT and its main role-players needs deep and thorough consideration.

The main reasons for the Christian beliefs that the NT rejects the Torah, Rabbinism, and Oral Torah interpretation by the Rabbinic order, are contained in the following popular concepts:

1. Christian teachings of 'Grace versus Law', 'once saved always saved', 'the Law has been nailed to the Cross,' etc.

2. Harsh words and statements used in the NT against the Pharisees and scribes.

3. Seeming rejection of the Torah (Law) by the Nazarene in the NT.

4. Paul's teachings against the Law.

Against this we need to weigh the following factors:

1. The influence of Roman hatred towards Jews and Judaism on the early Messianic congregation.

2. Probable tampering with the NT writings under the influence of the Roman Church.

3. The influence of forces within Judaism of that time which sided with the Romans and betrayed their own people.

These influences which serve as driving powers for anti-Judaism and anti-Rabbinism, are so wide and encompassing that it underlies all and any discussion of the wider topic of this book. We have thus already discussed some of these influencing factors earlier in the context of other issues. We shall continue here with the rest of those listed above.

The harsh Rabbinic debates in and about the NT

Rabbis can be harsh and at odds with each other at times. The harshness in the recorded NT debating did not imply a hatefulness, or disqualification of the opposing side in the debate, but was merely a reflection of Jewish religious tradition and scholarship by the Jewish role players in the NT.

What could be the motive behind the seeming rejectionist attitude of the Nazarene towards the teachers of Judaism in some of these NT statements?

"War over a book ultimately leads to love" (*Talmud*). Argument for the sake of heaven is valid and good and will stand in a place of righteousness, to paraphrase the Mishnah.

Debate in Talmud and in all Rabbinic literature was an expression of passion and love between the Sages arguing for G-d, the Torah and the Jewish people, even though it could sound nasty at times. It was very important not to blur the issues at hand; not to take an ambiguous word that could have a possible contradictory application and turn all points of differentiation in that Divine Word into confusion.

One of the teaching methods of the Sages was to use jokes and laughter to start off a lecture for many deep reasons (*Brachot* 31a, *Sabbath* 30 b, *Taanit* 22a). They also would start a discussion with bitter criticism (censure) and end the discussion with encouragement, support and praise. Once Rabbi Tarfon bitterly attacked Rabbi Akiva and screamed, "I can't take it any longer. How long will Akiva keep developing his worthless teachings? It's intolerable!" However, when he was sure of the validity and solid logic of Rabbi Akiva's position, he humbly retracted. "By the holy Temple service, you did not make this up. Be happy, Avraham our father, that Akiva came forth from your descendants. Whoever departs from the teachings of Rabbi Akiva is as if he departs from his own life" (*Sifri Numbers*). Both of these Sages died a martyr's death at the hand of the Romans while defending G-d and country.

The Sages, at times, would fling arrows at each other ('empty vessels', 'you foolish Babylonian'). In accordance with Psalms 127, "As arrows in the hand of a mighty person, so are the children of one's youth. Happy is the person who has his quiver full of arrows. They will not be put to shame, even when they speak with their enemies at the gates." This means the arrows of intellectual analysis, fired at their enemies, in legitimate debate concerning the exact meaning of the holy Torah. Again, these people who are fighting with each other and arguing, throwing insults and barbed remarks were usually the best of friends. (*Kedushim* 30).

> Deuteronomy 6:5-9 says: "Teach the Torah diligently to your children ..." Your children are clearly considered your students, that means your students are like your children!

Each group of Sages move to an opposite side, thereby creating in the middle of this forum of inquiry room for creation to emerge with finite bounded dimensions, enabling a practical, physical and corporeal application of the Divine Word in question; giving it height, width and depth, thereby clothing it with physical application in this physical, finite, corporeal world in which we live.

The form and outer structure of the Oral Torah is in itself a reflection of godliness and G-d in His transcendental aspect of existence. With this in mind, one can better understand that expressions of harshness between the positions of the Jewish Sages are crucial to create different sides to the in-depth examination of Biblical texts – as the lyrics of a popular song "I can see things from both sides now, from up and down ...."

The Mishnah states: "Warm yourself by the fire of the Sages; but beware of their glowing coals lest you be burned. For their bite is the bite of a fox. Their sting is of a scorpion. Their hiss like that of a snake and all of their words are like fiery coals." In ancient references to traits of animals were used in a positive way. E.g. when Jacob blessed the Tribe of Dan as 'a snake', it was a positive parallel.

It's OK and acceptable to shape your intellectual G-d-given logical analysis of verse and Word into a sharp, well-defined arrow-like point that can fly over a great distance. G-d gave us a mind not as a stumbling block, but as a tool to discover Him. We need to use the mind's logical and intellectual capacity to the nth degree in order to understand G-d's wisdom to the nth degree.

The Rebbe who authored the dictum stated: "I learned much from my teachers, more from my colleagues, but most from my students". He still was able to say, half jokingly, of his brilliant disciple Levi, "It appears to me that he has no brains in his skull." Meaning, he is so open-minded that his brains have fallen out.

Sages have called each other (despite unanimous agreement on their respective piety, intellect and scholarship), the following epithets: cowards, troublesome fellow, empty bottles, a hard man – as hard as iron, a black pot, earthen vessel, untrained judges (literally untrained at arbitration); foolish Babylonian; or the opposite, namely that one Babylonian scholar is worth two in the land of Israel, they being more analytical, the Israeli ones being more encyclopedic. All of the above examples show that harsh words and strong images and adjectives can be used by Sages. This in no way implied that there was any lacking of legitimacy, holiness, piety or wisdom. The point being made here is that it is normal to have harsh words between the Sages for the purposes of clarification, examination and analysis of a text, thereby 'drawing to the sides' in order to capture the minute nuances, depths and wisdom of the Divine Word under debate

CHAPTER 13

The Apostle Paul's anti-Rabbinic teachings in the NT

It is hard for anyone to admit the possible error of one's most cherished theories. To most NT believers, the apostle Paul's instructions seem to have taken precedence over the instructions of G-d. It is the NT teachings of the apostle Paul, who regarded himself a Pharisaic Jew, that have caused much of the anti-Judaism, anti-Rabbinism and anti-Torahism which is so prevalent in the Church – even amongst ardent Hebraic Roots Restorers who have returned and accepted so much of Torah Judaism, that they live and even dress like Jews. 'Rabbinic authority' and acceptance of the Oral Torah, even for these to-Torah-returned and Torah practising non-Jews seems to present the final insurmountable stumbling block. It remains an obstacle to the ultimate goal of Prophecy, namely, reconciliation between the two divided Houses of Israel and Peace in the House of G-d.

The reader should withhold judgment on this issue of the correctness or not of Paul until having carefully perused and considered the content of this chapter. The prevailing popular misconceptions concerning Paul will become clear, especially if considered in the light of the other convincing evidence presented in this book, viz.:

- The Halachic Jewish foundations hidden in the NT.

- The clear evidence presented in the NT that the Nazarene himself was a traditional Jew connected to the culture of Rabbinic Judaism.

- The phenomenon of the current Hebraic Restoration movement across the entire earth, confirming the fulfilment of the main Prophecies of Scripture and the ultimate Divine Goal for humanity.

Any justification of Paul's anti-Rabbinic teachings should be weighed up against these confirmations.

Taking a sobering look at Paul, the main spokesman in the NT

The author of the thirteen Pauline epistles plainly admitted that he had not reached perfection; and it is a gross injustice to his character to present him to the world as infallible and the author of a "new Gospel".

A diligent search through all thirteen of the epistles of Paul will show that he was every whit as subject to the weaknesses and prejudices of mankind as is any other human being in this world This fact is thus emphasized, NOT because we have any desire to belittle this apostle; but rather that the false over-rated image of this man might crumple and fall and the final obstacles to peaceful reunion in the House and Nation of G-d be removed so as to pave the way for the establishment of the re-united 12-Tribed Kingdom of G-d.

It is regrettable that popular, traditional NT interpretation have so wrested the words of a man of G-d, that he has become a substitute for the Word of G-d. Thus, the instructions of Paul, when colliding head-on with the clear Command of G-d in the Tanach (O.T.), is taken above that of G-d! For this purpose, many Christian teachings have openly done away with the 'Old Testament' in defence of Paul's reasoning's! Consequently, the Rabbinic interpretations are discarded as man-made Laws, while Paul, just another man, is regarded as infallible and above the spirit of the Word of G-d as founded in the Jewish Tanach.

Surely it is high time that the authority of the Word of G-d (Tanach) be restored, and the inflated image of this admittedly 'carnal' man (according to his own admission in Romans 7:14) be deposed from the minds of G-d-fearing individuals. Let the faithful and true Jeremiah's dare "to root out, and to pull down, and to destroy" this mistaken impression of the apostle Paul, and "build and plant again in the hearts of G-d's people the true Word of G-d".

At the outset of this overview, let us realize, that what we have today in the 'New Testament' and which is attributed to the Hebrew apostle Paul, sections which are very 'un-Jewish' for a learned orthodox Jew such as Paul, may never have been written by him. One such instance is the whole Church leadership system of 'elders and deacons' - a system which is in contradistinction to the historic Judaic transmission, management and teaching process. He is closer to the pagan concept unknown to the initial Messianic Faith. Sections like this may well have been inserted by the Roman Catholic establishment which had almost exclusive rights over the original NT Scriptures (which are 'lost' to this day) and during a time when there were no printing presses or means of copying outside of the powerful hold of the Church.

The utterances and Commands of G-d never change or become obsolete - His admonitions and precepts are everlasting - they shall endure forever, The NT itself has this to say concerning them:

> "Heaven and earth shall pass away, but My words shall not pass away" (Matthew 24:35)

The Nazarene proclaimed: "Till heaven and earth disappear, not one yud (the smallest letter in the Hebrew alphabet) not one little stroke shall disappear from the Law until its purpose is achieved" (Matthew 5:18).

Yet, we have to conclude that the Scriptures contain an account of many of man's words, as well as a record of the Words of G-d. Consider, for example, the classic advice offered to Job, by his wife, when she saw him sitting "down among the ashes", covered with boils, and scraping himself with a chunk of broken pottery: her cheerful recommendation was that he should "curse G-d and die" (Job 2:9) - obviously not a G-d-inspired utterance!

No believer would dispute the fact that G-d's Words are perfect. If the record of His words bears any imperfections, they result solely from man's clumsy handling of the material. This is made evident in the many conflicting translations of and commentaries on the Bible, which are widely circulated at the present time.

The sober answer to the question: "is all Scripture Truth?", must be "No". for although all Scripture does give a true account of what took place, there are actually numbers of statements and quotations in 'The Book' which are merely a record of what someone has thought or said - and many of these, while accurate quotations of man's remarks or reflections, are actually in their content and meaning, Untruths: "You shall not surely die" (Genesis 3:4), the serpent breathed beguilingly to the woman - but she did die!

The discrepancies noted in the above-cited Words of man are glaringly evident - but there are many instances where the inconsistency is not so obvious. Many of the "dark sayings" of the prophets are truths which are veiled in the aura of metaphor and symbol. When these are taken out of their place or context they create no end of confusion. Peter said, concerning the writings of Paul, that there were some things hard to be understood, "which uneducated and unbalanced people distort, in the same way as they distort the rest of Scripture" (2 Peter 3:16).

"Rightly dividing the word of truth" (2 Tim.2:15), is an exact science. The apostle here advises that believers should study to show themselves "approved unto G-d".

It should not be difficult for anyone to believe that only G-d's words are the infallible standards: His Word is always Truth. Neither should it be confusing for anyone to accept the fact that the words of man are often one-sided and obscure.

Much of the darkness and error rife among many professing believers today, is largely due to unstable doctrinal foundations, a great number of which are unwittingly based upon distorted views and misconstruction of statements found in the epistles of Paul.

No one searching for Truth should be offended by the declaration that the Words of G-d are superior to the words of Paul. Yet, some may contend that G-d was the Author of every word which Paul wrote. But by studying Paul's own words, such a position can be disproved "I speak not by Commandment ... and herein I give my advice" (2 Cor. 8: 8-10). Paul's 'advice' undoubtedly was good, but it certainly was not always the Word of G-d.

Now notice the two different sources of the commands which Paul has written: "Unto the married I command, yet not I, but the L-rd .., but the rest is from me, not from the L-rd" (I Cor. 7:10-12). The apostle here makes it plain that he sometimes wrote what G-d commanded; and sometimes he wrote his own advice. The apostle himself is showing that these "Words from the L-rd" are superior to his own remarks.

Here is a quotation which definitely tells us that some of the apostle Paul's utterances and admonishments were of his own making: "Now concerning virgins I have no commandment of the L-rd: but I give my own opinion" (1 Cor . 7 : 25). Is the apostle's 'opinion' to be considered on a par with the Tanach and the Torah G-d? Surely not!

One other line from Paul's epistles should settle forever that his writings were not verbatim Inspiration of G-d: "What I am going to say now, is not prompted by the L-rd, but said as if in a fit of folly, in the certainty that I have something to boast about" (2 Cor, 11:17).

The wonderful thing about the Bible is that it does not hide the frailties of the men who were "subject to like passions as we are". We read of Adam and Eve's failures right at the outset – Paradise Lost! Noah's drunkenness, of Jacob and Rebecca's scheming, of Moses' mistake in striking the rock instead of speaking to it – he missed entry to the Land, king Solomon in his old age making a series of mistakes, and of the failings of many others. None of these great men were angelic or superior to the Word of G-d. For those who believe in the NT, why would the same not apply to Paul?

It would be well for people everywhere to examine the writings of Paul with unbiased minds, taking into consideration what they were, and realizing also what he was – simply "a man with like passions".

This misrepresentation of the True Purpose and Plan of the Creator G-d for man - as embodied in the 'New Gospel of Grace', which is accredited to the apostle Paul, who seems to have strayed from the original Hebrew roots of it all.

It is claimed that Paul wrote 13 letters, and each one of them started with his own name! He used the personal pronoun 'I, me, or my', 949 times! In the twelfth chapter of 2 Corinthians, the big personal pronoun was used seven times in the sixth verse alone; 60 times in the same chapter of 21 verses!

Certainly no other Hebrew teacher has displayed so much egotism, in so many different ways, as the apostle Paul has exhibited throughout all of his writings. We find that the apostle Paul declared that he was "not a whit behind the very chiefest apostles" (2 Cor. 11:5); and again: "In nothing am I behind the very chiefest apostles" (2 Cor. 12:11). Masses of Christians today regard him as just such - and even more, considering that they allow Paul to have authority over the Law of G-d, claiming it to have been replaced, done away with, nullified, "nailed to the Cross!" As such, they regard him as author of a 'New Gospel'.

Devotees of the theology of 'grace unlimited' find abundant support for their teachings in the epistles of Paul. It is this teaching that has opened the door to the world for unrestricted license, freedom and liberty from all law to any who will accept and believe the new Gospel. It is this interpretation which has contributed to these present times of lawlessness and crime without proper judgment in the world.

The thirteen epistles of this proponent from Tarsus representing Nazarene teaching are written in a style that is like an amazing obstacle course: Truth angled in such a fashion that it freely yields to the manipulations and devices of the triflers.

Here are some further audacious claims by Paul: "According to my Gospel" (Rom. 2:16; 16:25; 2 Tim. 2:8). No other NT contributor ever spoke of the Messianic Gospel as 'my' Gospel. Even the Nazarene himself never referred to it as 'My' Message.

It seems from a NT perspective, that it would be uncalled for, for anyone to attempt to introduce another Gospel. This is even contrary to Paul's own teaching.

Those who rebel against G-d, despise the Divine Commandments and rebel against Go-d's Law - eagerly grasp at Paul's teachings which apparently sanction lawlessness.

Doctrines related to the Law seem to have been the most confusing issues in the mind of the author of these thirteen letters to the Messianic congregations. At times he wrote one thing to a congregation in one city, and then again, he would write just the opposite letter to another group: "A man is not justified by the works of the Law" (Gal. 2:16) he told the Galatians - but to the Romans he wrote; "For not the hearers of the Law are just before G-d, but the doers of the Law shall be justified" (Rom 2:13). Surely the man was not double-minded? Could it have been that he was in confusion on this subject of Law?

Consider the following quotations, taken from two different epistles, written by this same man: "Once, when there was no Law, I was alive; but when the Commandment came, sin came to life, and I died. The Commandment was meant to lead me to life, but it turned out to mean death for me" (Rom.7:9,10); and, "... if the administering of death, in the written letters engraved on stones, was glorious ... if there was any splendour in administering condemnation, there must be very much greater splendour in administering justification ... if what was done away with was glorious, there must be much more in what is going to last for ever" (2 Corinthians 3:7-11).

If words mean anything, then the author of these epistles is saying that the Ten Commandments were done away with, abolished, ended. At least, this is the meaning as it appears on the surface and as it has been accepted by most of Christianity: but remember, that the words of this scribe are tricky and they are especially designed to trap the carnal mind which rebels against the Truth.

Paul said that there was a veil upon the hearts of the Jews when they read Moses (2 Cor. 3:15); but that veil, he claims, created upon the hearts of those Pharisees of old by the writings of the great patriarch is as nothing compared to the covering which the works of Paul have effected to envelop many hearts in our generation. The words of Moses never offered even any remote excuse for carnality; no way out for those who would try to dodge the Divine Command - but many of the things set forth in the epistles of Paul are loaded with bait to snare the hypocrite and the rebels against the Law!

If the following words are to be taken literally, consider the latitude they offer for licentiousness: "All things are lawful unto me ... all things are lawful for me" (I Cor. 6:12); and again, "All things are lawful for me" (I Cor. 10:23). Add to these, the verse, "Happy is he that condemns not himself in that thing which he allows" (Rom. 14:22). If this combination does not offer a license to sin, then words have no meaning!

If NT believers insist that it is Divinely inspired, then they have to conclude that G-d allowed the above seeming misinformation to be in it. Yes! The Most High has designed many snares and set numerous traps for the feet of the deceitful: The NT itself confirms "G-d shall send them strong delusion, that they should believe a lie" (2 Thess. 2:11).

The attitude of every sincere seeker of Truth should be one of prayerful caution with regard to the writings of the apostle Paul. No explanation in his messages should ever be accepted as valid, unless such conclusions can be confirmed by the Word of G-d as contained in and guarded in the Tanach (OT). How is it possible that this apostle so often appears to be misquoting, and even misrepresenting the Scriptures as interpreted by the Guardians of G-d's Oracles (the Jews - Romans 3:2) in such a seemingly careless manner?

Many of the statements in Paul's letters are extremely misleading. Examine this apparent contradiction concerning those who died in the plague of Midian. In Numbers 25:9 we read: "And those that died in the plague were twenty and four thousand." Now compare the above statement, made by Moses, with that of Paul's in (1 Cor. 10:8), "Neither let us commit fornication, as some of them committed, and fell in one day twenty three thousand". Did Paul miss the number by one thousand?

With several direct statements Paul intimates that the Law no longer exists:

- "We are now dead to the Law" (Rom. 7:4)

- "We are now rid of the Law ... free to serve in the new spiritual way and not the old way of a written Law" (Rom. 7:6)

In his contradictory way he then continues in the next few paragraphs (Rom. 7:7-25) to uphold the Law with statements like:

- "The Law is sacred" (Rom. 7:12)

- "The Law is spiritual" (Rom. 7:14)

- "he dearly loves G-d's Law" (Rom. 7:22)

- "he serves the Law" (Rom. 7:25)

In 1 Cor. 7:25-40, Paul embarks on a further contradictory advisory position regarding virginity and intimate practices of married couples. It is a perfect doctrinal essay for Catholic Celibacy - which makes one think: who really wrote this section of Scripture? Judaism advocates celebration not celibacy, in other words, active reproduction of life according to G-d's Command in Gen. 1:28: "G-d blessed them saying: 'Be fruitful, multiply, fill the earth and conquer it'". Isaiah says that world was created to be inhabited, not desolate. Paul prescribes non-marriage and even withholding of intimate relations within marriage. G-d saw that "it is not good that the man be alone, I will make him a help mate ..." Gen. 2:18. So G-d created a female partner for Adam! Paul says it is better to stay single and not give your daughter away in marriage! He puts marriage as a good second, as a fatal alternative because of reigning immorality. In other words, "O.K. rather than immorality, if you cannot exercise self-control, then get married!" Intimacy between married partners is sin - is the loud and clear message of this section.

> Paul's unadulterated egotism is clear from his arrogant statement in1 Cor. 4:16, when he boldly says, "I beseech you, be ye followers of me," and again in:

> Phil. 3:17 and 2 Thess.3:7. "Be ye followers of me even as I am also of Messiah" (1 Cor. 11:1).

Yet, Paul admitted to "sin that dwelleth in me" and he talked about the evil which he would not do, and "that I do" (Rom. 7:19). He stated that in his flesh "dwelleth no good thing" (Rom. 7:18). Can a NT follower really take this man as their perfect example and allow him to declare the Law of G-d as 'abolished' while the Nazarene himself declared the Law "has NOT been abolished" Matt, 5:17.

Over the matter of the doctrine of circumcision. he bragged to the Galatians that he had dressed down the apostle Peter:

"I withstood him to the face, because he was to be blamed ... I said unto Peter before them all ..." (Gal 2:11-21). "Behold I Paul say unto you, that if ye be circumcised, Messiah shall profit you nothing ... ye are fallen from grace" (Gal. 5:1-4). Nowhere did the Nazarene ever indicate that circumcision would be done away with – while he and all the apostles were circumcised themselves "on the 8th day" as the Torah requires. Is Paul inferring here that the apostles, followers of their Messiah, do not profit from their Messiah?

But the astonishing thing about this whole matter is that a number of years after he publicly withstood Peter to his face over the matter of circumcision, he himself circumcised a man! The father of his friend Timothy, was a Greek - so, before he took this young preacher with him on his missionary journeys, Paul himself, performed the Abrahamic Covenant rite upon him. "... and Paul, who wanted to have him as a traveling companion, took and circumcised him. This was on account of the Jews in the locality ..." (Acts 16:3).

In Galatians 2:7 Paul recognizes his mandate: "I had been commissioned to preach the Good News to the uncircumcised..." and then he makes an astonishing statement in total contradiction of what the NT states about the mission of the apostle Peter, shown to Peter in the Vision of the unkosher animals. Paul erroneously concludes in this text "... just as Peter had been commissioned to preach to the circumcised." Clearly, by insisting to go "to the Jew first" with the Gospel, Paul was either confused - or else he challenged his Divine mandate!

Doesn't anyone else find it incongruous that not a single utterance from the Nazarene's teachings in the Gospel accounts are found in Paul's many letters? If the apostles were handpicked and trained by the Nazarene, it was obviously in order that their witness would be full and superior to others. Then it should be incumbent on Paul to learn from them. Yet, by Paul's own admission, he fails to do so for years. How then can Paul form the greater body of NT Scripture when his ideas are not based on the Nazarene's teachings? When his teachings so often oppose and overthrow the Torah and Tanach (OT) teachings? Christianity is being expounded by someone who never spent any extended time with the Nazarene, never trained under him, and whose writings are devoid of utterances of the Nazarene - except for one small unique aphorism and only one inaccurate quote from the Nazarene's Last Supper (Pesach Seder) account.

Other respected thinkers have been astonished by Paul's lack of mentioning any lessons of the Nazarene. Albert Schweitzer once said: "Where possible, he (Paul) avoids quoting the teaching of Jesus, in fact even mentioning it. If we had to rely on Paul, we should not know that Jesus taught in parables, had delivered the Sermon on the Mount, and had taught his disciples the 'Our Father.' Even where they are specially relevant, Paul passes over the words of Jesus.". *Refs.: Albert Schweitzer Library: The Mysticism of Paul the Apostle (John Hopkins University Press: 1998). 28. Hans van Campenhausen, The Formation of the Christian Bible (J. A. Baker, trans.) (Philadelphia: Fortress Press, 1972).*

Paul shows himself up by his final blunders

Driven by an over-zealous self-determination to accomplish what G-d had said could not be done, Paul still believed that he could convert the Jerusalem Jews to Messianism. Shortly after Paul's conversion on the road to Damascus, the Nazarene told him plainly: "Hurry, leave Jerusalem at once; for they will not accept the Testimony concerning me ... Go! I am sending you to the Gentiles far away." (Acts 22:18-21).

However, after many years of preaching, he must have felt that he had acquired persuasive powers sufficient to open the eyes of the most stubborn Jew. At any rate, "Paul purposed in the spirit ... to go to Jerusalem" (Acts 19:21). Only a thoroughly self-willed, headstrong person would brush aside so many warnings such as Paul were given on his way south: "The Holy Spirit, in town after town, has made it clear enough, that imprisonment and persecution await me". (Verse 23). But blind self-will is a deceitful thing. He thought that he was doing G-d service; he purposed in his spirit to go, and that was that!

At the city of Tyre, he found certain disciples and "stayed there a week. Speaking in the Spirit, the disciples kept on telling Paul not to go on to Jerusalem" (Acts 21:4)... Notice that this instruction came through more than one disciple. According to the NT, the Living G-d was speaking "through His servants" to this headstrong, misguided servant.

On his way to Jerusalem, Paul simply ignored all warnings and all Commands "through the Spirit". He had only one thing in mind: he must convert the Jews to Messianism.

The question may arise, "Why was Paul not stopped in his tracks because of his wilful disobedience to the Divine Command?"

Paul, accordingly, was in fact severely punished for his rebellion. From the very day that he turned from the Divine Commandment which he perceived, he was very much on his own. His six days in the big city are a disgrace upon his ministry. He compromised his whole message against priest craft in an abortive attempt to reach the Jews. He did the very thing for which he had openly rebuked his brethren.

He discarded all that he had preached and taught, by offering an animal sacrifice! Hear these words from the records of the book of Acts (*with our comments in brackets to emphasize the essence of this amazing section from the NT*):

We read from Acts chapter 21:19 onwards about Paul's arrival and meeting with his Messianic brothers in Jerusalem. "After greeting them, he gave a detailed account of all that G-d had done among the pagans through his ministry. They gave glory to G-d when they heard this. 'But you see, brother' they said, 'how thousands of Jews have now become believers (*in Messiah*), all of them staunch upholders of the Law (of Moses), and they have heard that you instruct all Jews living amongst the Gentiles, to break away from Moses (*admitting therefore that Paul did teach "doing away with the Law". The New Testament writings of Paul abounds with such instructions*), authorising them not to circumcise their children or to follow the customary practices (*Rabbinic Halacha*). What is to be done?"

The leaders of the Messianic congregation at Jerusalem then arrive at the following solution: Acts 21:23, "We have four men here who are under a vow. Take these men along and be purified with them (*a ritual process according to Jewish Law*) and pay all the expenses connected with the shaving of their heads. This will let everyone know that that there is no truth in the reports and that you still regularly observe the Law. As for those Gentile believers (*who have accepted the Messianic Faith*) we wrote them and told them our decisions (*regarding the need to keep the Law*), that they must abstain from things sacrificed to idols, from blood, from the meat of strangled animals and from fornication (*This according to a prior ruling which they had made and in line with the minimum requirements set by the 'Noahide Covenant' - Acts 15:19*)."

"So, the next day Paul took the men along and was purified with them, and he visited the Temple to give notice of the time when the period of purification would be over and the offering would have to be presented on behalf of each of them. The seven days were nearly over, when some Jews caught sight of him in the Temple and stirred up the crowd and seized him, shouting, 'Men of Israel, help! This is the man who preaches to everyone everywhere against our people, against the Law and against this place!'"

In a hearing against him, shortly after, Paul admitted: Acts 24:17 "After several years I came to bring alms to my nation and to make offerings. It was in connection with these that they found me in the Temple."

From this time to the end of his life, Paul remained a prisoner. NT readers may contemplate whether it was the 'Rod of G-d' that had fallen on his back as punishment for his stubborn rebellion against the advice of G-d?

Conclusion

Paul's teachings have also been rejected also by the Ebionites and the Nazarenes who were the Hebraic rooted Messianic community of that period. They regarded Paul as an imposter, as a Gentile who tried to marry the daughter of a Jewish priest, got circumcised but was still rejected by her family. According to this rejection belief, he went out with a chip on his shoulder to argue against the Sabbath, circumcision, which he called in Greek 'mutilation' and the laws of Torah.

Eusebius, a Roman bishop who canonized the NT, describes the Hebrew rooted Ebonite community negatively, because "the Ebonites thought that the letters of Paul ought to be wholly rejected and called Paul an apostate from the law" (*HE* 11 127, 3-6 - translation of Eus, *HE* by K.Luke in the Loeb series).

The 'saved by Grace' believers have the foundation for their belief based upon their own interpretations of the writings of Paul. Take these epistles away from them, and in the rest of their Bibles they have no foundation for their teaching of "Grace which has done away with the Law". These teachings of Paulinism have influenced the teachings of most of the denominations of Christianity and it forms part of the 'pagan baggage' which the noble Hebrew Roots Restoration Movement has not fully recognized yet for what it really is. To these people, Paul has virtually superseded the Nazarene whose servant he should have been. Paul's words and interpretations are taken above the Word of G-d as defined in the Tanach and the Torah.

On the positive side though, there is a wide awakening amongst re-awakening Ten Tribers of the Hebraic Roots Restoration awareness. This process has received fiery momentum by the knowledge explosion of the last few decades, true to the prophecy in Daniel 12:9, "These words are to remain secret and sealed till The Time of the End ... the learned will understand". The advent of the technology revolution has made knowledge available on a scale never imagined before.

Out of this has grown a gradual movement amongst serious and sincere Christians, back to the True System of G-d. Seventh Day Sabbath churches popped up as early as the 19th century and restored the true 'Jewish Sabbath'. This was followed by the restoration of the Sacred Feasts of G-d ('Jewish Feasts') as was powerfully promoted by Herbert Armstrong's 'World Wide Church of God' movement.

Then followed the Sacred Name Movement, restoring the original Hebrew versions of G-d's Name. And of late, there arose "The Restoration of Hebrew Roots Movement" amongst dedicated Christian sectarians. This movement promotes the original Biblical ('Jewish') customs and Hebrew language terms are used freely and intermittently. For many Restoration believers, this has led to a desire for full conversion to Judaism - which completes the full circle back to the original – as foretold in numerous Prophecies of the Tanach (O.T.).

These Hebraic Restorers and Returnees to Torah had to, and continue to 'wrestle' with the writings of Paul. Notwithstanding the positive denunciation by Paul of many true tenets of Judaism, many of these Returnees, while defending Paul, are nevertheless progressively returning to the Law and Customs of Judaism, the Original True Faith.

The contents of the study above and its headlong confrontation with 'Paul's written statements', should shed much light on the true facts, namely, that only G-d is infallible and mankind, including the powerful apostle Paul, are merely beings 'of like passion'.

May this realization give a further and final boost to the Restoration of the re-united 12-Tribed Kingdom of the G-d of Israel.

CHAPTER 14

Pagan influences in early Christian theology

Rick Richardson in *Origins of our Faith – the Hebrew Roots of Christianity* brings many examples and sources to elucidate the above heading. Prof. Howard Vos, in his book *Exploring Church History*, points out that, though Christianity was winning a victory of sorts over paganism, paganism won victories of its own by infiltrating the Church in numerous subtle ways. Large segments of Constantine Church membership consisted merely of baptised pagans. Distinctions between Christianity and paganism became blurred, as the State church was established under the authority of the emperor – who was considered "G-d on earth".

We need to remember that in the early Church there were not just new believers in the Nazarene; there were also brand-new believers in regard to Avraham, Isaac and Jacob. Before this time, these new members were worshipping many gods and viewed worship of the G-d of Avraham in a way that was natural and familiar to them. In this way, Christianity also developed as a 'watered-down Judaism.'

John Selbey Sprung, in *The Hebrew Lord*, says that the Christian faith was born in a Hebrew context, serving a Hebrew G-d Who was One: life-giving and life-loving. It eventually confronted the dualistic mind of the Greek world. The Hebrew view of the goodness of creation and the wholeness of life, with its underlying unity, was forgotten. The Hellenization of the Gospels had begun and many were the outgrowths of neopolitan Greek philosophies. The Church Fathers were not educated in the Torah but in Greek philosophy. Because the Gentile had a different paradigm, the manner in which they viewed what the earliest followers had written led them to an entirely different conclusion. For example: Mervin Wilson in *Our father Avraham* writes: "Platonism holds that there are two worlds – the visible and the invisible. The visible world is a source of imperfection and evil. Salvation comes at death when the soul escapes the body."

Origen, one of the important 'fathers' of Christian theology, was a Platonic philosopher. ("*The Greek ideas of Immortality*" – Harvard Review 52:1460). The Hebrews viewed the world as good, though not yet redeemed. It was created by a G-d of pure spirit and absolute Oneness who designed it with humanity's best interest at heart. So, instead of fleeing from the world, human beings experience G-d's fellowship, love and saving activity in historical order within the world. Dr. John Garr gives a glimpse at the ideas that were being promoted during this early point in Christian history.

Marcion, son of the bishop of Sinope in Pontus, joined the Syrian Gnostic credo in Rome in developing a dualistic view of sacred history. This postulated the existence of two 'gods', the good and gracious 'god' of the Nazarene and the demiurge 'god' of the Jews. He taught an irreconcilable dualism between Gospel and Law, Christianity and Judaism. The demiurge of the Jew's religion was seen as harsh and severe; therefore Jews were thrown into Hades by the Nazarene who was the 'Good god.'

Marcion established the 'New Canon of Gospels': an abridged Gospel of Luke and ten of Paul's epistles. He twisted the words in Matthew 5:17 to say, "I am not come to fulfil the Law and the Prophets, but to destroy them." Ref. www.marcion.info/

Marcion believed that Christianity had no connection whatsoever with the past, but had fallen abruptly and magically from heaven. The Nazarene was not born nor did he die. His body was a phantom to reveal the 'good G-d' and his death was an illusion. This Nazarene was not the predicted Messiah. He was a totally new and unforeseen manifestation of the good god of Greek dualism. The rest of the apostles were corruptors of pure Christianity. The Nazarene appointed Paul to be the apostle to preach the truth of Marcion's anti-nomianism and anti-Judaism.

Marcion was the first to create a 'New Testament' and believed that the 'Old Testament' should be discarded! The Church excommunicated Marcion because of lunacy and heresy, but even so, they incorporated his collections of Gospel texts and the epistles of Paul into the canonised, official 'New Testament'.

As we mentioned earlier, some Christian scholars point out that the anti-Semitic aspects of the epistles are from Marcion, and the pro-Jewish sentiments are original Paulinian. There was a great influx of Gentiles into this new Hebrew sect at the same time that Roman oppression was growing and would wipe out a generation of Jews. Therefore, the ensuing wars between Jews and the Roman Empire removed the Sadducees from history along with the small Hebrew Messianic community. It also blotted out the righteous school of the House of Shammai. During the wars against Rome, Jews fought against the pro-Roman Sadducee Jews. In brief, the ensuing wars between the Jews and the Roman Empire knocked the Sadducees right out of history along with many small contradicting Hebrew sects, including Hebrew Christian sects.

As a result of the destruction of the 2nd Temple and other wars against Rome, the righteous school of Shammai was obliterated. So, again, the people that would have created a pro-Roman court, to sit at night, namely the Sadducees, no longer existed. In other words, the Sadducees who sentenced the Nazarene were actually wiped out by the Jewish Pharisees against Rome and its collaborators. The majority of arguments between the Gospels and the Pharisees were actually arguments between the schools of Hillel vs. Shammai (schools of legitimate Biblical thought). So, many of my Christian friends have been wasting their time being angry at groups of people and blaming present day Jews in the name of opposing Jews who haven't existed for over 1900 years.

Prof. Vergilius Ferm, in his *Encyclopaedia of Religion*, brings numerous proofs of the rampant pagan ideologies that surrounded and intertwined with early Syrian-Roman Christianity. Pagan ideologies frequently had a holiday around Dec. 25th, celebrating the winter solstice. Another example is SUNday, which was so named because it was dedicated to the pagan sun god. Under Constantine, it became the day which replaced the Sabbath for the early Church.

The important early Christian sect called Arians, held that the teaching of 'A Trinity' is illogical and impossible, and denied the claim that the Nazarene was equal to G-d. However, they were outvoted in the Council of Nicaea in 325 CE. The majority opinion forced the minority to submit to their views at the risk of torture and death. Constantine's Christianity sought to be all things to all people and needed to incorporate what started out as a monotheistic Hebrew sect into a pagan, Roman, world religion.

PART 4

GENERAL - RELATED ISSUES

CHAPTER 15

Who is to blame for the death
of the Nazarene?

Let us examine another great misunderstanding which is commonly embraced by the Christian faith: one which developed from Hebraic foundations. I wish to paraphrase a quote from Earl Doherty's *"The Nazarene Puzzle,"* regarding the historic reality of the existence of the Nazarene:

> "The book of Mark makes Pontius Pilate act in a way that contradicts the historical record and Roman imperial policy, by having the demands of the Jews to kill the Nazarene nullify his attempts to exonerate him. Roman authorities would never have allowed a crowd to choose Barabbas over the Nazarene. An event of this sort has no precedent in Roman policy. As the NT reads, Mark places the responsibility for the conviction and execution of the Nazarene on the Jews."

It does not require a theological thesis to establish the clearly-defined bias from the New Testament itself, in which it presents the true guilty party for the execution of the Nazarene. The NT places this guilt squarely on the shoulders of his followers – which thus excludes the Jews as a religious entity which rejected the Nazarene as Messiah.

1 Cor. 2:8,

"Which none of the princes of this world knew: for had they known (it), they would not have crucified the Lord of glory".

Luke 18:31-33,

31 "Then he took (unto him) the twelve, and said unto them, 'Behold, we go up to Jerusalem, and all things that are written by the prophets concerning the Son of man shall be accomplished. 32 <u>For he shall be delivered unto the Gentiles</u>, and shall be mocked, and spitefully entreated, and spitted on 33 And they shall scourge [him], and put him to death: and the third day he shall rise again'."

The former Catholic Pope, present Pope and a host of Protestant theologians acknowledge that Rome fought wars against the Jews:

- The revolt against Rome 66 CE resulting in the destruction of the 2nd Temple.

- The revolt of Jewish slaves in the Diaspora.

- The Bar Kokhba rebellion, a.k.a. the Hadrianic Wars in 132 CE, which culminated in the destruction of Jewish settlement.

- As well as several mini-wars against the Jews.

Early Christian Messianism, which was destined to grow under Roman rule, was therefore exposed to, and virtually forced to put up with Roman hatred of Jews, as well as Roman influence of and tampering with texts. Either this, or Mark is guilty of blatant misrepresentation of historical facts.

This also reveals the source of a serious problem that occurred during the infancy of Christianity – hatred of Jews. Implanted into the formative years of the infant Christian Church, ancient Roman hatred of Jews seems to have been a major cause of the great misunderstanding by Christianity of Judaism. This applies also to children, where the first 7 years are regarded as the formative years of their future culture, from which the future mature person will always have difficulty extricating himself.

Similarly, the great phenomenon of late, the Hebraic Roots Restoration among Messianics of Christian origin, may be regarded as the mature stage of this religious 'infant', during which he is 'thinking for himself', asking questions and making his own conclusions – in this way returning to his original heritage. It is to be expected that during this progressive spiritual process, many of them would still be captured along the way by this hidden power of deceit from which these faithful are striving to extricate themselves.

Matthew's report added another blood libel, by putting into the mouth of the Jews, "Let His blood be upon us forever". Upon means a covering that is a form of atonement. The literal word here, atonement - *kappora*, in Hebrew literally means something that covers i.e. a Kippah which is a head covering or a Chupah which is a wedding canopy!

King of his beloved Jewish people? This would make him an enemy of Roman imperial rule and a target for arrest, trumped-up charges and execution.

According to *A Christian Reading of the Gospels* by Rev. Elmer A. Josephson. *Israel God's Key to world Redemption*, Bible Light Pub., Hillsboro Kansas:

> "It was at the Temple at Chanukah where every vestige of the Christ-killer charge against the Jews was punctured. The occasion was a celebration of the Jewish Maccabees victory over the Greek Hellenists, called the Feast of Dedication (John 10:22). According to the NT, the Nazarene, referring to his coming death, declared, 'Therefore does the Father love me, that I lay down my life. No man takes it away from me, but I lay it down of myself. I have the power to lay it down and to take it up again'".

John 11:50 says that the Nazarene was to die for the people – and not just for the people of that time, but also that he should "gather together in one, the people of G-d being scattered abroad." This seemingly refers to the gathering of the Lost Ten Tribes of Israel in the latter times, thus implying that Christianity would be a tool in this process.

Rev. Josephson points out that the Gospels cite crucifixion as a method of Roman execution. Crucifixion was never used by the Jews; stoning was more applicable. However, the Torah courts of the Pharisees refrained from declaring death penalties. They did not execute anyone in those days because the corrupt, pro-Roman Sadducees often were part of the court.

The cruel Roman occupation disrupted the entire public Jewish legal system.

Those who hate Jews for 'having killed Christ', and who base their well- formulated accusations on NT information, should consider the following historical fact: the Jewish religious authorities were never in the business of punishing Jewish heretics. You will have to look far and wide to find another religious leadership that was as tolerant towards strange thoughts and heresies as was (and still today is) Jewish leadership. They simply did not kill people for their warped religious ideas – not then, and not now.

These self-same haters of present day Israel, might like the version of the Nazarene that offers an instant free pass from their sins and perceived salvation, but I bet as Rev. Josephson asks, "how many would vote for him?"

A superficial reading of the Gospels will result in the conclusion of a horribly unfair prosecution of a good person by bad people. Such a terrible happening would have been engraved into the minds of early Christian preachers and codifiers who were also (just the same as most of today's Messianic teachers) uninformed and misinformed about Jewish Halacha and Oral tradition which underlies so much of the NT statements (as we have shown in our discussions above). This resulted in further misinterpretation, thus leading to anti-Judaism and anti-Rabbinism.

In Romans 8:32, Paul proclaims for all to hear and know: "The magnanimity of G-d Who did not spare His own son but delivered him up for us all". Ephesians 5:2 "It is the Nazarene himself who, in love delivered himself up on your behalf as an offering and a sacrifice whose fragrance is pleasing to G-d."

Why then blame and hate the Jews for it?

Betrayal and arrest or self-sacrifice?

Matt 11:23 "On the night of his arrest and betrayal ..." Translators have the tendency to present this episode as an arrest following a betrayal. Christian tradition views this from a highly anti-Jewish perspective. Understanding the correct verb lightens up and decreases the gravity of the arrest and betrayal since it could also mean 'delivered up', 'handed over' or 'sacrificed of own volition'.

All translators use the terms 'arrest and betrayal' (alluding to Judas) in rendering *para didomi'* in this part of the verse. The verb, in its basic sense, means: 'to hand over' or 'deliver up' and is a technical term in the context of justice or martyrdom. The usage by the translators of "betrayal" in this verse is governed by their preconceptions against the Jews, in this way rendering a Gospel with a clear anti-Semitic spirit. In the Gospel story it can take on the meaning of arrest or betrayal as in Mark 14:21, but in Paul there is no need to see it this way. He uses the same verb in Romans 8:32 "He (G-d) did not spare His own son but delivered (the same Greek word) him up for us all." Here it can hardly imply betrayal or arrest. In Eph. 5:2 & 25 it is the Nazarene who "gave himself up (same Greek word) on your behalf." No thought of Judas or an arrest or Jewish betrayal on Passover eve would be present here.

We might also note that the Greek shows a curious use of tenses. The verb "was handed over" (*para didoto*) is in the imperfect, which literally makes the meaning "on the night he was being 'delivered up'". This implies that the act of surrender was going on all through the supper. It seems that Paul could hardly have had the Gospel scene in mind, and scholars who had noticed this (e.g. Robertson and Plummer – 'International critical commentary') suggest that Paul is taking a broader meaning, perhaps as "surrender by the father" as in the passage in Romans. (As explained by Earl Doherty in *The Source of Paul's Gospel*).

CHAPTER 16

The Lawgiver Controversy

The need for approved Bible interpretation

Our tracing of the hidden 'Jewish' Halachic foundations contained in the NT statements of the Nazarene, is centered on many issues for which neither the NT nor the Torah offer any specific directives. The interpretation or directives for these religious procedures and requirements are therefore left to the interpretation of the reader and observer of these scriptures. The question now arises: who are truly qualified for this wider oral interpretation of issues regarding the nation of the G-d of Israel?

If the word of G-d is truly divinely inspired, then, no doubt, it should also contain the specific divine directives and mandates for the authoritative interpretation of these all-important living standards and guidelines. These guidelines, which in fact are no less than divine requirements set by G-d Himself for His true followers in His written Word, are known in Judaism (the most long standing proclamation of His Word) as 'the *Torah*'. The way of life the Torah proclaims is known as '*Halacha*'.

Like any law on earth, it requires both promulgation and publishing of a law, as well as interpretation of its finer application for various circumstances which it has to control. On many divine requirements (like the mezuzah on the doorpost of a Torah-believer's home or business, tallit, Sabbath observance, etc.), the written word is severely limited and devoid of specific details. It requires wider interpretation and specifications. Specific provision has been made in the text of the Written Torah for this wider interpretation and enforcement through the appointment, by divine declaration, of appointed 'guardians' of Torah. We will discuss the appointment of the Tribe of Judah as His Lawgiver or Judicial arm ('the Mechoqeck') in detail in this chapter. The NT clearly confirms this in Romans 3:2 and Matthew 23:2.

Divine Mandate for true interpretation

The Torah, in Deut. 30:12, makes the point that Moses received the Torah and brought it down to earth. "The Torah is not in the Heavens ...", which means that Moses explained the Torah to the Hebrews. It does not say that another 'future' Moses would bring them another Torah from heaven. That is, nothing of the Torah has been left behind in the heavens.

It is clear from Leviticus 18:30, that the Sages and judges were the 'managers' of the faith system. They were instructed and given authority to make protective decrees in an effort to guard the values and the directives of the Bible. These injunctions of the Oral Law are not new Biblical laws but rather Rabbinic interpretations and guidelines to protect Biblical legislation; to save individuals and the entire community from violating divine principles and values. As the verse says: Lev. 18:30, "And you shall keep that which I have entrusted you to guard."

186

Lev. 26:46, "These are the statutes (*chokim*), judgments (*mishpatim*), *Torahs* (teachings of a Torah that has multiple dimensions) that HaShem established between Himself and the children of Israel, by the hand of Moses, on Mount Sinai."

- Statutes refer to directives for which the reasons are not completely comprehendible by man and the details of which are derived by principles of exegesis, because they are not clearly stated.

- Judgments imply laws that are more explicitly stated. The word 'judgment' in Hebrew implies laws that have more obvious logic and logos, therefore being more understandable to man's mind.

- The Bible uses the term 'Torot' (the plural of Torah), translated 'teachings'. This indicates that Israel received two Torah's - one Oral and one Written.

Some amazing revelations await us as we delve into the Hebrew Scriptures surrounding the topic of the Law of G-d and Judah's designation as the Mechoqeck (Lawgiver) of G-d. May the contents of this section assist in bringing some agreement and unity by demonstrating the Divine appointment of Judah as the Mechoqeck of G-d, i.e. the 'lawgiver' or 'law interpreter' and divinely mandated authority.

The Christian world has studied much, but not enough of the original religious Hebrew heart and mind set of these very Jewish Messianic writings. In addition they have neglected the 24 books of the Tanach and separated it from its original environment of harmony between Oral and Written Torah.

In general, Christians and 10-Israel have room to grow regarding their respect for Judah as the authority on the practical application of Commandments. Hopefully this section will bring greater understanding.

Elders and teachers were always with us throughout the history of Judah. We know who's who, right through from Moses to today and back again! We have always maintained a Chain of transmission. We know who our major players were and are. We of the Covenantal faith community are intimately aware of who our torchbearers are.

The Hebrew word 'elder' - 'zakein', is related to the word 'kaneh', to purchase with blood, sweat and tears. Who is an Elder? One who has purchased wisdom; who has paid his dues by a lifetime of dedication. If someone tells you, "I have not toiled and have accomplished, do not believe him," advise our Sages. The Torah is attained only by one who totally dedicates himself to it.

"'The Men of the Great Assembly' were a council of 120 Sages (10 for each of the 12 tribes). They contained the last of our Biblical Prophets. Daniel tells us that his book closes Prophecy the way it had appeared in the Hebrew Scriptures. 'Close the words ... Daniel, go on your way, for the words are closed and sealed until the end of time'. (Daniel 12). Afterwards we have basically only divine inspiration ... This illustrious Assembly led us after the Babylonian Exile. Many challenges faced the fragile, recovering nation, ravaged by ....displacement.... (They) applied their knowledge of Torah to address the needs of the time ..." (*Permeations@6pointmedia.com* - vol. 3 no. 3 Sivan 5765).

Numerous times the Torah says to the Rabbinic leadership (Moses, Aaron, the Elders, Joshua, Kalev, Etamar, the Judges, etc.) to keep and guard that very self-same Torah (Ex. 22:2, Lev. 19:3, Deut. 5:8).

Now you know that the Hebrew alphabet, like ancient Egyptian and Chinese, is pictorial. The holy letters have a graphic dimension. This is in addition to the sounds, vowels and consonants. The sounds and pictures described by our holy letters go together like "love and marriage – you can't have one without the other".

The very pictorial representation of the Biblical word 'Guard', is a picture of a simple handmade corral or fence. A field fence made of inter-connected branches of sticks of thorns and thistles. Our Torah leadership are comparable to shepherds who need to fence-in their beloved sheep 'from fear in the (dangerous) night' (Song of Songs 3:7).

Thus, the very concrete, physical black ink of the shape of the letters cries out for our leadership to protect and tangibly guard the Torah. That's not adding; that's just protecting. No Rabbi ever calls a protective measure a Torah law. They are merely placing a hedge of roses around to protect and guard the Torah laws from being carelessly trampled. Thus, it is a Biblical directive to erect fences around the Laws. The Torah commands us in no uncertain terms to take whatever protective measures which those in authority deem necessary. The fence made by the shepherd for his herd, is man-made for a specific purpose, utilizing the shepherd's intelligence, creativity and wisdom. Now we can see, touch, feel and hear the deep Biblical basis for the following Mishnah:

"Moses received the Torah from Sinai and transmitted it to Joshua; Joshua to the Elders; the elders to the Prophets; and the Prophets transmitted it to the Men of the Great Assembly. They (the Men of the Great Assembly) said three things:

- Be deliberate in judgment; [fair, honest, careful and just].

- Develop many disciples; [to an independent level], and

- Make a fence for the Torah. [Enact provisions and cautionary rules to safeguard against transgression]. (Art Scroll Siddur pg. 545).

Divine appointment of Judah as ruling authority

Throughout much of this section of the book we will be referring to the following Scripture as our primary text:

Gen. 49:10, "The sceptre shall not depart from Judah, nor a lawgiver from between his feet, until Shiloh come; and unto him shall the obedience of the peoples (*the nations*) be." See also 1 Chronicles 5:2, "For Judah prevailed over his brothers and of him came the chief rulers... "

The Hebrew word translated 'sceptre' here, is 'shevet'. *Shevet* means 'tribe, rod'. In modern Hebrew it mainly means 'tribe'. In the Tanach it is used 143 times to denote 'a tribe'; a division of a nation. It is the preferred term used for the twelve tribes of Israel (Gen. 49:16; Ex. 28:21). *Shevet* is also used to denote 'rod'. As a 'rod', the word *'shevet'* is used to denote **'a symbol of authority in the hands of a ruler'**. As such it is translated *'sceptre'* as in Genesis 49:10 and Amos 1:5, 8. And, it is used as an 'instrument of warfare' by Messiah at the establishment of His Kingdom. "But with righteousness shall He judge the poor, and reprove with equity for the meek of the earth: and He shall smite the earth with the **rod (*shevet*)** of His mouth..." (Isaiah 11:4).

In Genesis 49:10, '*shevet*' is generally translated **"sceptre"** – depicting the **rule and authority of Judah**. The blessing declared by Genesis 49:10 upon the tribe and the descendants of Judah was part of the blessings pronounced by Jacob under Divine inspiration, on his death bed, over his twelve sons (fathers of the twelve tribes of the nation of Israel which would proceed from them). It was defined as being a declaration of 'what lies before them in time to come'. (Genesis 49:1). According to this prophetic blessing, Judah would retain the ruling authority (sceptre) amongst the twelve tribes of Israel 'until Shiloh comes', to whom the ruling authority over the nations belongs. Unto Shiloh shall "the obedience of the peoples (the nations) be." The word 'until' does not mean 'up to and **ex**cluding', but rather 'up to and **in**cluding'. In terms of Torah wisdom and direction, *Shiloh* (Messiah) shall then rule over the nations **with** Judah who will be directly under his direction.

Now referring to our primary text, we will add the translation and bold for emphasis to give the reader a better understanding:

> Gen. 49:10, "The **sceptre (*ruling authority*)** shall not depart from **Judah**, nor a lawgiver from between his feet, until Shiloh come; and unto him shall the obedience of the peoples (*the nations*) be."

> Psalms 114:2, "When Israel went out of Egypt ... Judah became His sanctuary..."

G-d set up His true system of worship amongst Judah and settled them in the Land of Israel, controlling the city which bears

His Name and His favour - Jerusalem. His Temple would be in Jerusalem, controlled by Judah. This would be His abode; His sacred dwelling-place while the Temple was there. Judah was the principal or leading tribe, recognized as the tribe where power and leadership were to be concentrated and from which the ruling Messiah was to proceed. The rest of this verse says, "... Israel His dominions." (The Stone Edition Tanach). This is referring to 'Israel' (Ephraim, 10-Israel) receiving the promise of multiplicity and, when exiled amongst the nations, they would rule.

G-d's choice of Judah as 'His sanctuary' or holy dwelling denotes the tribe of Judah's separation from the world and consecration unto G-d. "In Judah is G-d known..." (Psa. 76:1). Judah is chosen as being, from the time of the carrying away of the Ten Tribes onwards, the surviving heir of the ancient Divine promises belonging to all Israel. Judah alone remained as 'the Kingdom of G-d' (1 Kings 11:13 12:20; 2 Kings 17:18). Throughout the ages, Judah would not lose its identity and indeed would be known as G-d's people, guardians of the Torah, and keepers of the faith.

Messiah may very well be our head Rabbi, but there will always be a law system under the leadership of Torah leaders. Even with an evil inclination subdued and Satan, so to speak, vanquished, there will still be a need for law and spiritual order. Much like traffic laws, even without drunk drivers and speeders, people need a certain amount of direction. Thus, even with the advent of Messiah, we will still need a system of justice for the sake of good order and success.

Of course, Christianity, in their endeavours to proclaim the Torah as 'done away with' and 'nailed to the Cross' of their Messiah, claim that Judah's Lawgiver status has been cut off by the 'Coming of Shiloh', which they claim is their Messiah who came 2000 years ago. We read the following interesting confirmation of Judah's Divine Mandate

We can all easily accept that G-d is our Judge and Lawgiver: "For G-d is our Judge, G-d is our Lawgiver (Mechoqeck), G-d is our King; He will save us." (Isaiah 33:22). The NT agrees with Isaiah, that "there is only one Lawgiver and Judge, the One who is able to save and destroy. But you - who are you to judge your neighbour? Anyone who speaks against his brother or judges him, speaks against the Law and judges it. When you judge the Law, you are not keeping it, but sitting in judgment on it." (James 4:12).

Even opposers of G-d's Law (Torah) would not think of denying that G-d is the Lawgiver, as the above NT quote confirms. They would however take exception to the following Scriptural statement and undoubtedly find or create reasons for arguing it away. The onus is on you, as the individual reader, to consider this Scripture and decide how you will interpret and accept it.

The following Biblical texts use the exact same Hebrew word, **'Mechoqeck'**, when referring to **Judah as lawgiver**! In Psalms 60:7 G-d states: "Judah is My lawgiver (Mechoqeck)." In Psalms 108:8, G-d repeats that "Judah is My lawgiver (Mechoqeck)."

The word "Mechoqeck" appears only six times in the Tanach. Once it refers directly to G-d Himself as quoted above in Isaiah 33:22. Twice in Psalms 60:7 and Psalms 108:8, quoted above, it refers clearly to Judah (the Jews) as "Judah is My lawgiver." Some English translations render it 'My sceptre'. Of the three remaining instances, twice it is a vague reference, and the final instance is an equally bold declaration regarding Judah - our primary text:

Gen. 49:10: "The sceptre (*ruling authority*) shall not depart from **Judah**, nor a **lawgiver (*Mechoqeck*)** from between his feet, until Shiloh come; and unto him shall the obedience of the peoples (*the nations*) be."

Let us continue with the word study of our primary text above. This next piece of information should be a new and interesting revelation.

As stated previously, in Genesis 49:10, 'shevet' is generally translated 'sceptre' – depicting the rule and authority of Judah. However, this interpretation results in **duplicating the 'ruling' aspect** of this Divine mandate in this Scripture, "The sceptre (**ruling** rod) shall not depart from Judah, nor a lawgiver (Mechoqeck) from between his feet, until Shiloh comes to Whom the **rule** belongs." We may therefore consider using the alternative and more often used meaning of 'tribe for 'shevet', in the first part of the text. Thus: **"The tribe (tribal identity) shall not depart from Judah**, nor a lawgiver (Mechoqeck) from between his feet, until Shiloh comes..." This would be valid in terms of the historic fact that, while the Ten Tribes of Israel disappeared into the nations, Judah remained identifiable throughout the 2000 years of their dispersion – all the time retaining and expounding their Mechoqeck (lawgiver) mandate.

The word 'shevet' has a synonym, 'matteh' meaning both 'rod' and 'tribe'. It occurs 251 times in Tanakh. As 'rod' it signifies authority or power over another nation. And as such is used in reference to the Messianic rule as in Psalms 110:2. It refers to 'tribe' 183 times. The 'tribes' of Israel are each designated as 'matteh'.

This dual meaning for 'matteh' therefore validates the probability that the Divine mandate to Judah in Genesis 49:10 could well refer to the maintenance of Judah's tribal identity as the 'lawgiver' of G-d, who would be recognized for it by the return-ees of the Lost Ten Tribes of Israel.

The prophets predicted the re-identifying of the Ten Lost Tribes of Israel in the End Time. 10-Israel would return to Torah and to the Land, by their own free will due to their love and obedience to Torah and the Prophets. 10-Israel's return should be preceded by true repentance from their original sin of idolatry and rejection of the authority of Judah, and a recognition and willingness to come under the authority of Judah's Divine mandate as lawgiver of G-d. In turn, Judah needs to diligently pursue its role of lawgiver and specifically engage in teaching 10-Israel.

Jurisdiction of the lawgiver (Mechoqeck)

Judah's responsible guardianship and interpretation of the Torah has been steadfast for thousands of years. Winner by default, there simply were no Catholic Bishops or Southern Baptists, or Canadian recently new-born, self-proclaimed Bible experts, to tell us why not to keep the Torah which G-d in His wisdom entrusted to Judah to keep, to cherish, to pass on to the world and to have the final mandate of interpretation and authority for.

The Church basically did away with any notion of systematic observance of the Commandments. Only in very recent modern times has there been a desire to check out and get in touch with whatever the Hebrew Roots are all about. Along with this, came a growing appreciation of, and the wish to participate in some actual Commandment observance - but not to extreme; not in-depth, but simply: however 'the spirit moves one'. Well, my dear, dear brothers and sisters: We of Judah did not have such luxury of picking and choosing. We received marching orders from our Commander-in-Chief, our Teacher, the Almighty. We were told to report directly to the Sages that would be in each successive generation (Deut. 17, etc.) for clarification of any orders. We have always done our homework plus extra credit assignments. We have sacrificed great wealth to do all of this and often our very lives.

Many times our Gentile neighbors have legislated against our observance of a host of Commandments that aggravated them. They would even attach a death penalty to such observance! Guess what happened? We died horrible deaths, went underground or waged desperate wars. Sometimes we won against vastly superior forces. But win or lose, we never lost our direct participation in observing those Commandments and learning, loving and living Torah!

What does the Law of G-d (Torah) entail – of which Judah has been declared 'the *Mechoqeck* (lawgiver) of G-d'?

In its broader sense, the Law of G-d is referred to as: The Torah – 'law, teaching, direction, instruction.' This noun occurs 220 times in the Hebrew Tanakh. In Judaism it entails the first five books of the Bible which specify the 613 Laws of G-d, often referred to as 'The Laws of Moses' – meaning: 'as given through Moses'.

Psalms 119:1 defines the Torah in finer detail: "Blessed are the undefiled in the way, who walk in the Torah of G-d". This is followed by 176 verses praising the Laws, Statutes, Judgments, Commandments, Decrees, and Precepts. This wide embodiment of His Law gives clear indication of how shallow the reasoning goes, which claims that G-d has only Ten Commandments which have to be observed. G-d's laws and system are for the purposes of running a country and a nation – and this requires as wide a set of laws, rules and regulations as any country requires. G-d gave Israel the Torah in order that they might observe it and live. "And what nation is there so great, that has statutes and judgments so righteous as all this Law which I set before you this day?" (Deut. 4:8).

The Torah, the Law or Way of life, needs Sages, Judges, Scribes, and Teachers as the Bible repeatedly confirms (elders are mentioned over a 100 times as being the leaders of legal spiritual direction). The authority regarding the spiritual operation and determination of this much wider embodiment of His Law has been given to the spiritual leaders of Judah ... "Until Shiloh comes, to Whom the rule belongs,..." when nations will be subdued to His rule of Law – as in any government in the world.

It also is a Command that the Hebrews should optimally use men of the Tribe of Judah to rule. When, on some occasions, they did not pick such teachers from the Tribe of Judah, bad things transpired and we ultimately lost sovereignty.

In any event, Shiloh has not yet come, for the nations are in more turmoil than ever before and certainly not under such universal control as our primary text predicted. It also speaks of a triumphant nation which we are not as yet or ever have been.

It is not common knowledge among non-Jews that the Torah is also understood and interpreted by the Rabbis on a mathematical level. G-d gave the Hebrew letters assigned numeric values. As such, by analysis of the various ways or of methods of numerical evaluation, you can see amazing Bible messages. We also see the internal perfection and balance that is the hallmark of the Hebrew Bible. I can think of fifteen systems of numerical insights that are used.

Pertinent to our present discussion, comes to mind a beautiful numerical level of meaning. The term 'Children of Israel' (*B'nei Yisrael* in Hebrew) has a numerical letter value of 603. This becomes 611 when you use the method (*im ha osios*) that also adds to this total word value the number of actual holy letters that compose the very word in question. *B'nei Yisrael* has a total of 8 Hebrew letters. 603 +8 = 611, which is the numerical value of the Hebrew letters for 'Torah'. This gives us a Scriptural hint that there is a special relationship or meaning between 'Torah' and the "Children of Israel'. One may combine various systems in searching to grasp the deep mysteries of Torah. Thus if you count the actual words (according to *im ha teivas*), not only the letters or their assigned value, you have two words in the Hebrew term *B'nei Yisrael*. So now we have 611 plus 2 = 613. Thus, our hint refer to the children of Israel being the representatives of the Commandments and Torah in the world – or that there is a special relationship, bond or responsibility between the two.

Our Oral tradition offers the following interesting confirmation. According to Deut. 31:25 we are told to safeguard a copy of the Torah. Our ancient teachers said that altogether Moses wrote 13 Torahs - one for each tribe, and one in the trust and care of the Cohanim and Levi'im, which was placed inside the Ark of the Covenant ... "that it may be for a witness against thee". These scrolls were the source documents to compare and transcribe future scrolls from!

Jeremiah prophesied of a future time when G-d would renew His eternal Covenant with His people (not a new Torah - there are many covenants). According to this 'New' (perhaps rather 'Renewed') Covenant, the Torah would be internalized. G-d's people would willingly obey Him, according to a loving spiritual obedience of their hearts and minds. "I will put My Torah in their inward parts, and write it in their hearts; and I will be their G-d, and they shall be My people." (Jer. 31:33). In Malachi 4:4, the closing paragraphs of the Tanakh remind and challenge G-d's people to remember the "Law of Moses" in preparation for the Coming of Messiah.

It is readily evident in these current times, that HaShem is causing 10-Israel and foreigners (Gentiles) to return to Torah in preparation for the Messiah:

> Isa. 56:3-7 "And the foreigners who join themselves to G-d, to serve Him and to love the Name of G-d, to become servants unto Him, all who guard the Sabbath against desecration, grasp My Covenant tightly. I will bring them to My holy Muntain, and I will gladden them in My House of prayer; their elevation offerings and their feast offerings will find favour on My Altar, for My House will be called the house of prayer for all peoples."

Within the meaning of the word 'Torah', to which the people are admonished to return, we will demonstrate that Judah, as Lawgiver, is to teach the Torah, and as we will suggest, specifically to those returnees to Torah.

The word 'Torah' is derived from the Hebrew root verb 'yarah' (2 Chron. 26:15) meaning, "to show the way, to shoot, to throw (like an arrow), to pour water, to point out (as if by aiming the finger), to teach, archer, direct, inform, instruct, to lay a cornerstone". The word for a teacher, in Hebrew 'moreh', is a direct derivative of the verb 'yarah', from which the word 'Torah' is derived. We could conclude that this is an indication that by being appointed and declared the 'Mechoqeck' (lawgiver) of G-d, that Judah has been divinely intended to be the Law teacher of the twelve tribes and of the world.

Psa. 147:19, "He issues His Commands to Jacob, His statutes and rules to Israel." So, we see that the legal system given to the Hebrews is that which expresses G-d's Will, not just man-made laws. Gen 18:19. "For I have singled him out, that he may instruct his children and his posterity to keep the Way of HaShem by doing what is just and right." This implies that HaShem Himself has a personalized justice system which He gave over to Avraham and his seed for the purpose of keeping it, guarding it and doing it. Exodus Rabba 30 says, that a human being may instruct others what to do, but often does not comply personally. Not so HaShem. What He does, He expects Israel to do. Judah is the bow and Ephraim is the arrow. It is self-evident who is leading who. Jehoshaphat spoke to the judges upon their taking office: "Consider what you are doing, for you judge not on behalf of man, but on behalf of the L-rd and He is with you when you pass judgment. Now let the fear of the L-rd be upon you. Act with care for there is no injustice, favourites, or bribe-giving with the L-rd our G-d." (2 Chron. 19:5).

Now you can finally understand why the Torah calls judges and courts 'Elohim' (G-d). In Exodus 22:7, you should not revile G-d by speaking of the judges and courts, because they simply represent G-d's Divine Justice and therefore are called by His Divine Name (Sanhedrin 72a). The Rambam, in the Mishnah

Torah (*the Laws of Sanhedrin 23*) clearly states that any judge who doesn't act properly, causes the Divine Presence to leave Israel. On the other hand, any judge who does true justice is like one who sets right the entire world and causes the Divine Presence to dwell in Israel. As the Torah says, G-d stands in the Divine Assembly (of judges). Genesis calls the Temple, 'Mount Moriah' - which means 'a place where instruction is'. '*Hora'ah*' means 'religious awe'. 'Moriah' also contains the word '*orah*' which means light, meaning the place from where the light went out to the world. The verse says, "From out of Zion shall go forth the Torah". This implies from out of the Jewish faith community, not Johannesburg, Kansas, or Rome, etc.

The jurisdiction of Judah's Rabbinic authority also is confirmed in the NT from the point of view of its Messiah:

> Romans 3:2, "They (the Jews) have been entrusted with the very Words of G-d."

> Acts 15:21, "For Moses has been preached in every city from the earliest times and is read in the synagogues on every Sabbath." Note the distinction made here between Oral explanation (preaching) and the Written text which is read. This subtle distinction is presented in typical Rabbinic fashion.

> Matthew 23:1-3, "Then the Nazarene said to the crowds and to His disciples: 'The teachers of the Law and the Pharisees sit in Moses' seat. **So you must obey them and do everything they tell you. ...**'"

The criticism of hypocrisy against the Pharisees that follows is very Jewish. No nation has more self-criticism and constructive criticism than the Hebrew/Jewish people and Judaism. It only sounds anti-Semitic when it is taken out of the true context which is a same-team, intra-family rebuking, correction and constructive criticism. Only when divorced from an in-shop, family criticism and presented by the pagan Nazi-like Romans, do those words take on an anti-Semitic spin. If your own loving family members criticise you, it is called loving constructive criticism, of which Proverbs say, "Criticize the wise and they will love you." However, if you are harshly criticized by a bitter enemy, then it is called a character assassination.

Matthew 23:1-3 closely relays the Torah instruction of Deuteronomy 17:8-13 with its directives to turn to G-d's appointed Mechoqeck, Judah, for Law interpretation, and then to strictly abide by it.

> Deut. 17:8-13 "If a case comes before you ... any dispute at all ... you must make your way to the place that G-d, your G-d, chooses and approach the Levitical priests and judges that will be in those days! (*For in truth, we only have the Judges of our respective days*). They will ...give a decision for you. **You must abide by the decision they pronounce for you ... you must take care to carry out all their instructions. You must abide by the verdict they give you and by the decision they declare to you,** swerving neither right nor left of the sentence they have pronounced for you. If anyone presumes to disobey the priest who is there in the service of G-d, your G-d, or the judge, that man must die. You must banish this evil from Israel. And all the people shall hear of it and be afraid and not act presumptuously a second time."

Messianic Hebraic Roots Restorers who are in the process of returning to Torah (as prophesied in Ezekiel 37:15 and elsewhere), should thoughtfully consider that Matthew 23:1-3 validates the Nazarene's sanction of Deuteronomy 17's Divine declaration of Judah's authority. Could it really be coincidence that the Nazarene's instruction echoes the Deuteronomy 17 directive?

There are several other confirmations in Scripture of this essential concept of Oral interpretation and transmission of the intent of G-d (Ex. 13:9, Deut. 8:3, 12:21, 17:8-11, 30:1-14; Isa 55:11, 59:21; Jer 31:33 -36; Dan 1:3- 18; Ezra 7:25; Pro 1:5,8, etc...).

Historic rejection of Judah as Lawgiver

Let us quickly review the conditions surrounding the historic rejection of Judah and its divinely mandated lawgiver status by the Ten Northern Tribes of Israel.

In the time of King Solomon (970 - 931 BCE), the ancient Kingdom of Israel split into two opposing factions:

- 'Israel' - the Northern Kingdom, Ten Tribes, with their main city Shechem;

- 'Judah' – the Southern Kingdom, two tribes, with their main city Jerusalem.

After this, the Tanakh specifies and refers to the two factions as 'Israel and Judah'. It also refers to the Ten Tribes as 'Ephraim' or 'Joseph'. The alert reader should bear this division in mind and steer away from the general concept that the Jews of today

represent all twelve tribes of Israel, "because the Ten Tribes
have already returned after the Babylonian exile", with Judah.
The fact is that only a remnant of the Northern Ten Tribes
escaped to the south as refugees to join Judah. The Bible record
is very distinct, not only in its reference to this historic division
of the Hebrew nation, but more so in its multiple Prophecies
and Divine assurances that the Ten Tribes shall "return to the
Land of their fathers" and be reunited again with Judah – in the
distant future, in Messianic Times!

For purposes of our topic, we are particularly interested in the
historic cultural and rebellious religious attitude of 10-Israel
towards Judah's 'lawgiver' leadership which, along with idolatry, led to their rejection by G-d. When one is aware of this great
rift between the two Houses of the divinely elected 'nation of
G-d' and the reasons behind it, the culture and attitude of these
re-identifying Ten Tribers today is almost identical.

The seldom-read books of Kings and Chronicles record the history
of the two greatly divided Kingdoms in a very interesting style:

1 Kings 11:9 records how G-d became angry with the Judean
King Solomon because his heart had turned away from G-d.
As a result, G-d undertook to tear the entire Kingdom away
from Solomon. One tribe only would remain under the rule of
Solomon's son "for the sake of David and Jerusalem."

> 1 Kings 11:12, "For your father David's sake how-
> ever... I will not tear the whole Kingdom (away).
> For the sake of David, and for the sake of Jerusalem
> which I have chosen, I will leave... one tribe..." –
> Judah v..20; 2 Kings 17:18.

The awesome conclusion that must be drawn from this - **Judah represents the Kingdom of G-d** because of this historic Divine Decree!

G-d's purpose for retaining one tribe is explained in 1 Kings 11:36, "So that My servant David will always have a light in My presence in Jerusalem, the city I have chosen as a dwelling place for My Name." This links up with His Divine intention of selecting Judah as His ruling *Shevet* (tribe) and *Mechoqeck* (lawgiver). This is part of the fulfilment of the Divine blessing of Judah to remain an on-going, identifiable tribe before Him who would be responsible for guarding the Torah over the millennia. This Divine blessing to the tribe of Judah is reaffirmed in 2 Chronicles 13:5, "Do you not know, that the G-d of Israel, has given the sovereignty (Kingdom) of Israel to David forever? **It is an inviolable (everlasting) Covenant!**"

The reality and implications of these statements, hidden in the seldom-read books of Kings and Chronicles, are staggering – for it **confirms that Judah would retain the rule and the sovereignty – the authority and control - of the Kingdom of G-d on earth "until Shiloh comes to Whom the rule over the nations belong."**

Both houses contributed to the ultimate division of the Kingdom of Israel. However, Scripture records in 2 Chronicles 10:15-16 and I Kings 12:1-17 that G-d allowed a situation to develop whereby Israel angrily removed itself from Judah's authority and the tribes were divided. Why? To fulfill the purpose of **G-d to establish His Word that the Kingdom would be divided.**

Scripture records the events and attitudes of Judah and 10-Israel that contributed to the dividing of the Kingdom of Israel:

- 1 Kings 11:1-9. The Judean King Solomon loved many foreign women and when he grew old, his wives swayed his heart after the gods of others. G-d became angry with King Solomon because his heart had turned away from G-d. 1 Kings 11:11-13. G-d tells Solomon that He shall tear away the kingship from him and give it to his servant. However, G-d would retain one tribe for Solomon's son, Rehoboam, for the sake of David.

- 1 Kings 11:40 – Solomon sought to kill his servant, Jeroboam, who was destined to lead the Northern Ten Tribes, but he escaped to Egypt and remained there until Solomon's death.

- 1 Kings 12:1-4. Jeroboam came to Shechem to meet with King Rehoboam of Judah. Jeroboam, along with the Congregation of Israel, asked that the King lighten the tax yoke and they would serve Rehoboam.

- 1 Kings 12:10-17. King Rehoboam responded that he would increase the tax load. Instead of listening to the wise elders/Rabbis who counselled tolerance, he listened to his young, ambitious friends. He did not listen to the Sages of that time which brought calamity on the Kingdom. When all of Israel saw the King did not listen to them they rebelled and responded to the King, "What share have we in [the house of] David? We have no heritage in the son of Jesse! Back to your homes, O Israel! Now see to your own house, O [Kingdom of] David!" Thus, Israel rejected the House of Judah and made

Jeroboam King, thereby dividing the Kingdom into two, as prophesied by G-d.

- 1 Kings 12:28. King Jeroboam set up false idols for the ten Northern tribes (House of Israel) to worship, so they wouldn't go to the Temple in Jerusalem. They rejected the Torah of G-d and His system of worship by driving out the priests of G-d to make priests of their own liking. Note: The priests who were serving in Northern Israel and who wanted to serve G-d in sincerity, returned to Judah and Jerusalem to serve G-d with Judah. They were joined by "members of all the tribes (10-Israel) who were whole-heartedly devoted to the worship of G-d." (2 Chron. 11:13-17). But this was a minority of Israel only.

- 2 Chron. 10:19 - "Thus Israel rebelled against the House of David, to this day."

In 1 Kings 12:26 onwards, we read about 10-Israel's King Jeroboam, how he declared his anti-Judah religious practices, after rejecting Judah's leadership – for fear that 10-Israelites would return to the Jewish faith and thus cause his demise and death:

- He appointed priests from ordinary non-Levite families.

- He erected idols for the nation to worship.

- He moved the 'Jewish' feasts a month forward - like the Sadducees who collaborated with the Nazi-like Romans tried to do unsuccessfully and like the confused, self-hating Karaites tried to do as well. Both groups simply fizzled out.

This sounds peculiarly familiar to the attitude of some modern 10-Israelites who reject the lawgiver leadership of Judah and insist on having their own separate identity from Judah, their own Beith Din, their own temples, distinctly separated from Judah, their own 'corrected' Biblical calendar, and their own appointed teachers and priests.

It is also conspicuous how some modern 10-Tribers often deny that it was their rebellion against the Lawgiver status of Judah which was the main reason for G-d's rejection of 10-Israel from His Covenant. They simply reject the overwhelming evidence given by the Bible (as summarized above) that the G-d of Israel has given the sovereignty (Kingdom) of Israel to David forever. **It is an inviolable (everlasting) Covenant!**

Because the House of Israel has been estranged from the House of Judah and its authority for thousands of years, it is difficult for them today to appreciate and come under the leadership of Judah. With education and repentance, they will return to G-d's true system of worship which includes its priests and Biblical calendar.

Hidden in these books we find another example of 10-Israel's rejection of Torah and Judah as lawgiver, yet it ends with a wonderful prophecy:

> 2 Chron. 15:3-4, "Many a day Israel [10-Israel] will spend without a faithful G-d, without priest [Cohen, Rabbi] to teach, without Torah [for they have rejected and pulled away from the Lawgiver of G-d]. But, in their distress, they will return to G-d, the G-d of Israel. They will seek Him, and He will let them

find Him." (But it will be in a time of trouble among the nations – verses 5-7).

There will be those who try to twist these Scriptures as applying only to Judah. However, an astute reading of verses 1-3 of this chapter and the context of previous chapters, will define that Judah and Israel (10-Israel) are at war, and that 10-Israel, according to verse 3 is without G-d, priest, and Torah.

Is it not clear, in light of the prophecies of re-uniting 10-Israel and Judah into one nation and one house again, that the Divine intent, according to this inviolable Covenant, must be to join re-identifying 10-Israel to His Kingdom, which has been allotted to Judah – the Kingdom of David? Is this not the Kingdom which the Nazarene told his followers to pray for: "Thy Kingdom come ..."? (Luke 11:12). There is no other Kingdom, no other inviolable Covenant.

Returning 10-Israel today has a vital decision to make - who will they join?:

- That faction of re-awakening 10-Israel that is rebelling against Judah's Lawgiver appointment? Or,

- The faction of 10-Israel that is returning in humility to Judah to learn from its teachers?

Many of returning 10-Israel emphasize the importance of the Prophetic Scripture that confirms the authority of Judah in Zechariah 8:23, "Thus said HaShem, Master of Legions: In those days it will happen that ten men (10-Israel?), of all the languages of the nations, will take hold of the corner of the garment of a Jewish man, saying, 'Let us go with you, for we have heard that G-d is with you.'" (*The Stone edition Tanach*).

Psalm 78 gives a lengthy overview of the history of Israel's provoking of G-d and concludes with G-d's election of Judah in preference to Israel (10-Israel). Yet, in this, He provided a way of escape for 10-Israel.

> Ps. 78:67, "Moreover He refused the tabernacle of Joseph, and **chose not the tribe of Ephraim (10-Israel):** But **chose the tribe of Judah**, the mount Zion which he loved. And He built His sanctuary, a copy of High Heaven, founding it firm like the earth which He established forever. He chose David also, His servant, and took him from the sheepfolds: From following the ewes great with young, He brought him to **feed Jacob His people, and Israel His inheritance/heritage**."

Judah would oversee His Sanctuary on Mount Zion, where His holy city, Jerusalem is built. By maintaining the Sanctuary of G-d and its inherent religious system, Judah would spiritually lead, feed, teach, and care for Israel (10-Israel) – His heritage or dominion. This is confirmed in Psalms 114:2, "Judah was His sanctuary, and Israel His dominions (pl in Hebrew)." This phrase "Israel His dominions" – refers to 'over whom, or through whom, He would rule His Kingdom.' The Hebrew word used here for dominion, is '*memshalot*', the plural form. This denotes 10-Israel as being 'many nations' according to the promises to the patriarchs - Avraham, Yitzchak and Ya'acov.

Psalms 114 is a much-quoted portion in the Jewish Pesach ceremony, saying that at the sight of the twelve tribes leaving Egypt during the Exodus, "the mountains and hills skipped like rams" (verse 6) because they could see that the purpose of G-d was in process, to rule through His elect over the world. Of course, we know today, that the final fulfilment cannot be achieved without the Second Exodus of the return of all twelve tribes from across the world where they have been exiled and dispersed among the nations!

> Jeremiah 16:14, "However, behold – days are com-ing – the word of HaShem – when it will no longer be said, 'As HaShem lives, Who took out the Children of Israel for the land of Egypt, but rather, 'As HaShem lives, Who took out the children of Israel from the land of the North and from all the lands where He had scattered them.' And I shall return them to their land which I gave to their forefathers." (*The Stone Edition, Tanakh*)

Until Shiloh comes … Who is Shiloh?

There can be no doubt that one of the main reasons why Jews (descendants of the tribe of Judah) are disliked by other nations is because of their image of representing the Torah and religious legalism. This dislike certainly emanates from many Christians who regard themselves as "free from religious legalism by the grace of their Messiah". Even a major part, if not the majority, of Hebraic Roots restorers protest against what they regard as "the man-made legal obligations that the Rabbis place on people", though they are gradually par-taking more and more of these Hebraic legal responsibilities themselves – like the Sabbath, feast days, Jewish customs, etc. However, in their restorative drive, many of these returnees select only those laws which they believe they are obligated to, and even then, they choose to interpret and define these laws according to their own understanding or, as many claim, "according to the leading of the Holy Spirit." Notwithstanding this claim, which should logically require that they should all be in perfect agreement, they still vociferously differ with each other. This results in discord and disunity in the Hebraic Restoration movement because of the great confusion among its adherents regarding interpretation of these Jewish laws and practices and their rejection of Rabbinic interpretation of the issues about which they cannot even agree about amongst themselves.

Let us consider at the onset, the claim of Messianics that the Christian Messiah who appeared 2000 years ago, was 'Shiloh' who, according to the Genesis 49:10 Prophecy, would replace the ruling authority of Judah. They believe that the Messiah came to rightly interpret the Law in place of the Rabbinic authority. This is the position also held by the greater majority of the Messianic Hebraic Restoration movement, who proclaim a far more authentic Jewish version of the Christian Messiah whom they refer to by his Hebrew name 'Y'shuah' rather than the name 'Jesus' which they regard as pagan

Let us recall here our earlier review regarding Judah as the Lawgiver (Mechoqeck) of G-d. Has the Nazarene now replaced Judah as the Lawgiver, thereby ending Judah's Divine mandate? Adherents of this claim are unanimous in their strong denial and rejection of what they term 'Rabbinic authority'.

The NT however, often claims that its hero is not a law giver but that "he came to save from sin," etc. If you think Shiloh came 2000 years ago, read these:

> Luke 12:13, "And one from the crowd said to him, Teacher, tell my brother to divide the inheritance with me. **14** But he [the Nazarene] said to him, 'Man, who appointed Me a judge or a divider over you?'"

> John 3:17, "For G-d did not send His Son into the world that He might judge the world, but that the world might be saved through him."

> John 12:47, "And if anyone hears my Words and does not believe, I do not judge him; for I did not come that I might judge the world, but that I might save the world."

> Does he sound like a lawgiver here?

The scriptural authority of Judah as the Mechoqeck of G-d entails the Divine Mandate for interpreting the Law. If the Nazarene replaced Judah and its Rabbinic interpretation, who should Jews now turn to for Torah interpretation since the Nazarene is not physically present. Before the Nazarene's time, G-d was not physically present either, hence Judah's Divine aappointment as 'Lawgiver'. Since the destruction of the Temple, the Rabbinic order is fulfilling the role of judges as set down in the Torah, to rightly interpret Torah and its requirements. With more than three thousand years of practical experience in Torah study and observance, there is no other group of law interpreters more experienced in Torah guidance than the Rabbis. In 'Old Testament' times ample Divine provision was made for the nation of Israel for Torah guidance:

> Deut. 17: 8-13, "If a case comes before you...any dispute at all...you must make your way to the place that G-d your G-d chooses and approach the Levitical priests and judges that will be in those days! [For, in truth, we only have the Judges of our respective days]. They will...give a decision for you. You must abide by the decision they pronounce for you...you must take care to carry out all their instructions. You must abide by the verdict they give you and by the decision they declare to you, swerving neither right nor left of the sentence they have pronounced for you. If anyone presumes to disobey either the priest who is there in the service of G-d, your G-d, or the judge, that man must die. You must banish this evil from Israel. And all the people shall hear of it and be afraid and not act presumptuously a second time."

One of the remarkable features of the Hebraic Restoration movement is its gradual return to Torah observance - which is one of the greatest prophetic fulfilments of all time! These Messianic followers are also faced with this same Torah instruction of Deut. 17 above, now that they are becoming Torah observant. Who should they turn to for interpretation and guidance in those day to day events and problems for which the Written Torah gives no information? Also about the long standing Torah directives which they have lost during their 2800 year exile, like Shabbat, Feasts, Sacred Calendar, rituals, religious apparel, etc? If their Messiah is truly Shiloh, the 'new' Mechoqeck (Lawgiver jurisdiction) – how unfair that they are left without a Deut. 17 source of Guidance from which they should not deviate?

Hebraic Restorers who have not yet returned to Rabbinic authority would respond that "they are led by the Spirit", guided by their own interpretation and "just sticking to the Written Law", etc. They turn a blind eye to the fact that on many things 'there just aint ANY written directives for!' They self-assuredly ignore the fact that their 'Spirit Guidance' vary from person to person and from group to group!

Stalemate! – and they cannot contact their 'Shiloh Messiah' on a direct basis just as even Moses could not contact G-d on a constant basis, from case to case. Logically, G-d in His Wisdom foresaw this and installed a Mandated System.

It is this 'Mandated System' that became the source of all anti-Semitism, anti-Judaism and anti-Rabbinism. Resultantly, various 'replacement theoilogies' evolved.

The implications for Judah now, is that it is incumbent upon them to respond to 10-Israel and to actively take up this responsibility to teach and interpret Scripture.

Let us continue with our primary Scripture study of Genesis 49:10 now, and consider the **"until *Shiloh* come"** portion of this Scripture. Most commentators simply refer to *Shiloh* as a place or name. However, that '*Shiloh*' refers to the Messiah is agreed to by Jewish commentators throughout the ages as a possible position "despite the fact that nowhere in Scripture is that term (Shiloh) applied to the Messiah." (Rav Dr. J. H. Hertz, *The Pentateuch and Haftorahs*, Soncino Edition). By the way, if this refers to Messiah, it is telling you something about

Messiah. One possible root of that word means 'placenta', indicating that the Messiah would be born as a normal human birth. Even so, the word 'until' does not imply that Judah will in anyway be forcibly retired, but simply that it all will continue under the leadership of the King Messiah.

Shiloh is also written without a Yud in some ancient Jewish versions (Septuagint, Targum, Saadyah, Gaon, Rashi, etc.) 'SHLH' an archaic designation for 'his' (Sheloh); or, as if it were a poetic form for 'peace'. Thus, "the sceptre shall not depart ... till all that is reserved for him shall have been fulfilled" (derived from the Septuagint "until that which is his shall come").

Another rather ingenious way of interpretation of this Scripture brings into our discussion the topic of the beloved Ten Tribes. "... till Shiloh cometh, and the obedience of the peoples be turned to him". This is a hint (prediction) of 1 Kings 11: 29. where Ahijah, a prophet in Shiloh, explained to Jeroboam that Solomon's Kingdom would be broken, i.e. that 10-Israel would break away from the House of David. 10-Israel is called 'peoples' here, as they were referred to in Genesis 48:4 (R. Hertz, Pentateuch, Soncino Press, London, 5740).

Even if the Messianic claim that 'their Messiah is Shiloh and that he replaced Rabbinic authority' were valid, then, by their own interpretation, he is not 'ruling over the nations' until his 'Second Coming'. Therefore, Judah is still the judicial authority until the 'Second Coming'. Remember, any fair explanation of a complex nature must fit in and not contradict the rest of the Bible. Some texts are purposely vague and no fair or honest explanation should take off on a trip to outer space, turning over, nullifying and disregarding the rest of the Bible.

Jewish and non-Jewish commentators consider '*Shiloh*' as a possible reference to the Messiah – and this confirms Oral interpretation anyway! Both Jewish and Ten Triber Messianic teachings refer to 'two' (events) in their understandings of Messiah.

- Christian Messianics believe that Messiah will come on two occasions, returning at the End of Time in a second coming to rule as King on earth.

- Jewish interpretation is also explicit about the existence of two Messiahs:

  - <u>Messiah ben Yosef</u> – Who, according to the great Jewish Sage, the Gaon of Vilna, has the sole mandate to regather Israel, returning them to Torah observance, and

  - <u>Messiah ben David</u> - Who will **reign as King** over Israel and the world.

Here are some sources for further details on this subject:

- Chabad.org – with a most comprehensive review, at http://www.chabad.org/library/article.asp?AID=101747

- Aish.com with an enlightening review, also regarding the Redemption, at http://www.aish.com/h/c/t/dt/48918582.html http://www.torah.org/learning/ruth/class34.html#

- The orthodox Jewish commentator and researcher, Yair Davidiy, mentions several Jewish sources in his studies on his website: http://www.britam.org/messiah.html

In both of the above teachings of Two Messiahs, "Shiloh, as Messiah, must be **reigning as King** over Israel and the world" - which is what our primary Scripture says:

> Gen. 49:10: "The sceptre (*ruling authority*) shall not depart from Judah, nor a lawgiver (*Mechoqeck*) from between his feet, **until Shiloh (*Messiah*) come**; and unto him shall the obedience of the peoples (*the nations*) be (***The King Messiah ruling the nations***)."

"A Lawgiver from between his feet"?

Closer investigation of this commonly quoted English translation (even in Jewish publications) which does not make much sense, provides a highly viable interpretation which confirms Judah's Law Mandate and Rabbinic Oral Torah interpretation. An alternative English translation of *"mi'bein ruglaiv"* is: "... from between (or amongst) his legs.". The word *"ruglaiv"* can refer to both his two feet or legs. For obvious reasons, the Hebrew publications render the less coarse English alternative of "feet".

Upon questioning the validity of this general translation, the following revealing alternative meaning was discovered - a meaning which makes far more sense and which, in fact, would confirm overall Truth in general. A meaning which also would give depth and correct guidance to especially the returning 10 Tribers. It would also be perfectly in line with the Mechoqeck theme that we have analyzed thusfar. Most of all, it gives credence to the very sole fundamental source of anti-Rabbinism - i.e. the Oral Torah, or Rabbinic interpretation of the Torah. The latter being the final obstruction in the way of re-awakening

10-Tribers and Hebraic Roots Restorers. While this may be the very reason why this alternative meaning would therefore be objected against and rejected by the opposers and rejecters of Oral Torah, it will also serve as the convincing factor to serious returning 10-Tribers who struggle so much with all the confusion caused by resistance against this very Key factor on HaShem's List of Truth Secrets!

So, what are we referring to? What is the alternative, hidden meaning of *'ruglaiv'*?

In Hebrew, there is a word referring to "traditions, customs." It has the same roots and the same spelling in Hebrew as our textual word under discussion. It is related to the same basic *"regal"* which, has an English alternative: "regular". Can you grasp the association already? - regular - habitual - customary - traditional. The same applies with the Hebrew alternatives of the same root format "r-g-l". It refers to "(walking) according to traditions" as well as to physical feet and legs. Thus, our Hebrew word *"ruglaiv"* could refer to "his customs", "his regular habits, traditions". The Alternative word in Hebrew for "Traditional Jewish/Rabbinic religious Custom" is "Halacha" (lit. The Walk) - from the root "to walk". The overall relationship is clear!

We therefore submit an alternative and, most likely, closer translation of the text as follows: "The Sceptre shall not depart from Judah, nor the Mechoqeck (Law Giver faculty) based on (or from amongst) his customs and traditional interpretations..."

Conclusion

The conclusion, from any fair-minded point of view, is that 'Shiloh' must therefore refer to Messiah's yet **future** coming (whether for Judah the first time, or for Christians the second time), when He will truly reign as King over the nations. Until then, according to Genesis 49:10, Judah will still retain its authoritative legal rule, having duly been mandated for this by G-d "until Shiloh comes - unto whom the nations would be obedient."

The Rabbinic Sages knew that the ancestral right to kingly leadership rule, resting in the Davidic line of the tribe of Judah, would cease at the coming of the "Messiah, the son of David" (a common appellation of King Messiah found in Rabbinic writings). However, **kingly leadership** does NOT equal **Torah leadership**. Under King Messiah, Judah will retain the Torah leadership - lawgiver mandate. Messiah 'himself' will be the agreed upon Chief Rabbi, the Ruling King of the Universe.

Though the 'Root of Jesse' is claimed by Messianics to refer to 'Messiah at his first coming,' a prophecy from Isaiah clearly refers to a yet future event - a time when Judah and Ephraim will be reconciled to each other. Until that time of Reconciliation of the two divided Houses of Israel, Judah shall retain its Lawgiver (Mechoqeck) leadership through its Rabbinic authority over Torah interpretation.

> Isaiah 11:10-13, "In that day the Root of Jesse will stand as a banner for the peoples; the nations will rally to Him, and His place of rest will be glorious. In that day G-d will reach out His hand a second time to reclaim the remnant that is left of His people from Assyria, from Lower Egypt, from Upper Egypt, from Cush, from Elam, from Babylonia, from Hamath and from the islands of the sea. He will raise a banner for the nations and gather the exiles of Israel; He will

assemble the scattered people of Judah [Jews] from the four quarters of the earth. Ephraim's [10-Israel's] jealousy will vanish, and Judah's enemies will be cut off; Ephraim will not be jealous of Judah, nor Judah hostile toward Ephraim."

Just as any country, Kingdom, or domain has to have a legal judicial body, in the Kingdom of G-d on earth, it is and will remain Judah. Just as the citizens of any country will have criticism and dislikes with certain issues of the ruling law system, so, in the Kingdom of G-d, there are many citizens who criticize, object, and even reject the judicial rule instituted by G-d Himself. Just as citizens in any country take the rule of law in their own hands, so some citizens of G-d's Kingdom try to get away with making their own adaptations of the law of the land.

The re-awakening House of 10-Israel is in the process of learning to be 'citizens' of the Kingdom. With the help of G-d they are coming out of Christianity and paganism, learning Torah, keeping Shabbat (along a Noahide way), observing Sacred Festivals and crying out to HaShem to be allowed to return home to the Land. Mostly, they are doing this on their own, some with an arrogant attitude and some with a humble attitude.

We have the additional issue and valid complaint from 10-Israel, that they are not being invited to come home to join their big brother Judah. Their rightful heritage is being withheld from them by their brother who sees them as unfit for citizenship. Truly, it is time for their return and the G-d of Israel says He will purify 10-Israel, also when they are in the Land, similar to Judah's process of return (Ezekiel 36 clearly confirms this while it is also implied in other Scriptures).

In the Tanakh and in the Oral Torah's elucidation, we see that getting back to the land has a lot to do with return to G-d and Torah. For example:

> Ezekiel 36:24, 25, "... and I will bring you to your Land. And I will throw pure water on you and you will be purified – from all your impurities and your idols I will purify you."

This implies that coming back to the Land is part of the Redemption process and that the process of purifying them more fully from their pagan baggage will only occur when they are in the Land.

Those of Judah, who set such high demands on the spiritual and religious status of these Returnees, should take note of this and be more tolerant in their demands and considerations.

According to the NT the true and ultimate charge was that of rebellion, a political charge alone. "Here lies the King of the Jews a potential rebel leader against absolute Roman Imperial authority."

CHAPTER 17

The Oral Torah Controversy

Much of the opposition by re-awakening 10-Israel today is directed at the Oral Torah concept which underlies the Rabbinic Order. This Oral controversy then also is the final obstacle for Hebraic restorers to overcome on the way to Reconciliation with Judah. Ironically, the use of the word or concept of 'write' in the Written Scriptures, is limited to some 25 times only, while the Oral communication, e.g. "Speak, say, said, by the word of his mouth, command," etc. is used untold times. It is very clear from the Written Torah that a huge amount of G-d's instructions and explanations were never written down. The ONLY part of the Bible, written by the 'Finger of G-d' on the stone tablet, was smashed anyway. The Tablets that survived were hewn by a human. The 'Written' Torah which developed in 'partnership' with G-d, which we have been left with, is the product of Moses and the elders of Israel (Deut. 27:1). "The Torah that Moses commanded us, is the **Heritage** of the congregation of Jacob" (nation of Israel) (Deut. 33:4), for them to be "A Light unto the Nations," 'Heritage' means: an inalienable possession of the Covenantal Faith Community of Israel given over from one generation to the next. It is their property! They are the heirs.

It was the Divine intent therefore, to convey His Word to the nations. through the Oral transmission of Moses from the outset. The very concept of Torah (Word of G-d) entails 5 Books only, while the Oral communication on this topic across the world is immeasurable.

Much as anti-Torah Bible believers, even modern Torah favouring Hebraic Restorers, reject Oral Torah as 'man-made Rabbinic Judaism', yet, there are many instances where there very faith is dependent on the directives of Oral Torah.

So, for instance: the descendants of Moav (Moab) and Amon were forbidden to ever be allowed into the congregation of the Hebrew nation. If not for the overruling interpretation of the Oral Torah, then, just on this one point, the legal Biblical entitlement of the Nazarene to True Messiahship could have been nullified. For King David descended from Ruth the Moabitess, "Rehoboam, his grandson from Naamah the Amonitess!" Thus, their dependents, which includes the Nazarene, would be regular Gentiles, with no share or part in Israel! But, the Oral Torah ruled that the Torah always meant to forbid only the Moabite. - not the Moabitess. Only the Amonite, not the Amonitess. No prohibition was ever intended by G-d on the females who were good people in contradistinction with the barbaric and cruel menfolk. Thus, according to Oral Torah only, can Christians lay claim to any valid Biblical and Prophetic identity of their Messiah.

Even the Written Torah is Oral Torah

"Let my teachings drop as the rain, let my _speech_ distil as the dew." (Deut. 32:2)

"And on them [the Tables of Stone] was written
according to all the words which HaShem spoke to
you on the Mount." (Deut. 9:10)

From these texts we learn that G-d taught Moses the finer
details of the Law (*Megillah* 19 b), The Written Torah exists
"according to all the Words that HaShem spoke with (Moses)."
In other words, the Oral Torah decides and gives guidance on
how the Written Torah should be interpreted. G-d ordained
Moses to record his written version of His spoken words. And
indeed, every detail of the written Word exists according to
the understanding of the Oral Torah. Originally, ONLY the
Ten Commandments, were written "by (G-d's) Own finger on
tablets of stone." – these G-d - written Tablets were destroyed
and all the rest was communicated to a man (Moses) who was
instructed to write part of this Revelation down and to teach
(Orally) its finer details and implications of that which was
written, to the nation.

After Moses smashed these Tablets at the sight of the Israelites
dancing around the golden calf, he rewrote the "Ten Words" on
tablets of stone. In both cases there was a transmission of oral
into the Written Word. G-d spoke, and then it was written only
afterwards - and even long after! It took Moses forty years in the
desert, carrying the "orally transmitted word from G-d" around
in his mind, as received by him directly from G-d during the
forty days he spent in heaven and during his judgment rule for
forty years over the Israelites on their desert journey. Moses
was constantly consulting G-d directly in problematic practical
cases before completely transmitting them to parchment.

Moses completed this massive task just before his death. We
see the first Tablets of 'The Ten Words' were the work of G-d's

hand. The second set was engraved by Moses. G-d had obviously decided that human involvement and partnership is what He wanted in the giving, teaching and transmission of Torah. Before, the Torah was entirely a work of the Almighty. Now, with the second set of Tablets, it was a work of a divinely inspired man. And the rest of the 613 Laws and Regulations, were Moses's renderings anyway, of what G-d had verbally instructed him.

From here and henceforth, connection and understanding of Torah would depend on the engraving process of sincerely devoted people involved with the practical enforcement and interpretation of the Law according to the needs of the nation. In this way, creating a 'community of the children of Israel', a Covenantal Faith community, where Torah would be understood and lived in daily life.

Hence Moses did not remain on Sinai, as he well could have done, in an austere way, saying that the Torah is too holy for common man. "I will keep it safe up here, with me and the angels." Instead, he hurried down to begin a process of teaching which the Elders continued until this very day. All of us should be trying to engrave that same Torah in our minds and hearts and in our actions.

That process of revelation demands extreme active participation in understanding and communicating the overwhelming masse of information of that awesome Revelation. Indeed, this is the way the Almighty G-d, Lo-rd of the universe, decided it to be. It is G-d Himself Who set up the system of transmission from one generation of Sages to another, thereby firming up righteous Torah observers in learning, living, managing, dying if need be, for it, cherishing the Torah which demands our engraving it upon ourselves, in order to be the vessels, the receptacles to receive and pass it on. In this way, communally, we will be 'a Light unto the nations.'

The shape and the size of the letters of the Hebrew alphabet, the sounds to these letters for their pronunciation, the style of script from a specific historic period – all of this underlies the Oral Torah.

Who decides about this? The entire five books of Moses were originally written without vowels. In numerous instances, different vowels used with the same set of letters yield different meanings, concepts and directives. Who decides about this differentiation and all the rest? From whence does this information come? It comes from all the words which HaShem spoke and which precede the Oral Torah. The Written Torah itself (as we show in our discussion of the Mechoqeck or Lawgiver review) places the authority for these decisions in the hands of "judges, elders, scribes who will be in your time" (Deut. 17).

So the Hebrews themselves, though many nations deny this, have some national special expertise when it comes to interpreting and recognizing the Hebrews' national way. Israel's ancient Oral Law, the Oral Torah, the Written Torah's 'other half' provides a key - the master key - to unlock the myriads of secrets in the Bible. The Written Torah is an outline, the diaphragm - the chassis, the Oral Torah adds the detailed specifications.

The revelation at Sinai confirms the teachings received from the great mentors with prophetic understanding. They passed on a heritage to their descendants. See Genesis 26:5; *Mishnah, Kiddushin* 4:14; *Talmud, Kiddushin* 82a, *Berachot* 26b, *Yoma* 28b. (*The Rainbow Covenant* by Michael Ellias Dallen, Lightcatcher

Books and *The Rainbow Covenant Foundation*, New York, New York, 2003, Website: www.rb.org.il Page 29, 36 and 37).

Both sisters, Leah and Rachel, were needed to create the 12 Tribes. Similarly, both Written and Oral Torah are crucial in creating a deep knowledge and attachment with G-d and the Hebrew Tribes!

Today, Hebraic Restoration leaders and groups zealously define their own version of 'restorative' theology – all of which smack of 'Rabbinic' Judaism. They are supported in this by their followers, who generally reject Orthodox Jewish Rabbinic authority because "it represents the Oral ('man-made') interpretation of the Rabbinic order."

In this review I will show that the Gospel writings, through their silent and often hidden (to its readers) Keys to unlock greater Truths, actually confirm Rabbinic Halachic Oral Torah Judaism. As pointed out by the *Dictionary of Biblical Imagery* (A Christian publication). "Their possession of the Law, which instructs them in the very will of G-d (Rom 2:18), convinces them that they are a guide for the blind, a light for those who are in the dark, an instructor of the foolish, a teacher of infants." (Rom. 2:19-20). "....G-d's fatherly rejection of Israel is only apparent, not real." (Rom. 11:1); "it serves the larger purpose of the Reconciliation of the world." (Rom. 11:15.) (*Dictionary of Biblical Imagery*, Intervarsity Press).

The Gospels also bound to Oral Transmission

Christians find the concept of an orally-transmitted Torah disturbing. Christians and Messianic Hebraic Roots Restorers generally maintain that the Rabbis have added their own man-made version of Oral Torah in addition to the Written Torah. These 'restorers of the original,' insist on "sticking to the Written Torah only." However, I would like to demonstrate that the Gospels themselves follow similar Oral transmission.

Even a casual consideration of oral interpretation will confirm that every reader has to apply his/her own *oral* interpretation of what has been recorded in the Bible, in order to understand its overall Message and to draw personal conclusions.

Starting from the beginning, Genesis 1:1 says, "In the Beginning G-d created the heavens and the earth."

- When and what was the 'Beginning'?

- Who and what is G-d?

- How did He create?

- How long did it take Him?

- Why did He create it?

- What do 'the heavens' entail?

- You know, the Mishnah says that if you search the Torah, you will find everything in it. So perhaps, we can ask, where do we learn baseball from the Torah? Nu, from the 'big-inning!'

- Since the Torah is our users' manual on how to live in this life, should not the Torah have begun from the first commandment as opposed to the story of creation?

- Why start: "In the beginning G-d created?" Should we not start off more properly by saying G-d created in the beginning etc.

- Why does the Bible not start with the first Commandment given to the Hebrew nation?

The above and another 1001 fair, logical and rational questions need to be answered! The written Scripture, in its entirety, is not very explicit on most of these questions and we are only at verse 1. The Oral Torah provides the detailed answers to these and many more questions, according to the understanding and traditional teachings which have been carefully preserved in Judaism by faithful students of the Torah who dedicated their lives to the study of Torah. These teachings stem from Moses himself, who personally received it from G-d. It has been debated in great depths throughout centuries of practical administering of these Torah principles.

Another Scriptural example of the need for Oral Torah occurs in the time of Noah. Noah was called 'righteous' sixteen generations before the giving of the Torah at Sinai. He was told to take pure and impure animals onto his legendary ark. The Bible goes into some detail about the dimensions of the ark but does not specify the terminology of 'pure and impure' animals to be taken on the ark. Noah complied, according to the later written Bible record, and ushered in a slew of animals according to the divine instruction. Our first conservationist, Noah, of necessity had to be instructed regarding the detailed definitions of these terms. His relationship with G-d depended solely on oral instruction. It is unthinkable that he would not have passed this information on carefully and precisely to his direct descendants. Thus, long before Sinai, G-d interacted with humanity through oral, verbal and inspired dialogue. Twenty-six generations related to the Will and Wisdom of their Creator in this Oral mode and interface. Centuries later only, the foundational framework of these comprehensive directives and communications were committed to writing, leaving much of the technical aspects of those long-ago communications in their original oral mode.

Regarding the Gospel texts, one needs to remember that the final canonization of the NT took place in 393 and 397 CE (Synods of Carthage and Hippo). Therefore, the principles of the new faith contained in the Gospels were being similarly transmitted **orally** throughout the first few generations of disciples. There existed many manuscripts and texts. It was the oral decision of Church officials that ultimately decided which to keep and what its final edition would be and which to burn and who to burn along with the rejected versions!

The original Messianic congregation consisted almost exclusively of traditional Jewish believers. The interpersonal relationships and communications of the initial followers of the Nazarene were based on their Jewish religious culture and upbringing. This was all well-established by **oral** transfer throughout the centuries, right back to Moses.

I personally found over 600 references to Oral Torah and Rabbinic literature in the NT letters of the Apostles. Peter J Thompson (Christian theologian) found over 700 references according to his book, *"Paul and the Jewish Law, Halakha, in the letters of the Apostles to the Gentiles"*, (Fortress Press, Minn. 1991).

The teachings/guidelines of the Nazarene's disciples took on an oral mode through what they termed 'the guidance of the Holy

Spirit', and only much later were these encounters recorded. It was centuries later that they were canonized into what became the New Testament, under the directions of Constantine, through Eusebius and the early Catholic Church fathers. They were strongly opposed to the original Jewish faith of the early Messianic congregations. The NT was edited by Eusebius and his supporters, who hunted down and annihilated both the teachers and the texts of those who disagreed with them. Just go to any good library and look up this fellow; all that he recorded have been translated into a host of languages. Open up the Catholic Encyclopaedia on 'the canonization of the Gospels and the NT' and you will be astonished! They used, as did the Spanish Inquisition, a literal distortion of John 15:6 which states: "If anyone does not remain in me, he is like a branch that is thrown away and withers; such branches are picked up, thrown into the fire and burned." They frequently literally burned their theological opponents. However, in Talmudic thought or from a Hebrew mind-set, being burnt and fire meant embarrassment and shame.

Oral transfer of the Gospel of the Nazarene, therefore, forms the entire foundation of the New Testament. Oral transfer of the Torah, as practiced by the Nazarene's Jewish followers and compatriots of his time, was similarly transmitted to major portions of the Gospel records. What a pity that the Church authorities did not ask the Jewish spiritual leadership what possibly could be the meaning of this line in John. After all, it is part of Jewish Messianic literature. At first glance (Greco-Roman glance that is) it seems way out of pace with a document calling for "turning the other cheek"; "loving your enemy and neighbour"; "forgiving gross sins in others" and general passivity in confrontation. Had they asked and listened, they would have learned that no doubt the intention on that line is of emotional and spiritual 'fire' i.e. shame or embarrassment! Tens of thousands of lives could have been saved!

The question that arises is: what then is so strange to Christians about the concept of **orally transmitted Torah**? To early Messianism, a transmission process without a system of elders was not conceivable! Paul and Barnabas appointed elders, Acts14:23. Peter refers to himself as a 'fellow-elder'; in 1 Peter 5:1-3, John the apostle calls himself 'the elder' in his 2nd and 3rd letters, 2 John 1:3; Guardians (teachers) are found in the NT; Gal. 4:1, Gal. 3:24-25 and 4:2, 1 Cor. 4:15-16. Peter exhorts them to use their gifts as good stewards (managers), 1 Peter 4:10. (*Dictionary of Biblical Imagery*, Intervarsity Press, pp. 59-60).

To this day, the entire Catholic denomination refers to the church fathers for their authoritative understanding of the Bible. They kept it locked up for hundreds of years, even after it was finally canonized and written down. Even after the printing press was invented, laypersons could not have a copy. Hundreds of years would pass, right up to our modern times before a written text would be made available to the average churchgoer! In Judaism, throughout the centuries, even before the printing press, careful reproduction was an art practised by the Scribes and regulated by the spiritual leaders to ensure the absence of even the slightest mistakes in copying. These scrolls were read publicly in synagogues and studied in learning institutions by all who were interested.

Many Protestant denominations have likewise created a body of elders who passed judgment on all questions of theology and practice within their church organization. Similarly, since the great Reformation, Martin Luther and Calvin are taken as official guides for Protestant theology through their oral inter-pretation of the Bible! In fact, the entire Reformation came about on the basis of a difference of opinion with the Catholic Church regarding the oral interpretation of the Bible. Much of Protestantism holds to the changes brought about by the great Reformers of those centuries, while for others, reformation has continued to this day.

Currently, this continuing Reformation is spearheaded by the Hebraic Restoration movement – which is all based on oral interpretation of the Scriptures. Yet, the Oral interpretation of Judaism, dating back to the time of Moses, remains a bone of contention for most. They have no problem referring arguments back to their respective fellowship-church elders, but they get peeved when Jews refer back to their Hebrew prophets and Sages, their scholarly, pious teaching leadership.

The process and apparatus of transmission was Biblical in nature. G-d Himself ordained a system of transmission of His instructions. The prophets, Scholars, Sages or elders in their role as teachers, interpreters and transmitters, are clearly rec-ognized and discussed over one hundred times in Torah. The severe criticism of the Tanach was only levelled at 10-Israel's assimilated and rebellious leaders and not the spiritual leader-ship of Judah!

Further, the present day Restoration movement seeks to follow the Written Torah in such a way as to live a lifestyle that is as close to what the ancient Israelites lived as possible, while liv-ing in the Diaspora. Many of these people (i.e. 10-Israel, Lost House of Israel, etc), in order to get back to what they call 'the Hebrew or Torah way of living' inadvertently refer to the Oral Torah and other Jewish sources for information on how to keep and live the Written Torah (i.e. keep the Commandments). Because the Restoration movement is unfamiliar (although this is changing) to a large extent with the Oral Torah and Jewish writings, they do not always know that what they are referring to for information, is in fact the Oral Torah and/or Jewish sources e.g. the Talmud.

The Restoration movement leaders are viewed by 10-Israel in much the same way as Judaism view their Rabbis and Sages. These leaders expound on the Written Torah (much of the time from a Jewish perspective) either in writing or orally, and 10-Israel view these 'teachings' as the proper way in which to follow and/or keep the Written Torah – while consciously rejecting the Oral Torah of Judah, founded on the interpretations of an academy of Jewish Sages compiled over a period of nearly 3000 years, right back to the time of Moses. Much of the confusion within the Restoration movement is both the unfamiliarity with Jewish writings and uninformed perspectives in regard to the Oral Torah, as well as the failure on the part of its leaders to educate the people about the Oral Torah. Some examples of how 10-Israel has incorporated the Oral Torah in their re-identification process, are Kashrut, the Festivals, Shabbat, marriage, Hebrew study techniques (i.e. PaRDeS), tzit tzit, kippot and mezuzot, to name but a few. The Jewish way of observance based on Oral Torah interpretation in many cases has been adopted by 10-Israel, making it their own tradition as well!

CHAPTER 18

The Karaite Movement – eternalizing '10-Israel's Original Sin'

As shown in chapter 16, the 'Original Sin' of 10-Israel for which they have been cut off from the Covenant, was their rejection of Judah as G-d's 'official Lawgiver'. For this reason, the teachings of the Karaite Movement find fertile grounds for conviction amongst re-identifying Ten Tribers and Hebraic Roots Restorers today, thereby keeping them bound to the sins of their forefathers.

In this chapter we will address one of the many opposing forces against this Divinely mandated authority of Judah as Lawgiver - i.e. the Jewish Karaite movement. Karaite teachings have today become a very popular haven of retreat for the booming Hebraic Roots Restoration movement across the world. This movement identifies itself by the sincere attempts of its adherents to break loose from their spiritual captivity 'in Egypt' - which remains evident as a hangover from their ancient forefathers' rebellion (as the Northern 10 Tribes of Israel) against this very Torah authority centered in the Tribe of Judah in ancient Jerusalem. Unfortunately the Karaite rebellion against Rabbinic authority and the Oral Torah serves as very fertile ground for eternalizing the ancient 10-Triber rebellion for which HaShem rejected them, leaving just ONE Tribe to continue His Kingdom, i.e. Judah, the very Tribe against whom the Karaites rebel, replacing themselves as the interpreters of Torah above G-d's mandated appointees, the Rabbinic institution, which dates right back to Moses.

Since the symbol of the *Nachash* (snake) in Genesis, there has been a spirit of rebellion against what are obviously G-d's Words and Instructions, and against the pious representatives of His unbroken transmission of those Words - the Rabbis. Numerous times the Torah says to the Rabbinic leadership (Moses, Aaron, the Elders, Johsua, Kelev, Etamar, the Judges, the Prophets, etc.) to keep and guard that very selfsame Torah (i.e. Ex. 20:2; Lev. 29:3; Deut.17; Deut. 5:8).

Through Biblical analysis we learn that the Jewish sages reviewed the Torah many times. They taught three main guiding principles:

- Be exact (deliberate) in judgment - fair, honest, careful and just;

- build up many students, (develop to an independent level), and

- make 'a fence for the Torah.' Enact provisions and cautionary rules to safeguard against transgression (*ArtScroll Siddur* pg. 545).

If the prophet calls Judah the bow and Ephraim the arrow, it means that Judah by necessity needs to be intuitive, creative and active in explaining the Torah - just as an archer must be with his students and when out on missions. An Archer is no good as a mindless robot. He needs to use his G-d given mind and body to the N'th degree.

Because of the Torah positive Command it was incumbent on each Israelite to write his own Scroll of the Torah (5 Books). Whereas this was impossible for every individual to do, they would group together and hire a scribe to write a Scroll for public and private reading and studying. In ancient times already, they were counting the letter and word values for wider and more intellectual interpretation and understanding of the Bible. (Deut. 31:19 - *Footnote Herz Pentateuch*)

Compare this to Christianity though, where the Bible Scriptures were hoarded by the spiritual leaders and teachers. The Bible was locked up and available to the priests only for centuries until the advent of the printing press. Thus, Christian believers were dependent on the Oral teachings of their priests - but, according to the Church views. The Church, born from Roman Empire times, was strongly anti-Jewish and anti-Semitic and followers had no insight into the Scriptures itself. Hence an entire anti-Jewish and anti-Torah religion was instituted to oppose the Rabbinic interpretations. History abounds of how followers of the Original Bible Faith and of Jewish principles were persecuted by the Roman Empire. The monumental buildings testifying to these persecutions remain to this day in Rome as tourist attractions amongst the palatial buildings of the new Faith of Catholicism which replaced the Jewish Faith with a new totally anti-Torah religion. This new religion, though claiming the same Bible of Judah as its foundation, was based on the oral interpretations of the Popes and bishops of Rome.

It took more than a millennium for the average Church goer to find the Bible Truth for themselves. Throughout this great time period, the liberal accessibility of Torah and its oral interpretation by Jewish sages and wise teachers continued unabatedly since the days of Moses - though unwontedly for non-Jews.

Home schooling exists in Judaism since the days of Abraham. Only because of Roman persecution which disrupted Jewish home schooling, did subsequent Jewish enactment of mandatory education become necessary. This was like a tragic step backwards for the faithful, while to other nations it is a step forward.

The Written Torah is similar to the magnificent skeleton of the human body. The Oral Torah fills in and out the body, giving skin, eyes, body systems, hair-colouring, personality etc. Together they make the Hebrew people with the Bible the longest living faith.

Remember in the book of Numbers, Korach and disgruntled company attacks the authority of Moses, Aaron and the Elders. Well, that was not the last attack but merely one of the first attacks upon the Rabbinical guides, the spiritual leadership of the covenantal faith community. The Karaite schism likewise has character traits of that same old rebellious serpent and Korach and company. Korach was brooding, filled with jealousy and hate for not getting a promotion in the priesthood. His supporters, Dothan and Aviran had similar complaints. They were first born and were skipped over for promotion. The first born had lost a possible aliya potential (not a right but a possibility). Because of the sin of the Golden calf fiasco (only the Tribe of Levi was completely clean of it) they had one down many levels. Still they felt they deserved an upgrade and hated, despised and nursed envy and jealousy against the Torah leadership of that time.

Likewise the essential founder of the Karaite movement. Anan, lost the position of Exilarch to his younger brother Hananiah. This petty envy and jealousy led to open confrontation. Instead of accepting the majority decision of the Geonin [the undisputed spiritual leadership of the nation], Anan and company opposed the decision and fomented rebellion.

Ten Tribers and Hebrew Roots folk today, who so eagerly though blindly are following the modern Karaite movement, should know that the Karaites immediately declared themselves a new religion and were so recognized by the Muslim Shihite Caliph as a new separate religious faith and people. Many of them are actually non-Jews and are proud of it. They were defined by Saadiah Goan (a great Torah authority) as total apostates and heretics and not as another misguided sect. They agreed that they were different and often sought from gentile powers recognition as a new/old religion, completely distinct from Torah Judaism, with many elements of replacement theology.

For a few examples of Karaite non-Jewishness and replacement theological tendencies, we have the following historic evidence:

In 1795 they convinced the anti-Jewish Empress Catherine II, to drop the double tax that Jews had to pay and were allowed to buy land. Because they were not really Jewish, even though they claim to have the real 'Jewish' tradition, these Jews are similar to imposters.

In 1827, they [in Crimea] were exempted from army service by the Jew hating Czar Nicholas I and then exempted in

Lithuania. At the same time Jewish kids even as young as eight, nine and ten were forcibly inducted for periods of 20 to 25 years. Unbelievable horrors were being suffered by the Jewish Kehillah. All the while the Karaites bad-mouthed us and so proved their hatred towards the nation of Israel, that these murderous despots felt so comfortable with them thus granting them favors. They claimed to have great qualities while the general Jews were full of the worst character deficiencies.

They were successful in even causing the forced exile of a holy, good and ancient Jewish community of Troki gaining sole rights to livie there. By 1840 they were officially called 'Russian Karaites', with no reference to their former status as 'Jewish - Karaites'.

These kind of tactics helped them become landowners and wealthy while the Jews were only allowed to be artisans and peddlers.

In 1840, in Russia, the Karaites became equal to Muslims in the law of the land. Also independent Church status was accorded them. The Karaites always did things to promote estrangement from the Jewish nation and to prove to gentile powers how non-Jewish they themselves really were. We find this in all of Russia and Poland for example. \

During WW2 their attitudes 'vacillated between indifference to the Jewish cause and some cases of actual collaboration with the Germans [Nazis] 'ibid *Encyclopedia* pg. 776. The Einsatzgruppen gave them positions of trust, authority and favor. The Nazi Ministry of Interior said that the Karaites were not Jewish and were of a different 'racial psychology' [*The Phases of Jewish History,* Devorah Pub. 2005, pg. 148]. The point is they always had the wrong spirit and the enemies of our people were quick to spot it and therefore felt and treated them as allies against the eternal Jewish people. "The enemy of my enemy is my friend," the Arabic saying goes. The very worst enemies of Torah and of those charged with keeping and transmitting it (namely the Jews) saw in the Karaites, friends in their wars against Am Yisrael. (*The Ben Zvi Institute* of the Former President of Israel was very helpful with a wealth of documents, as was Hebrew University's Givat Ram Campus Library).

The Karaite rendering of history has largely been recognized as "unhistorical, fanciful and biased Karaite sources"\ (*Encyclopedia Judaica Jerusalem*, vol. 10pg. 766, *The Rise of the Karaite Sect*, Barron, and many other sources). In addition, Karaitism was also influenced by Islam i.e. Abu-Hanifah, the founder of the Muslim school of Hanafite jurisprudence, was a great influence for the formulation of the Karaite legal system (which often opposes the Torah).

The same *Encyclopedia Judaiuca* (pg 763) and many other sources point out: "The (Karaite) sect ... (is) the result of a combination of factors:

- the amalgamation of various heterodox trends in Babylonian – Persian Jewry;

- the tremendous religious, political and economic fermentations in the entire East, resulting from the Arab conquests and collision of Islam with world religions;

- social and economic grievances of the poorer classes of Jewry, particularly those ... migrated to the sparsely settled frontier provinces of the caliphate ...' Thereby (being) rural and out of touch with the centers of Torah learning and authority."

The Karaite sect absorbed both such Jewish sects as the Isawites (adherents of Abu Isa al Isfahani) and Yudghanites (who were influenced by East-Islamic tendencies and small remnants of ... Boethusians'). "Innumerable groups ... were formed. It became impossible to find two Karaites who held the same opinion on all religious issues" Al Kirkisani (founder of a Karaite sect).

We find a further example of the great internal division in Karaitism, in Ishmael of Ukbarte sect who was violently against Anan's followers and denounced him as a fool and ass, *ibid.* pg,766.

You have Karaite leaders at one point calling Anan the first wise man then later in their careers, I guess after feeling rebellious even against their own leadership, called him the first of fools, i.e. Daniel b. Moses al-Qumisi, first scholar to live in Jerusalem (*ibid* pg.768).

As usual despite their claim to reject Oral Torah they needed to invent their own whenever they wished to implement anything on a practical action, doing level. Without a central recognized leadership it all became a 'do your own thing' game in line with the rebellious attitudes of its founders. Without the Sages their observance led to anti-biblical absurd restrictions, anarchy and became a stepping stone for Jews to completely leave the faith and fold assimilation, intermarriage and finally extinction (Refer: *The Phases of Jewish History ibib.* Pg. 146).

Here, dear reader, for your interest are some offbeat non-biblical positions they take. They only have 8 accents of musical notation on the haftorah readings; they disregard the other markings [accents, cantillation notes]. They just swallow, gobble up or draw the rest of the text in an un-natural way into the 8 motives. By the way there existed no way to transmit sounds, pronunciations, vowels and melodies without an advanced Oral Torah transmission system! (Refer: Dr. S. Hoffman, in: *Leshonnenu 22* (1948), pages 264 - 265).

In attempts to create uniformity of observance they based themselves on exegetical methods they had previously bitterly condemned! (*The Phases of Jewish History, the Karaite Schism*).

A very crucial Karaite wise guy, Judah HaDassi, used 80 hermeneutical rules, the best ones coming right out of the Talmud (*Eshkol hakofer.* nos. 114, 168-73). This implies their applying their own Oral interpretation for their selective interpretation.

Anan and company wrongly translated a term in Leviticus 11:19 as 'chicken' and thereby listed it with impure, non – kosher birds. They further twisted and perverted texts leading to forbidding marriage between even the most distant relatives, and they complicated the Biblical circumcision procedure, while forgetting some of its crucial aspects. They made ritual purity between husband and wife much more rigid and severe, prohibited kindling light even before Sabbath but insisted on extinguishing it on the Sabbath [an older Karaite law]. This is nuts at best, rebellious, psychologically dysfunctional and hateful of self and family ties at worst.

Regarding Sabbath they even have themselves divided up between opposing camps of good/light verses evil/darkness! (Z. Cahan, T*he Halakah of the Karaites*, 1936). As mentioned earlier they could not function without any Oral Torah, so like the Catholic Church Fathers and the Protestant Church Elders they needed to invent oral explanations. Their own collection of traditions is called in a kind of negative way a 'yoke of inheritance', full of things not found in the TaNach. The book of Precepts is an outstanding example of their own mishmash of self-produced oral interpretations.

Very important to keep in mind is an inescapable fact, namely, many of their greatest leaders and founders, in their moments of truth, were forced to conclude how together, organized and reliable the Talmud is in general! They, for example, conceded that the prohibition not to 'boil a kid in its mother's milk' should be understood as relating to forbidding any meat cooked with milk.

The Mishawayh al-Ukbari sect of Karaites, although gone, has left its impact. Theyt held that inb all debates, disputes and uncertainties, they were to always follow the Jewish Rabbis. In other words they agreed on the logic and correctness of keeping the festivals in harmony with the rest of historic Jews and Judaism! Now get this: this principle included, as just stated, their confusing system of New Year and Calendar calculations! If in doubt, "go to the sages (Judges) who will be in your days", Deut. 17. Benjamin b. Moses Nahawendi of Persia is likened to the fathers of the movement: Anan, Josiah and Saul. He created a doctrine that has been in use for all sects right up to present times. The point is he, told his students to rely upon the Rabbis for all the times for which the Bible is unclear to them! (L. Nemoy, *Karaite Anthology*, 1952).

Along these lines, one of the greatest wise men and guides of all time Elijah Bashyazi, took a kinder, more respectful legal attitude towards the sages than these new guys, Johnny come lately, self-proclaimed recent Karaites. To paraphrase the chacam, Bashyazi: the overwhelming majority of Mishnah and Talmud is true and faithfully gives over the words, utterances and sayings of our Biblical fathers. 'Our people' must study the Oral Torah, it is an obligation and we need to study it with respect.

Moving along in this study, the Karaites reject many open practical Commandments, even those very well documented by history and archeology, as merely symbolic ideas e.g. Tzizit and Tefillin.

Hebrew Roots people today will, with a few fast facts, recognize the familiar spirit of rebellion, nasty gossip and slander of historic am Yisrael by this sect. Even a glance at the NT will yield boatloads of Oral Torah totally accepted by its main players. The ethical call not to wear Tzit Tzit and Teffilin in a show off way is very normal Rabbinic kind of censure; the sages always pushing and pulling the nation on to higher levels. Greater humility and service is what it is all about. No mention is made at all, that these ritual holy objects were inventions of the modern Rabbis of that time. All the ritual objects were assumed by the NT to be a logic part of the Faith, right back from the time of the revelation at Sinai.

What does "not a jot or tittle" mean? These are little lines, notes, decorations etc, written in the Written Torah, completely, 100% according to the ancient Oral Torah's directives! Whatever the NT is saying can only make sense with an Oral Torah explanation and understanding. Besides, after trying to trick the Nazarene, the Sadducees, who rejected Oral law, helped Nazi like Rome. They were the members of the puppet anti-Rabbinic court that sentenced the Nazarene illegally. They were basically wiped out by loyal Jews in the Revolt against Rome and were reprimanded by the Nazarene in the NT that they are ignorant, (being assimilated pro Roman), and that they do not know the power of Hashem!

Now let us address in a few words the noise that a few self-proclaimed Karaites leaders are making today. Often we have heard one fellow hailed as a great scholar. Not so in the least, by no academic standards is this fellow a great scholar of anything whatsoever. A degree of M.A. in any field does not a scholar make. He is hailed as having assisted on The Dead Sea scrolls project. This project spans many years. Hundreds of people have assisted the handful of big scholars over the many years. Assisting a professor never made someone, hocus pocus, a Professor. These people did numerous menial things for the real scholars, like bringing them lunch, tea, coffee, simple photo copying and basic back-up technical assistance. There is a huge amount of textual preparation work which is important, but takes no scholarship to perform. If a fellow was a scholar, he would not be merely another one from the scores of little helpers. He would be one of the professors with much post-doctoral work under his belt, not merely a student with a M.A.

This fellow was born and raised in an easy going modern orthodox religious Zionist way, not as a Karaite. So he had some issues with Dad, and has a bit of a rebellious streak. That's all there is to it. He found in some Hebrew Roots folk a similar bit of unresolved rebellion and also innocence and ignorance.

Now some interesting fast facts about the loud self-proclaimed recently made Karaites. Several of them were and are dear friends. The Ministry of Antiquities fixed up an old abandoned Karaite prayer center. The government then advertised to the general public the opportunity to come and take over the little facility. Eventually about five guys showed up to run the place.

My good buddy asked why I don't join them, just to get the keys to a tourist site is so cool. He was also working with Tourists and thought it amazing to be able to possibly take people into a site after hours. Wild and cool and convenient on so many occasions to have a little hall to use. This was a reason to start to get a little into some form of religion. He explained in detail how none of them were Karaites; they were merely secular regular Jews who saw an amazing chance to gain access to a small lovely facility. They did not keep any Karaite festival calendar, nor a dark, locked up Karaite restrictive Shabbat, nor did they keep any religious Torah Shabbos. They were secular, he told me. Get it! However, if some G-Man. a rep, from the Ministry of whatever came calling, he would swear that he is the most devout Karaite that you ever did see! Over the years he has kind of bought into his necessary con job on the Ministries. This fellow, like all the new Karaites that I know, also has a fun, rebellious energy. Hey, being a rebel can be very positive, when used in the right way.

Another guy [may he rest in peace] who was the leading scholar among them, actually worked against missionaries with Reb Shmuel Golding [may he rest in peace] and myself for many years. He came from a liberal traditional Sephardic background, not Karaite. He was a loner and had a serious rebellious personality. Now things did not work out for himself and his wife and child. The relationship dragged on; she wanted out desperately. He did not. She went to the courts, including the Rabbinical one. All agreed, it was time for him to give her a divorce and at least pay child support. He was very angry at everyone's interference and took off to Israel Where the Rabbis here, as did the ones there, wanted Shalom Bayit [reconciliation and family peace]. However it was not to be. Nothing was happening that could overcome the couple's personnel issues. So eventually the Rabbis told him to give a divorce and at least pay child support. Neither of which did he ever do. I tried to get him for many years to establish a relationship with the child despite the other problems. It was very intense and involved a great deal of personnel in-depth discussions.

The point here regarding our topic is his rocky road to Karaite conclusions did not happen in an intellectual vacuum. They rather partially grew out of the anger he harbored against the entire Jewish community on both sides of the ocean.

In brief, this is presented as a public service to the many up and coming 10-Israel as well as Hebrew Restoration folk. Forewarned is forearmed. We would not know even how to pronounce the Hebrew Alphabet if not for the Oral Torah. Similarly, in order to understand the Written Torah we have to rely on Oral Torah. Without such a practice, even the Written Torah would not be understandable. Check this out: 'You shall keep that which I have entrusted you to guard' Leviticus 18 ;30. The Sages are the management of HaShem's system.

Take a look at Daniel 1;3 -16 Where miracles were performed for him and his friends on the merit of keeping Rabbinic protective degrees.

Let it be known, that we, the manna eaters (the Jewish / Hebrew people), the children of our great ancestors, have never lost contact with HaShem, His Torah or our spiritual leadership. They, likened to angels, who so lovingly have passed it on in each generation from Sinai to desert drama and trauma, on through all our trials and tribulations. Through the blood, sweat and tears, glory and joys, we have always had a living, dynamic relationship with our righteous remnant, the giants of mind and spirit, our Sages.

CHAPTER 19

Obstacles in the way of Reconciliation and Redemption

The saintly and great Chassidic Rebbe, Rav Menachem Mendel of Kortzk, once explained; just as people look so different, and their appearances are varied, so are their ideas and overviews not alike. As one is not bothered by differences in appearance, so one need not be disturbed by differences in the way others think.

There can be little doubt that the current movement toward the original Jewish religion and culture among an ever-growing mass of non-Jewish Bible students across the world, must be the fulfilment of the multiple Prophecies contained in the Bible regarding the future re-identification and return of the Lost Ten Tribes of Israel. This group is referred to throughout the Tanach as "the House of Israel", as opposed to "the House of Judah." (Refer to the Addendum (Chapter 25) section "Scriptures that confirm the Restoration of the House of Israel" for a comprehensive list of these Scriptures). Further confirmation can be found in the commentaries and interpretations on this topic by Jewish Sages throughout history. It would require an entire publication to review these Jewish sources. Our Rabbinic readership is no doubt well acquainted with those writings. Readers may also turn to our website for more information at http://www.kolhator.org.il or to the Brit Am website and publications - www.**britam**.org.

This Return would have been much faster had it not been for major obstacles which strain closer relations between the two greatly-estranged Houses of Israel. The following paragraphs will help explain some of the complexities involved in uniting these two Houses.

The House of Israel (meaning the Lost Ten Tribes of Israel) currently consists of many people with Christian backgrounds who are experiencing a strong awareness and interest in Jewish religious tenets and culture. These people are gradually adopting various great teachings of Judaism, while many of them are totally unaware of the Prophetic reality of such a turnaround. Through their study of the Bible, these people are all in a process of adopting and practicing the ancient and eternal principles of Judaism. This spiritual evolutionary process, when they do become aware of its nature, draws them to learning about their biological, historical, cultural and religious heritage while developing the realization of possibly being part of the ancient nation of Israel. They are often totally unaware of this possible Hebraic heritage. These people are part of a movement that is known as Messianic Israel, Two-House, Hebrew Roots Restoration, Ephraim, Joseph, 10-Israel, etc. Many of these people are at different levels of coming out of Christianity and therefore are at different levels of understanding and of accepting or adopting their Israelite heritage.

In order to help both Judah and 10-Israel to begin to understand this process of Reconciliation, it is necessary to first identify and recognize the biases and blindness regarding this topic that is unique to each House. Once this is accomplished, then positive steps can be taken to work through and eliminate the obstacles that are present in both Houses, to reach a peaceful Reconciliation. This Reconciliation can then be founded on understanding and forbearing of each other while learning together and ultimately come to love each other. This will result in shaking off any biases and becoming enlightened and having the Torah heal and impart wisdom to all of us.

An important point to emphasize here, is how each House views Christianity. Judah is generally totally unaware of the vast religious theological segregation in Christianity and views this pro-Judaism Messianism with great suspicion as to its integrity. Judah is currently also very much unaware of this great non-Jewish swing towards Torah Judaism and the Land of Israel. Judah views all these greatly diverse factions under one umbrella, as being mainly Catholic or Protestant Christianity, and that 10-Israel somehow respects what these religious systems and their leaders have to say.

In this respect, Judah is totally off the mark. The Catholic system through its leaders and teachers, interpret the Scriptures through the Greek and Latin languages and everyone follows what the Catholic priests/leaders say and expect them to believe. In Judah's mind therefore, if you believe in the Christian Messiah, then you are 'Christian'. This mind-set stems from the fact that for centuries the Catholic religion has been the main dominant Christian religion which canonized the NT. Also, Catholicism and its religious branches were responsible for the major persecution that Judah endured throughout the centuries. Further, in the land of Israel, the dominant Christian religion is Catholicism.

The new reviving House of 10-Israel, however, strongly rejects any such references to them being part of Christianity. At the higher evolutionary stage of the re-identifying process, they no longer attend church services and do not belong to any organized church denomination. They are in fact rejected together with Judaism by mainstream Christianity and evangelicals. Judah does not recognize them either, since Judah views Christianity as a religion based on and infiltrated by pagan customs and teachings. What still identifies 10-Israel with Christianity, in Judaism's estimation, is their acceptance of the New Testament and its declared Messiah. Individually, as they progress in study and restoration, they accept more and more Jewish customs and teaching. As a result they move further and further away from a selective observance of Torah principles to progressively accepting and practicing more Torah principles and Jewish customs. As their studies progress further, where the NT seems to reject and/or contradict the Tanach, advanced 10-Tribers tend to accept the Torah and Tanach, while regarding the NT as simply commentary on the Torah and Tanach.

It is important to note, that while Christians have carried over a more spiritual interpretation of the Tanach, 10-Israel takes a more literal and Jewish interpretation of the Tanach. What is becoming clear is that 10-Israel is in a process of completely rejecting and repudiating all forms of Christianity!

The Restoration Movement faces one final obstacle to the complete fulfilment of the Return. It is the reluctance of progressive Ten Tribers to accept Rabbinic authority and its Scriptural interpretation as contained in Oral Torah. This stems from their background of anti-Judaism inherited from the Church culture from which they are busy extricating themselves. Years and years of Christian teaching against Rabbinic authority, defining it as 'man-made legalism', have left its marks almost indelibly on them. It also stems from the 'Original Sin' of the Northern Ten Tribes (refer "The historic Rejection of Judah as Lawgiver by 10-Israel" chapter 16) namely, rebellion against Jerusalem and its Temple institution and teaching by Judah. When this obstacle is removed or overcome, the re-identified 10-Triber then finds him/herself facing the barriers of conversion and physical return to the Land of Israel which they crave.

The following chart which appears on the Kol Hator website, explains this progressive spiritual Redemption process:

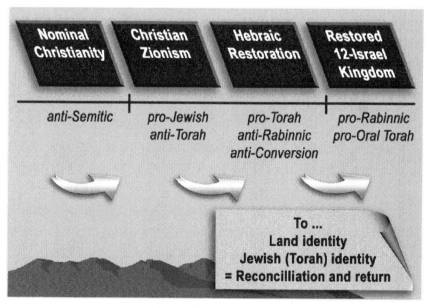

Source: http://www.kolhator.org.il

10-Israel does not respect what Catholicism has to say and in fact they have the tendency to do or believe just the opposite. 10-Israel does not like to be called Christian, or G-d forbid,

Catholic! They feel that they are in the process of coming out of pagan Christian indoctrination and are becoming the Israel that the Bible portrays and requires. Many Rabbis and Jewish scholars believe that the Lost Tribes will specifically emerge from Christianity. Many of the emerging returnees, at this advanced stage, feel that they are on the road to ultimately accepting historic Orthodox, Sage-led Torah Judaism. In the meantime, they appreciate and enjoy the status of being the sons of Noah, along with the rest of humanity. All Jews know and are very proud that they are descendants of Noah, specifically his righteous son Shem.

The Jewish people simply have more covenants: the patriarchal covenant, the Sinaitic covenant, etc., that impose more commandments, responsibilities, separateness and thus holiness.

With that said, the following is an outline of some of the obstacles between the House of Judah and the House of Israel. This list is difficult to compile for several reasons:

(1) Various Christian groups and their beliefs are represented in the Land of Israel and are negatively influencing Judah's view of 10-Israel. Because of this Christian influence, Judah erroneously thinks of 10-Israel as 'Christian'.

(2) 10-Israel does not hold to most of the tenets of Christianity and are in various stages of "coming out" of what they regard as paganism. Therefore, it is hard to articulate where exactly they are in the process. Their leadership is fractured and not in the Land. Therefore, they do not have a unified voice and cannot learn from Judah in a consistent, positive manner.

It is noteworthy to mention the efforts of the KOL HA'TOR VISION in this regard. Kol HaTor offers knowledge and guidance to both Houses in a sincere effort to promote and further the Prophetic Vision of ultimate Reconciliation – the very essence of the concept of Redemption (Geulah).

The Kol HaTor Vision presents an ideal vehicle to voice and promote such positive Action towards establishing Peace in the House, Family and Nation of the G-d of Israel (ref. http://www.kolhator.org.il).

In considering the obstacles listed below, the reader should consider his/her own share of either:

- Eternalizing this sad, ancient and persistent animosity between the two Houses of G-d's Elect Nation, or

- Positively working towards eliminating these obstacles.

Obstacles as seen by both Houses of Israel

Evidence of paganism - 10-Israel view themselves as coming out of paganism but resent it that, nevertheless, they are not being acceptable to Judah.

Judah views 10-Israel as still involved in some aspects of old world Church paganism, but it is evident that many of 10-Israel are quickly moving in the direction of a kosher Torah theology.

Traditional Concepts of the Origin of religious cultures - The concept prevalent among many sections of 10-Israel is that Judaism is not the original faith, but a religion which developed during the Babylonian exile.

257

As this entire book and many others prove: the NT is saturated with Oral Torah confirmations, unbeknown generally to its faithful readers and interpreters. The NT accepts at face value that Tefillin, fringes, kashrut, Shabbat, Feast Days, Temple purity rites etc., which are chock full of Oral Torah traditions, are correct. The accusation above is that Judaism was infested with Babylonian paganism during Judah's exile to Babylon centuries before. However, the NT never criticizes the apostles for celebrating at the wrong time, with a different calendric system. Neither is there any criticism of the NT of the Jewish Calendarbeing misleading to the people by using a Babylonian-influenced calendar or pagan influenced theology. Quite the contrary, it confirms the very traditional Jewish principles which had been formulated in Written Oral Torah format during and after the exile to Babylon. The above realization alone should be sufficiently convincing to end the misgivings surrounding the topic.

The Judaism of the first century (the birth era of the NT) is the exact Judaism that emerged from the Holy Torah-living-keeping communities of Babylon. In fact, the NT testifies to the fact that the Judaism of the NT times was kosher and based in Mosaic code. Had it been pagan influenced by Babylon, the NT would have pointed it out – not sanction it as this book proves.

In fact, the only NT criticism was, that at times, the common folk would be too ritually strict, forgetting the spirit of the Law. Not that they were lawless like Babylon, pagan like Babylon, and immoral like Babylon.

Paul claimed to be a proud, strict, devoted Pharisee, who held the Law dear (Phil. 3: 4-6). That is why Paul could say "... do not enter into quarrels about the Law ... "(Titus 3: 9). He knew that the spiritual leadership of the nation was completely reliable regarding the laws they had received and faithfully passed onward! No one knew better than the Rabbis as to what is permissible versus what is forbidden, what is pure or impure, who is obligated or exempt! Just the opposite. He was concerned that the early fellowships should fall to a host of pagan nonsense and fables! There were numerous myths circulating in the Near East at that time. Thus Paul's entreat of Timothy to avoid them (1 Timothy 1:3- 4).

The criticism of the NT is addressed to the Sadducees, a liberal Jewish sect, who were condemned for not knowing G-d's Word or Power (Matt. 22: 29). They collaborated with Rome; their kangaroo court rubber-stamped the Nazarene's sentence. The NT and history rejected the Sadducees' heresy as not being authentic Judaism.

Please, let's not forget Mathew 23 where the NT boldly and clearly claims that "the Scribes and the Pharisees sit in the seat of Moses"; meaning that there is continuity; that the Judaism of that time is the authentic Judaism of ancient generations of old.

Abraham came from Uhr of the Chaldees, a favorite city of his contemporary, Hammurabi. Abraham, Isaac and Jacob all lived in Canaan when it was under Babylonian sway (J. H. Hertz). Also, there was an Egyptian influence! But our patriarchs and matriarchs created a world of love and light in any place they lived, any corner they inhabited.

Now it was the Babylon creature that is depicted as evil NOT the Hebrew refugees - Gen. 10:8; Psalm 137: 1 , 8 ; Is. 47:6; Ezekiel 19: 9; 23:11-35 ; 24:11–12 ; Jer. 21:2 ; 25: 8; 27:1; 28:1; Jer. 51:7.

In the NT, Babylon takes on a giant role and personification of everything bad, criminal and fattening (1 Peter1:1; 5:13; Rev, 17; 19:6 -9; 21: 3-27 etc.).

Evidence of a formal religious system - Many of the House of 10-Israel still view Judaism as a formally organized religious system similar to Catholicism, from which they have disassociated themselves, sometimes at great social and familial cost. The traditional anti-Jewish culture in which these souls were raised regard Judaism as made up of man-made laws not found in the Written Torah. This sentiment is progressively changing with the growing awareness of 10-Israel's re-awakening and their subsequent increased exposure to true Jewish Torah culture and teaching.

Rabbinic Oral Torah - Some of 10-Israel have come to accept the 613 "Mosaic laws" but view the Oral Law, Mishnah, Talmud and Rabbinic rulings as 'man-made' and not binding upon them. They regard it rather as suggestions for divine service. They do consistently check-in and check-out what the Rabbis say and do in order to attempt some level of observance. As legal Noahides they are not obligated to numerous Rabbinic directives, and this is being understood more every day

Thus, the distinction in the NT was made between devout Jews, who are circumcised and debtors to all of the Laws and those uncircumcised, like foreign branches grafted on (Gentiles), who were exempt from all Jewish laws. What you essentially had before the Greco-Roman additions of hate and paganism, was pro-Torah, pro-Jewish, pro-reunification of the Tribes. It was in harmony with the Noahide system. A growing number of 10-Tribers are becoming increasingly open to Jewish teaching, Oral Torah and Rabbinic Halacha.

Judah views the Oral Law, Mishnah, Talmud, and Rabbinic rulings as vitally needed in order to rightly interpret the Written Torah. Judah is well aware that Christians and Messianics use the New

Testament to rebuke and reject Torah and Rabbinic authority. The NT has historically been misused to promote hatred of the Jewish people. Rabbi Yaakov Emden, more than 450 years ago, explained that Saul (Paul of the NT)) had as his mission, to differentiate the many Gentiles drawn to erroneous Jewish Messianic sects. As legal Noahides they are not obligated to numerous Rabbinic directives, and this is being understood more every day by both Houses.

Fear of a soulless, carnal and formal religion - Some of 10-Israel have little understanding of Rabbinic laws and are afraid of losing their new found spiritual joy of Torah, through Judah forcing them to keep a multitude of Rabbinic laws. Most of them, however, are not aware that Judah is not, nor ever was in the business of telling others what to do. No record in history has Torah Judah proclaiming, as Christianity has done: "Kiss the Mezuzah or kiss the sword".

Judah has historically been happy if their Gentile neighbours would only keep one of the seven universal Noahide commandments, viz "Thou shall not murder." These days, Judah is still getting used to increasing numbers of non-Jewish people wanting to embrace Torah Commandments. Indeed, Judah should make authentic Jewish Torah teaching more acceptable to re-identifying Ten Tribers.

Judah observes Rabbinic laws, but always distinguishes and draws a big distinction between Biblical laws and Rabbinic protective decrees. Those Gentiles who say otherwise are just uninformed, or, simply seething with replacement theology, envy, competition and baseless hatred.

Sincere urge to not deviate from 'The Written Word of G-d' - 10-Israel views giving up pagan customs of non-Hebrew origin as 'coming out of' Christianity and their adherence to

Torah as that which identifies them as 'spiritual Israelites'. However, there is a great element which regards "Torah observance" as having to be according to their own interpretation of the Written Torah. This element among 10-Israel therefore rejects the Rabbinic Oral Torah interpretation and replaces it with their own oral interpretation. It is for this reason that the twisted Karaite anti-Torah teachings find fertile grounds today amongst the re-awakening Return-to-Torah Gentile masses. (Refer chapter 18 for a comprehensive review of this movement).

Judah does not appreciate this anti-Rabbinic spirit – which in fact is simply the eternalising of the anti-Judah rebellion of the ancient Northern Ten Tribes of Israel which led to their rejection by G-d and their exile among the nations.

Judah needs to seriously reconsider and address the popular conclusion that persists among some of Jewry, that "once a Christian, always a Christian." It is encouraging to note that with the restoration of Torah principles by these 'returnees to Torah', this conclusion is changing.

Who is a true Israelite? - 10-Israel regard themselves as 'Israel' and not as ordinary Gentiles. They want to be recognized as such. 10-Israel understands that everyone has the legal status of descendants of Noah, but they regard themselves having a special status because they are not 'just another Gentile'.

Judah tells 10-Israel that only Jews are 'Israel', and that 10-Israel are only Gentiles who may or may not be of Hebrew origin. However, they are welcomed either as converts or as righteous returning sons and daughters of Noah, seeking greater identification with Torah. The concept of 'Hebrew Roots Restoration' is understood by Judah as a terrific motivating factor in pushing and pulling them onwards and upwards in service of HaShem. If things go well, then this perhaps is the Reconciliation spoken about in our Oral and Written Torah.

The concept of 'Easy Conversion' – Advanced re-identifying Ten Tribers are demotivated by the very strict Jewish Conversion requirements which they find hard, if not impossible, to comply with. They would prefer an easier, more lenient and receptive attitude from Judah.

Traditionally, Judaism for self-protection of their long treasured religious culture, had to apply restrictive conversion measures to ensure that only honest candidates would be added to the fold. Intermarriage with non-Jews has always been a serious eroding factor of the Jewish national and religious culture of the 'People of G-d".

Today in Israel, non-Jews who have Jewish relatives, even though they are 100% non-Jewish, are given a fast track on conversion and often special consideration regarding visas. Judah objects to such non-Torah fast tracking if it is not comprehensive and Halachic.

The Noahide concept of limited Torah responsibility - Many re-identifying10-Israelites think that they should keep the complete Torah. Judah's response in requiring them to do "only the Seven Noahide Laws" keeps them at arm's length, which does not promote reconciliation.

Some of Judah feel that Gentiles, in general, should not, or does not have to keep the Torah that was specifically commanded to the identifiable Hebrew nation. This is overcome if Judah is assured that this is a learning process leading to Noahide affiliation (when being of 10-Israel is then fine and dandy), or perhaps a process leading to conversion. In both cases, such a general outline assures Judah that it is not just some new religion or replacement fad. What is crucial in this general, open, wide and deep outline, is that Judah is reassured that they are dealing with good, sane folk who are anti-missionary and have Judah's best interests at heart.

Demographics - Scary Jewish population numbers at play in the Reconciliation - 10-Israel feels that their numbers will help Judah defend and hold the Land and that an enhanced Return of 10-Tribers will speed up the Messianic age. The Torah calls Judah the bow and Ephraim the arrow - like the song, "love and marriage goes together like a horse and carriage".

Figures speak for themselves. In Israel today there rages the 'Demographical Problem'. Leftist government policy makers use the very real specter of low Jewish population figures to back their suggestions for 'Peace' through withdrawing into smaller 'Jewish' strongholds in a much smaller land mass. 10-Israel promotors point out that Jewish population figures across the world simply do not allow for, and ridicules the Bible's stipulation of a far Greater Israel – hence the need for the Return of hundreds of millions of re-identifying (through renewed Torah observance) Ten Tribers from across the world. (Refer to the Map on the cover of this book and the front page Charts of the World Map. In chapter 20 we give a full review of Israel's Demographical problems).

Judah should recall that the Oral Torah records in the Midrash Rabbah that Rabbi Pinchas said in the name of Rabbi Shamuel ben Nahman: "We have a strong tradition that the evil Esav will fall only into the hands of Rachel's boy." (this refers to Joseph and

Benjamin – the consolidated Ten Tribes – to whom the credit of a final victory over Esav will be credited).

Judah feels overwhelmed with and threatened by the potential numbers of 10-Israel in the world, and because of their relative assimilated values, their lifestyle which seems so externally different from authentic Judaism and generally, their belief in a Messiah whom they want to enforce upon Jews who traditionaly have been strongly rejecting it. However, practically speaking, there are only very few of them here in Israel, with very little backing and means. Very important is their willingness to embrace all of Torah (orthodox) Judaism as quickly as they are made aware of it – and that they recognize a Torah obligation. Judah is reluctant to see the necessity for, or to admit to the demographic need for Judah to have multi millions of 10-Tribers added to their numbers in the Land. (Refer to ch. 20 for a full review of the Dmographics of Israel and the resulting implications for the Restoration of Israel).

Restrictive Viza control -10-Israel's return to the Land is hampered by the visa regulations of the State of Israel. The official practice has allowed Gentiles to enter the Land with permanent visa status to play sports. How much more should people receive lenient visa considerations, if they respect and honor Halacha and come to contribute and die, if necessary, for the State of Israel?

Judah should be exposed to and reminded of 'The Greater Israel' concept and what our Sages and Bible Prophecy have to say about this. If viza requirements can be alleviated for economic, domestic, sports and other commercial reasons, then why not for advancing the prime reason of Israel's existence: namely, to establish the Kingdom of the G-d of Israel and to be a Light to the World for His Torah?

Who killed the Nazarene? - At the higher evolutionary end, most of 10-Israel no longer believe that "It is Judah who killed their Messiah," This is found predominantly among those of 10-Israel who believe in a specific 'Ben Yosef Messiah' who came 'to reconnect them to their lost Hebrew roots.' Through the study of Torah, they are steadily being cleansed of this ancient resentment of their brother Judah. However, at the lower end of this spiritual evolutionary cycle, this resentment persists ... which gives the rest of 10-Israel a bad name among Jews.

Judah feels that it is customary for Christians and Messianics to harbour resentment against Jews for "having persecuted and killed the Christian Messiah." In today's world and amongst rejuvenated Hebraic Roots Restoration adherents, these are completely false charges (as clarified elsewhere in this writing). Judah does not recognize that there is a Messiah of 10-Israel who has specifically come. According to Judaism, he will be a mere human being, not Divine, as Christianity claims. He will make an international impact ... facts and action will be the hallmark of the day, not merely personal beliefs. Elijah the Prophet will likewise make a huge commotion "bringing back the hearts of the parents to the children ..." (2 Kings 1:8, 2:11; 1 Kings 17:1, 18:1-8, 17:2-16; 1 Kings 18:19 - 40, 19:10; Malachi 3:23-24, Psalms 29:6). Fundamentally however, Judah does agree that Christianity, in all its forms and in the big picture, has done its part of helping the world move forward.

Misunderstanding on both sides create great animosity - A great misunderstanding resulting from fermented anti-Judah Church teachings, is that Jews are unspiritual and unrepentant.

10-Israel should acquaint themselves with the true, deeply spiritual repentant spirit that Judaism in its teachings and spiritual guidance

constantly inspires. The reality of the Biblically ordained requirement and possibility of repentance is deeply ingrained in all of Judah.
As Rabbi Dr. Aryeh Kaplan z'zal (may the memory of the righteous
be a blessing) writes, "G-d created the universe for the ultimate good
(.., and He saw that it was good ... Genesis)." Rav Kaplan z'zal
clearly shows in his user-friendly 'Handbook of Jewish thought,'
(Moznaim Publishing Corporation) that: "Evil and sin only exist
in order to allow man to have free will, and therefore are neither
part of G-d's primary Purpose, nor do they have permanence." (See
Vol.1,3;5,x 3;26; 'Inner Space', pp. 71, note 51, 171.). The Rav goes
on to sum up all of our thinking, "All things that detract from man's
ultimate good are thus eradicable." Yes, we agree that G-d may have
permitted the existence of evil, but it is only a stain on the fabric of
creation, "and as such it is readily eradicated by repentance."

Yes, "sin couches at the doorway" (Genesis 4:7), but we have a
mezuzah there, and the Torah cries out: "but you shall rule over
it" (the very same verse in Genesis that raises a warning, also states
that victory can be yours!). The Torah is the antidote to the evil
inclination, the remedy and ultimate cure when rendered properly
to the image of the Divine, the good inclination, the rational soul
and the divine soul (spirit) which we all have within us! (According
to numerous sources in Oral Torah).

Thus Judah does not generally feel that it needs to pester others, for
they have their own dignified walk and growth process with G-d!

Judah is also so steeped in daily basic levels of survival, issues of life
and death, that there is simply no time, energy, funds or power left
to give to this involvement.

Historically, and even today, any outreach effort on the part of Judah
results in hostile reaction from anti-Jewish Christian communities.

As if it is Judah's fault that these good thinking folk will be leaving the Church and joining Judah – as if we have kidnapped them. In this way Judah becomes the convenient scapegoat for their own deficiencies. These reactions take many forms: from a gentleman's agreement to boycott us, to ugly violence in many manifestations.

Opposing views and solutions on either side need to find common understanding, communal acceptance and then solved - There are various schools of thought among 10-Israel concerning the role of Judah in G-d's Purpose.

Many of 10-Israel believe that Messiah will come for the Jews only in, what to 10-Israel will be, a Second Coming scenario. They believe that the Jews were blinded to his first Coming. In the latest and more advanced interpretation amongst re-awakening Ten Tribers, it is believed that their disputed Messiah, the Nazarene, had the Divine Mission to bring 10-Israel back into Covenant relationship with Judah; and that it is all in G-d's hands alone – not to be challenged by proselytizing Jews to "make them see something that was not meant for them anyway."

For Jews, according to the teachings of Judaism, it will be the first Coming, when an Orthodox Jewish person will properly fulfil the scores of prophecies associated with the Messiah of David according the their Torah leadership, this all in the spirit of Chazal, the wise Sages of blessed memory.

The growing awareness among 10-Tribers of the detrimental spiritual effects of Christian missionizing of Jews, has established the conclusion that Judah was divinely blinded from seeing the Messiah of 10-Israel. This, they understand, and experience has taught them (by observing the detrimental results of Jewish proselytizing when 'converted' Jews turn against Torah to accept general Christian Grace theology), was divinely intended for the spiritual protection of Jews. Their 'blindness' to the Reconciliation intended for 10-Israel, was caused in order for them to not fall into the false religions of Catholicism and Christianity and thus to preserve the Torah. According to this field-winning 10-Israel conclusion, Judah's realization of this fact will do much to remove their fear of proselytizing and to prepare them for greater acceptance of returning 10-Israel – and thus reconciliation and Peace in the Household of G-d.

This school of thought among advanced thinking 10-Israel, wants Judah to realize that they hold to belief in their Messiah as a path back to Torah. This is not relevant to Judah's Yiddishkeit.

Messianic 10-Tribers therefore cannot be expected, neither are they willing to ever deny "the One who has purchased them". They want Judah to understand and make allowance for this – for that is what brought them back to Torah; this is what brought them back from anti-Semitic hatred instilled by the Church (from which they have, or are busy, extricating themselves), to love Judah, the Land, Torah and its One only G-d. Some of 10-Israel postulate that without this realization and allowance by Judah, the Reconciliation and Redemption Process could be unnecessarily slowed down. Many of 10-Israel believe that the NT, the Nazarene and the Gospels was an aspect (*'bechinat'*) of 'Messiah ben Yosef'. This is in harmony with Jewish thought which looks at all Movements that moved the world forward in appreciating the Torah, are aspects of the concept of Messiah ben Yosef.

The leading edge amongst 10-Tribers do not want Judah to underwrite this tenet of their faith, but merely to understand "where they come from" – together, we have to trust G-d to do the final restitution.

Amongst the folk of Judah, there is the conviction that 10-Israel was still lost in paganism and needed a bridge back. Thus they see what Christianity ultimately became, with all its pitfalls and horrors committed in its name, as being used by HaShem as a kind of Messiah ben Yosef.

The bottom line is that all thinking and searching NT believers will ultimately find themselves standing with Judah. 10- Israel will find itself learning from Judah how to better serve HaShem and humanity! With this growth in Torah comes a willingness to reunite with their long lost relatives and to tread once again the ancient paths followed by their righteous ancestors! Seeing sincere non-Jews turn to exemplary Torah observers, will warm the heart of Judah and make them more receptive to receive their rebellious brother Israel back Home.

These advanced and mature spear point of returning 10-Israel sees the NT dispensation as being the fulfilment of the ancient Jewish dream, quest or hope for the Ingathering of 10-Israel. It was never meant to be a club to beat Judah, nor a mandate to convert Judah - nor a basis to make up and attach pagan Greco-Roman ideas on the Tanakh. Much rather, it was an attempt to give over the Torah Message of Noahide directives, to reach out to lost Israel and to offer them a bridge back home.

The mysteries of the Kingdom (Luke 8) meant something that the Romans feared. The Gospels were trying to hide the main Message, that of restoring the Kingdom of Israel. Such a thought would be treason in Roman eyes and punishable by death.

"Seek you first the Kingdom of G-d" (Matthew 6:33). Such a Kingdom is a challenge to Roman rule. Shortly before these words it is written "...Your Kingdom come, Your will be done on earth as it is in heaven" (Matthew 6:9). Now every Jew knows that Chazal teaches of a heavenly Jerusalem and Temple, just waiting to become a reality on earth. This would equal a colossal fall for the Roman Empire. Likewise, testifying of the Kingdom and preaching the Kingdom (Acts 28) - all have everything to do with fighting pagan Rome, and nothing to do with harassing Judah! All the talk about "open the door unto the Gentiles" (Acts 14:27), is relevant because 10-Israel was and still are officially Gentiles.

Judah is aware that the NT has been put into thousands of languages, thereby alerting billions of people to the existence of a Hebrew Bible, One G-d and an eventual Messiah to bring general and particular Redemption of Israel, a rebuilt Temple and world peace. This does not discount those aspects of Christianity which is still mired in various aspects of pagan confusion. However, this is not relevant to those of 10-Israel who are in a progressive state of rejecting these ideologies.

Judah is reluctant to be entangled in any complex dealings which have to do with people's personal growth out of religious systems which are alien to Judaism.

Judah has several reservations concerning the nitty-gritty of details of other searching people, even if they may be distantly related. This creates the impression among rapprochement-seeking 10-Tribers that Judah rejects them. To correct this misunderstanding of Judah's true motives, it is important that 10-Tribers realize that Judaism, first and foremost, believes that all people are intrinsically close to their Creator. As the great master teacher Sarah Schneider says ..."The human being is a microcosm, a miniature model of

Divinity." *The Talmud elaborates that the soul's presence in the human body parallels Divinity's presence throughout creation,*

She continues: "From my own flesh I perceive Divinity." (Job 19:2). In probing the mysterious depths of the human soul, one also discovers deep truths about the manifest nature of Divinity.

In other words, Judaism believes that humanity, and of course our own, lost distant Hebrew relatives, (10-Israel) are absolutely, automatically and extremely close to G-d by virtue of having been created in His image (Gen. 1:27). The Talmud teaches that the good of all people have a share in the world to come

Our mystical sources ask: "What do the good Gentiles have in the world to come?" These sources answer in symbolic language, that they will have a throne of gold. We now ask: "So what do they, the good of Israel, have? Why, they will have a throne of tears, until there will be universal recognition of the One HaShem and the brotherhood of humankind when it will be turned into a Throne of precious stones."

Judah is adamant that G-d is near to all who call upon Him; to all who call upon Him sincerely (Psalm 145). All Jews take seriously such verses as, "For You, HaShem, are good and forgiving, and abundantly kind to all who call upon You" (Psalm 86:5).

No Jewish person grows up without Noah and Jonah. In both cases the all-powerful Designer of the cosmos wants all people to return – and they would be accepted.

All Jews know that the Temple greatly benefited all of humanity, according to our narrative - for sacrifices were offered "on behalf of all the nations", and it was a "House of prayer for all peoples."

Elucidation

It should be expected that numerous hurdles will be put in the way of reconciliation and unity. It is only a test, a challenge, an illusion which is put before us to see what we are really made of. It is to separate the sincere and refined from the chaff; to demonstrate to the world and to the 'accuser', that we have the true inner qualities of faith and fortitude to return. Just as Joseph merely tested his brothers and G-d merely tested Avraham to show that he indeed had such depths of faith. The Talmud tells us that this testing process also purifies and brings atonement and merits to all of us.

It is the sincere purpose of this book to attempt to lay foundations for Reconciliation through better understanding of the Divine Purpose and, above all, our respective and individual spiritual obligations on both sides of the divide. Many of the obstacles in the way of the destined Reconciliation, and hence the resultant Redemption, may seem impossible to overcome. It would be presumptuous to suggest that the contents and message of this book could remove all the obstacles. But it is our conviction that a better understanding of the Halachic foundations of the New Testament could go a long way to plant and nurture the initial seeds to free people from Roman pagan ideas, to neutralize all missionary attacks, and to rescue the many Jews, who have become lost through assimilation with other nations, for an eventual Reconciliation. We shall concentrate mainly on the hidden Halachic and Oral Torah foundations of the New Testament Scriptures as they exist today.

These foundations are vitally affected by whether or not the general interpretation of the Gospels by these Returnees, is pro-Torah or anti-Torah, and specifically how they view the Oral Torah and acceptance of Judah as the Lawgiver.

CHAPTER 20

The Troubling Demographics of Israel

Hidden and forgotten Bible Solution holds the answer to the critical population imbalance in the contested land ownership in Israel

The subject of the "Ten Lost Tribes of Israel" has been filed away for so long, that we may have great trouble to uncover it from where it has been left untouched, discarded, under dust in the dark corners of the store rooms of our Jewish Temple library which contains the wealth of the world's religious literature.

Like the Scrolls of Qumran, it may require great care in restoring the dried-up pages of this Scroll to reconsider its Message which, after all, underlies one of the Main Themes of Torah, and indeed, of Tanach – if not the Main Theme itself.

As in the time of king Yoshi'Yahu, when the Book of the Covenant was rediscovered in the Temple, HaShem has His destined Time to restore and to uplift before His People, His Healing. It is the considered suggestion of this publication, that the opening of the Scrolls on this long neglected topic, contains the healing ingredients to prepare us more fully for the prophetically promised establishment of the 12-Tribed United Kingdom of Israel. If there ever was a Time when the nation of Israel required Divine Healing, it is now. The current international controversy over ownership of the Promised Land, threatens to tear the nation of Israel down the middle, like the father shredding his mantle at the sight of Cain slaying his brother Abel. While facing a nuclear armed 'Hitler' in Iran, Israel now stands alone - alone with the G-d of Israel, Supreme Creator of the limitless universe!

The long time onslaught by the ruling liberal leftist, anti-Torah and mostly anti-G-d controllers of Israeli government powers, has come into the open now with astonishing audacity. Their target is the small religious minority in the nation of Yisrael, who believe in, act on, and look forward with great expectancy to the Coming of the ruling Mashiach Ben David. To this ruling sector of the House of Judah, the prospect of the Rule of Mashiach presents a grave threat to their lucrative authority. They despise the image of the pious Jew, which to them represents a Message they prefer to for ever blot out in the minds of their subjects. It is the presence of this small and persistent group which has always prevented the ruling sector of Am Yisrael from fulfilling its craving of becoming intrinsically part of the world community of nations. These faithful have achieved this by persistently clinging to their Divine Mandate of being the 'Chosen' of the Creator G-d of Yisrael.

The enormous Event of the Restoration of the re-united, full 12-tribed House of David, has been proclaimed by ancient Bible Prophets and confirmed in the writings of ancient Jewish Sages, to happen in "the End Time", when the Lost Ten Tribes will be re-identified and re-united with the House of Judah into one Nation. It is referred to in the Bible as the *"Restoration of the Fallen Tabernacle of David."*

The Jewish Land of Israel is today standing at a dangerous crossroad. We have arrived at the moment where the fulfillment of the Divine Requirement of settling the Land which G-d had promised to the descendants of Avraham by Divine Oath, threatens to present the flint that will spark the international nuclear, bio-chemical holocaust of Gog and Magog (a.k.a 'Armageddon'). To make things worse for the small but persistent obstacle group, it is they, generally, who are the controversial 'settlers' of these disputed territories in the eyes of the jeering nations who despise Jews. It is they who take the Promises of HaShem regarding possession of the Covenant Land serious - serious enough to face all the risks of acquiring property in the so-called 'occupied settlement areas'. This small core is labelled by the secular rulers of Israel as presenting a "danger to the future peace of the Land." The world sees them as being the core danger to the future of the world, for representing, and causing the Middle East Crisis, which is regarded in upper political circles as the "gravest danger to international peace in the world."

The settlers number only some 400 000 in total, in all settlement areas, i.e. less than 6% of the total population. The total body of practicing, observant Jews in Israel today, which prevents the disintegration and assimilation of Am Yisrael, is possibly only double that figure. It is against this small sector that the ruling Israel government, representing the wishes of the masses (and indeed of the world), has now come down upon with crushing dictatorial powers in the name of 'democracy' – the will of the majority. Am Yisrael, to a greater extent than ever before in history, has now come to stand before the critical reality:

- to embrace the Promises of and the Protection of HaShem, insisting on taking possession of the Land irrespective of the wills and wants of the entire world outside of Israel and the pressures they present, or

- becoming a nation like any other, assimilating beyond any negative, disadvantageous trace of "The People of the Book."

The topic of the 'Demographics of Israel' is a vibrant and controversial issue in the Middle East Crisis. In presenting this 'Solution' to the demographics of Israel, the authors do not make any claims of 'new' light, or privileged insight into the Mysteries of Torah, which have been so insightfully been expounded on through the ages by our Jewish Sages. Our share is merely to have been observant of astounding changes in the ranks of the persecuting spirit of international anti-Semitism amongst the nations, where Judah and the Ten Tribes had been exiled. We do not believe that we are deluded in recognizing the engulfing good intent amongst a certain sector of the nations towards beleaguered Judah. We are equally aware of the continuing and even increasing anti-Semitism amongst the nations – and now, to much the same extent and intent, even from amongst the ranks of Judah itself.

Jewish continuity and demographic growth, even in its broadest sense and including the secular majority, is on a slippery slide of diminishing identifiable numbers. It has been so for a decade and more – and it is increasing in volatility. This subject has been the topic of many forums and conferences and most readers of will no doubt be well acquainted with the problem, its implications and suggested solutions. It is the intent of this publication to add what would be to many readers, a totally new (yet as old as the Torah itself) perspective. This may well hold the healing strokes of HaShem and much of the invigorating spiritual opium that will bring the high of the Final Redemption.

Even a superficial approach of this presentation should call for some enquiring interest from the observant reader. With the Scrolls of this subject filed away under dust, it has become a general tenet of interpretation that 'Am Yisrael' refers to the Jews only. For anyone holding this opinion, it should come as a first revelationary insight that Torah, when referring to 'Yisrael', always refers to all 12 Tribes of Israel and not to Judah alone. Yet, the common cliche amongst Jews who should know better is that "*Judah* came out of Egypt in the Exodus. The *Jews* stood at Sinai," etc. The entire Tanach presents a much broader spectrum of twelve Tribes of Israel (of which Judah was but one) that left Egypt, stood at Sinai, wandered the wilderness and eventually entered the Land. After the historic split of the 12-Tribed Kingdom of Israel in the 7th century BCE., the Tanach specifically and often uses a much overlooked termination, by defining "Judah <u>and</u> Israel", hence the Northern ten exiled Tribes of Israel ('Lost 10 Tribes') <u>and</u> Judah.

It is the Divine Promises regarding the sure future Restoration of these lost Ten Tribes that hold the key to Israel's otherwise insolvable demographics problem. Let the astute reader who immediately senses in this statement an underlying intention to establish here a suggested diminishing of the role of Judah, be assured that quite the opposite is true. It is an underlying precept of this publication, that Judah and the Rabbinical authorities fulfil an unchangeable Divine Mandate of authority over the divine Scriptures according to Bereishit 49:10, "The Sceptre shall not depart from Judah until Shiloh comes." Judah has its role to play - but so has 10-Israel. In fact, Redemption without the presence of the 10 Tribes is NOT possible. This is a fact to which the presence of the emblems of all 12 Tribes in every synagogue bears testimony.

This publication strives to present and identify what seems to be the current fulfillment of the re-identification and restoration of the Lost Ten Tribes in process all over the world. Even a casual observation (but for the dire reality thereof which is so unacceptable to Judah) should confirm it as the Divinely ordained solution in the face of the grave reality of international assimilation and the threatening imbalance of demographic ratios of the Jewish nation in the Land of Israel.

The latter problem has been the topic of the Jewish People Policy Planning Institute (JPPPI) in their annual assessment in which they outline the status of Jewish communities world-wide, describing trends that should be a source of concern; and proposing remedies for problem areas. We shall extract certain highlights from this Report and attempt to correlate certain staggering developments in the world amongst non-Jewish believers in the G-d of Israel, as a probable solution to Israel's survival Crisis – a Prophetic Solution which has been greatly overlooked by the religious leaders of the small and now persecuted core of Kidushim in Israel. In selecting these extracts, we wish to apply the recommendations thereof to our topic of the re-identification of the Lost Ten Tribes, now seemingly in process in the world and fast gaining momentum, and as such possibly being part of the Divinely ordained solution.

If this were at all true, then it would be vital that Jewish leadership of Judah now seriously and urgently consider, accept, cooperate and further this Cause.

Extracts from:

Jewish People Policy Planning Institute Annual Assessment

EXECUTIVE REPORT - 2005

FACING A RAPIDLY CHANGING WORLD

http://www.jpppi.org.il/main_projects/project. asp?fid=390&ord=1

"Essentially, the Jewish People continue a steady skidding down on a slippery slope. There is an acute need for radical and innovative counter measures, and the present absence of such measures is a significant negative finding of this assessment. Outreach efforts and the approach to broader demographic issues in the Diaspora continue to be fragmented and seem unable to reach a critical mass that could make a real difference." *(pg 6)*

"In an overview of the Internal scene in Israel in 2005, the reports comments:

"Nothing of major significance took place concerning trends of Jewish demographics and assimilation. In the absence of radical and innovative counter-measures, the continuing slippery slope reinforced previous worrying trends. Outreach efforts and the approach to broader demographic issues in the Diaspora continued to be fragmented and seemed insufficient for a critical mass." *(pg 10)*

Its 2013 Report concludes this update: "JPPI's 2012-13 Annual Assessment of the Situation and Dynamics of the Jewish People shows a deepening of the dilemmas and challenges confronting the State of Israel and the Jewish people globally we described last year."

In its Foreword, of the 2005 Report the following Vision is stated:

"Whether on demography, or affecting generational change in Jewish leadership, or investing in Jewish education, or better integrating the Jewish People as a whole, **it is clear that a hard-headed look at priorities is essential** … However, the measure of the assessment is not the discussion **but the actions that result from them**" *(emphasis ours).*

"A rapidly changing world requires the Jewish People to develop a combination of preserving continuity and creative adjustments to external and internal changes together with efforts to influence them." *(pg 5). (End of quote).*

To counter the negative factor of population loss through war & terrorism, the world today suggests better relations with Muslims, co-operation with the PLO, adjusting to USA democratization policies, handing over Biblical territory to the enemy by unilateral disengagement, etc. This is normally one-sided as Islam fundamentally rejects Judaism and the core Palestinian vision is the driving out of Jews from all the currently inhabited areas of Israel. Sharing the land with the enemy is also anti-Torah. The publishers believe that a serious consideration of, and a consorted outreach to the call of awakening 10-Israel, based on the Prophetic principles defined by the topic of the Ten Tribes of Israel, could ensure the invincibility of Israel

– and speaking of Israel here in the broader term as ordained in Torah Prophecy, the twelve Tribes as a whole.

The 'Disengagement' from Gush Katif under autocratic and draconic strong-armed, fascist-like enforcement by the Israeli government, has brought the contempt that the ruling authorities have for the Tzaddikim (righteous) and the Dati'im (religious) to a fore. The conditions not only in Gush Katif, but pertaining to all settlements, highlight the glaring shortcoming in the entire settlement project – namely, a shortage of numbers – people, souls. While volumes may be written in regard to the pro's and the con's, the why's and wherefore's, one salient issue is mostly overlooked by the Jewish Settlers and their leadership – **the lack of sufficient numbers of residents**, not only to make it a more viable economic issue, but in order to make it impossible for any ruling authority to displace and disenfranchise by brutal force, the property holders in these Divinely ordained territories of the Promised Land. There should be no doubts, that had the population of Gush Katif numbered a million or more (as the neighbouring area Palestinians claim they do), and not a puny 9000, then there would not have been a 'unilateral disengagement'- read 'forced deportation' or ethnic cleansing - of Jews from their Divine Inheritance.

In the aftermath of the eviction of the entire Jewish population from Gush Katif, commentators speculated that the Zionist Dream of a 'Greater Israel' (by Biblical delineation) could now also become abandoned. It appears that the total abandoning of Gaza had been a long time government consideration. Yitzchak Shamir in the early 1990's already, lost the elections against Labour because, against the advice of his advisers, he refused to abandon Gaza.

The successful settlement of the Greater Israel requires **settlers** – huge numbers of them. It has taken 57 years to raise up some 230 000 settlers only, in the West Bank and Golan. Many settlements have a few thousand and less inhabitants. In the West Bank, only 17% of the population are Jews – the rest are Palestinians. Measured against the entire Israeli Jewish population (which forms 80% of entire Israel population - 20% are Arab and Christian), the 230000 settlers represent 4% only. Less than half of the world's Jews live in Israel.

Now bring into the solution formula the fact of overall decreasing numbers, world wide, in the Jewish population; a drying up source of Aliyah (a mere 2100 in 2004, 16557 in 2012); the lack of direction and convicted leadership in any proposed solution as overviewed in the JPPPI Assessment; the fact that 96% of Israelis do not want to risk living in a settlement; the disinterest of world Jewry in the problems of Israel – and the issue becomes stalemate.

Another re-awakening factor which is becoming evident after Gush Katif, is that the 'closed house', highly selective strategy which many settlements followed, are to blame for their poor and almost stagnant growth rate over the 20 – 40 years of their existence.

This assessment reflects only negatives for the future of Am Yisrael and the physical Land.

Any future planners for Israel should be enlightened to the Prophetic provision of millions of true lovers of Zion and Torah in the reborn shape of restored 10-Israel. The struggling demographics of Israel should thrive on the abundance of prospective Settlers to turn the Greater Yisrael into its destined

Home and Kingdom for Greater 12-Israel. The onus rests on our Jewish cultural and religious leaders to guide and educate Am Yisrael and its authorities in this direction.

Another conclusion that the JPPPI Assessment presents, is the proven fact that minorities do not affect demographics. It concludes in response, that "therefore the primary relevant avenue for affecting population trends pertains to the domain of culture and identification." Thus, by steering the cultural and identification influences of the nation, the preservation and growth of the nation may be affected. Again, the current direction of the ruling authority in Israel is away from its Torah foundation, its Promises and its final Divine Redemption.

The acceptance of and the furthering of the 10-Israel Awakening (which is fast becoming a glaring reality in the world), could increase the physical numbers and the proportion of those who truly identify with the culture, the identity and the ultimate Plan and Purpose of HaShem for Judah and the wider Twelve-tribed Israel.

The question that remains, and which has to be addressed is this:

- Is the Lost House of 10-Israel identifiable in this day and age?

- If so, where are they and who are they?

- How will they ever integrate with the House of Judah to make up **one** re-united nation of Israel as per the Prophecy of Yechzekel (Ezekiel) 37:15 -23 "Take a stick and write on it: 'Judah and those Israelites loyal to him.

Take another stick and write on it: 'Yoseph, the wood of Ephraim and all the House of Israel loyal to him. Join one to the other to make a single piece of wood ... I shall make **one** stick out of the two and I shall hold them a one ... I am going to take the sons of Yisrael (12 Tribes?) from the nations where they have gone. I shall gather them together from everywhere and bring them Home to their own soil. I shall make them into **one** nation in My Own Land on the mountains of Yisrael and One King is to be King of them all. They will no longer form two nations nor be two separate Kingdoms."

Yeshiyahu (Isaiah) 11:12 "He will assemble the outcasts of Israel; He will bring back the scattered people of Judah from the four corners of the earth (note the distinction between Judah and Israel) ... Ephraim will no longer be jealous of Judah, nor Judah any longer the enemy of Ephraim." Note that 'Ephraim' is the collective term often used in Tanach to refer to the entire body of the Ten Tribes

With increased numbers of settlers in the settlements areas – millions of them - any withdrawal demands made on Israel will be superfluous and impossible, even for a dictatorial government, yes, even for the world's overpowering whims and wishes.

As religiously ethical as the strategies of many settlements areas may have been, namely to reserve domicile for 'the religious' only, it spelled the ultimate doom for these places. In much of the remaining territories of Judah and Shomron, today small limited numbers of almost stagnant population growth societies are desperately attempting to survive the mass onslaught by the Palestinians, backed not only by the world, but also given almost unconditional and certainly unearned advantage by Israel's government itself.

Unless the numbers of the Israeli minority, now under siege by their own Jewish government, increase explosively, they will no doubt face the same fate as Yamit in 1981, and Gush Katif in 2005. As the JPPPI Assessment and multiple other reports so convincingly conclude beyond any argument, "Jewish demographics are on the slide". Even if most of the Diaspora Jews immigrate to Israel, it is doubtful whether the volumes of population in the territories will grow substantially, especially in the aftermath of Sharon's onslaught on these brave citizens and the constant threat of 'returning Shomron to the Palestinians' (as if they ever owned it before), which makes contemplation of acquiring property in the territories an investment risk just not worth considering for even the bravest Kidushim.

How can one truly and convincingly object to the finger pointing of a hostile world which rejects the right of the extreme minority Jewish settler groups which desperately try to hang on to their sublime rights in a contested domain? What growth prospect do these settlements have in the face of a non-willing and declining number of prospective Jewish settlers?

In short: Where are the millions of Jews required to settle and develop these vast stretches of contested territory?

Can it be that G-d in His Wisdom retained millions of Israelites, unidentified under the cloak of ancient exile, for His ultimate trump card of Redemption? Informed sources and statistics refer to a group and a calibre of person out there in the world, lovers of Zion, who are prepared to and who are in fact craving for settling these Divinely ordained Territories to which they believe they also have part, with Judah - if it were only possible for them to be heard and accepted. Could these Bible believing people be the remnant of the Ten Lost Tribes of Israel, in who's souls a Jewish spirit has been kindled? – a yearning towards Torah observance? – a zealous identifying with the soul of Judah?

Surely, the flashing red warning lights bring with them very limited strategic options? Surely, Judah should recognize that by itself, refusing to broaden their perspectives, the Jewish leaders are facing the extremes of 2 options:

- Either lose the Promised Land to our enemies, bit by bit as has been the definite process to date:

- or consider the most likely Divine Providence of a re-awakening, Torah loving, Zionist inspired, 'Lost' but now yearning-to-Return 10-Israel of old.

Could this be the awakening of Ephraim and Yosef? The fulfillment of Ezekiel's "dry bones putting on flesh and spirit"?

If increasing numbers today is a problem for Judah to convincingly settle the territories promised by Divine Oath to Israel – that is, please note, to the broader 12-tribed Israel that it was promised - then where do the Prophecies fit in which tell of the Land being 'too small' for the returning millions?

> Yeshiyahu (Isaiah) 49:18 b "By My Life – it is HaShem Who speaks – your desolate places and your ruins and your devastated country will now be too small for all your inhabitants ... Once more they

will speak in your hearing, those sons you thought were lost [the 10 Tribes?] 'This place is too small for me, give me more space to live in."

ZacharYah (Zechariah) 10:6-10 – (*We will simply draw extracts from this section here – please read it in full context, noting the distinction between the Houses of Yehudah, Yoseph and Ephraim*). "And I will make the House of Yehudah mighty and the House of Yoseph victorious. I am going to restore them ... and they shall be as if I have never cast them off ... Ephraim will be like a hero ... I am going to gather them in ... They will be as numerous as they used to be. I have scattered them among the nations ... I shall lead them into the land of Gilead and Lebanon and even that will not be large enough for them."

Emphasising a Call in the Wilderness

No doubt, there will be those readers who will respond to these suggestions of involving strangers into sharing the Divine Promises for Judah, with the reasoning that Am Yisrael has proven throughout the ages that it is invincible, and that HaShem sees to this, and that He has been doing so throughout history.

We urge those to consider that, to totally eliminate the share that Am Yisrael itself bears in the fulfillment of the ultimate Plan and Purpose of HaShem, is to totally negate the responsibility of Am Yisrael to the Covenant. Was it not after all, the very failure of Am Yisrael to properly conform with their own responsibility to Dvar HaShem, that caused 10/12ths of the nation to be rejected and sent into oblivion?

If it is the Will of HaShem to re-identify the long lost Ten Tribes at the End of Time (as it is clearly prophesied as reviewed in this publication) and to re-unite them with Judah again to make **one** Nation (Ezek 37:15 onwards), then there surely must rest an obligation on us to recognize, accept and co-operate with such a Restoration when it takes place and not to obstruct it by our personal or organizational preferences in ignorance of the factual developments in this direction.

Because the authors are well aware of the development of this prophetic fulfilment, they are also well acquainted with the great clamour and outcry from the great wave of reawakening souls in exile, to be heard and accepted by Judah – a Call which is not only falling on deaf ears and unwilling hearts and spirits, but is in fact increasingly being obstructed by the leadership of Judah.

It is in this context and as healing Inspiration, that this Call is presented. We pose the likely probability, that HaShem in His Wisdom and Foresight, may have pre-ordained the ultimate Solution for the critical problem which is facing Am Yisrael today in all its stark reality – and that this Solution is embedded in the ancient Scriptural Message of the Ten Tribes of Israel which is now being uncovered from under the dust and restored to its glorious and wise reality, unknown in its true implication, to date.

The contents of this Message is therefore sent out as a Plea to Judah and its leadership, and to each soul in this great nation. Please consider seriously the signs and facts that abound around us, that one of the greatest Prophecies is in process of fulfilment – the Second Exodus of the entire 12-tribed House of Yisrael from the four corners of the earth – lest we are found to be obstructing the ultimate Redemption!

YeremiYahu (Jeremiah) 23:7 *"See then, the days are coming when people will no longer say, 'As HaShem lives, Who brought the sons of Yisrael* (12 tribes) *out of the land of Egypt', but, 'As HaShem lives, Who led back and brought home the descendants of the House of Yisrael out of the land of the North and from all the countries in which He had dispersed them, to live on their own soil."*

May the reader consider this message – for the sake of taking full possession of the Promised Land!

B'Ezrat HaShem

CHAPTER 21

Preparing for the Return and absorption of 10-Israel

Prophesied Restoration of the 12-Tribed Kingdom of Israel

The topic of the Lost Ten Tribes of Israel, their prophesied Return to the Land and their reconciliation with Judah (the Jews) to form one re-united nation which will become the Kingdom of the G-d of Israel to rule over all the nations in an era of Peace, is most controversial. Chapter 26 presents a comprehensive extract of all the Scriptures and their clear Promises of this Restoration.

Many commentators and researchers point out that these exiled and lost Tribes since 2800 years ago, eventually ended up in Western Europe and from there spread to England, the USA, Canada, South Africa, and Australia. Other commentators maintain that they also spread to the East where they integrated with the nations in great numbers.

Torah and Tanach prophecies are clear and emphatic that the Ten Tribes will "return" to their ancient heritage. Jewish sages throughout the ages have interpreted these prophecies to

293

indicate a return both to Torah observance and to the physical land of Israel. This process, which applies to both Judah and Israel, is referred to as 'the Redemption' (Hebrew: *Geulah*).

Ultimately, in the Final Redemption, we will all once again be joined in a covenantal faith community as it was before 10-Israel broke away from Judah 5 to 7 centuries BCE.

"The element of togetherness of G-d and man is indispensable for the covenantal community ...We meet G-d in the covenantal community as a Comrade and fellow Member. Of course, even within the framework of this community, G-d appears as the Leader, Teacher, and Shepherd. Yet the Leader is an integral part of the community, the Teacher is inseparable from his pupils, and the Shepherd never leaves his flock. They all belong to one group. The Covenant draws G-d into the society of men of faith ... G-d was Jacob's Shepherd and Companion. The covenantal faith community manifests itself in a threefold personal union: I, Thou and He." ('*The Lonely Man of Faith*', by Joseph B. Soloveitchik, Jason Aronson pg. 44-45).

By extension, this dynamic becomes family, friends, and community.

From authentic Torah sources we learn that:

- HaShem, for His own interest and purpose, will gather and return 10-Israel to their own soil in the Land of Israel.

- 10-Israel will be in need of proper Torah instruction because they will still be involved in false beliefs when they return.

- While in the Land, 10-Israel will be cleansed from all their contamination and idols.

- HaShem will cause them to follow His Decrees and guard His Ordinances and fulfill them.

- When in the Land, 10-Israel will remember their evil ways and deeds and will be disgusted with themselves.

- Ezekiel. 36:16-31 (The Stone Edition Tanakh).

"The Word of HASHEM came to me, saying, 'Son of Man, the House of Israel dwell on their land, and they have contaminated it with their way and with their acts; ... So I poured out My wrath upon them, because of the blood that they had shed in the land, and (because) they had defiled it with their idols. I scattered them among the nations and they were dispersed among the lands; according to their way and according to their acts did I judge them. They came among the nations where they came, and they desecrated My holy Name when it was said of them, 'These are the people of HASHEM, but they departed His land.' I took pity on My holy Name, which the House of Israel had desecrated among the nations where they came. **Therefore, say to the House of Israel:** 'Thus said the Lord HASHEM ELOKIM: **It is not for your sake that I act, O House of Israel**, but for My holy Name that you have desecrated among the nations where you came. I will sanctify my great Name that is desecrated among the nations, which you have desecrated among them; then the nations will know that I am HASHEM – the Word of the Lord HASHEM ELOKIM – when

I become sanctified through you before their eyes. **I will take you from [among] the nations and gather you from all the lands, and I will bring you to your own soil. Then I will sprinkle pure water upon you, that you may become cleansed; I will cleanse you from all your contamination and from all your idols.** I will give you a new heart and put a new spirit within you; I will remove the heart of stone from your flesh and give you a heart of flesh. I will put My Spirit within you, and **I will make it so that you will follow My Decrees and guard My Ordinances and fulfill them.** You will dwell in the land that I gave to your forefathers; you will be a people to Me, and I will be a G-d to you. **I will save you from all your contaminations;** I will summon the rain and increase it, and I will not inflict famine upon you. I will increase the fruit of the tree and the produce of the field, so that you will no longer be subject to the shame of hunger among the nations. **Then you will remember your evil ways and your deeds that were not good, and you will be disgusted with yourselves in your own sight because of your iniquities and because of your abominations.** Not for your sake do I act – the Word of the Lord HASHEM ELOKIM – let this be known to you! **Be embarrassed and ashamed of your ways, O House of Israel!'"**

(*For a comprehensive extract of the multitude of texts from Tanakh which define this Promise of Return and Reconciliation, refer to chapter 25*).

From these above explicit Promises it is clear that the honor of G-d's Name is a prime reason for returning the House of Israel in the latter days from across the earth (Ezekiel 20). Having desecrated His Name in the exile, He will return them to restore the honor of His Name before the Nations.

It is significant that the restoration of the Sacred Names is a prominent movement amongst re-identifying 10-Tribers. It is a highly controversial topic though with numerous research-ers delving for information and confirmation into whatever sources are available to them. As a result, it is a minefield of confusion with numerous varying versions of the Sacred Name being advocated by individual commentators.

The Restoration and its objectionable side-effects is also a great source of concern for Judah for whom the Sacred Name is a highly sacred matter. Judah regards the slap-dash approach of 10-Israel (generally) and their 'slinging around' of the Sacred Name, as a serious desecration. This issue seriously hampers Reconciliation.

As a Jewish fellow, my work is to prepare the tribe of Judah, the present day Jewish people, for this great Return. I base my belief on a host of Biblical and Talmudic statements that the Lost Ten Tribes will be coming home with all kinds of religious 'baggage'. It will one day become clear that it is not the place of Judah to judge them in this, but to reach out and teach them the Way of HaShem.

The prophet Ezekiel (Ch. 36 and 37) says that only at the time of their Return, the Tribes will put away their false beliefs and idols. It also shows how they will be led to return in repentance. "G-d is the Shepherd of Israel and leads Joseph like a flock," (Psalms). In Jeremiah 30:32, "At that time, I will be HaShem to all of the families of Israel." In Ezekiel 16:58, "Then shall

all of the House of Israel, all of you, serve Me." The use of the doubling phrase, "all of them", fortifies and proves that the Tribes will repent when they return home (see Rambam, 'Book of Redemption', Gate 3). So even when they are back they will still need personal shepherding. Zechariah 10:6 shows that HaShem will bring them back to the land and the relationship will develop to such an extent that G-d will never cast them out again, thus proving that a lot of spiritual work will come to pass even **after** the Tribes have returned.

Judah is experiencing this same spiritual rejuvenation as well. The community in modern Israel was like a desert in terms of Torah institutions - but now there has been, thank G-d, tremendous growth over the years of those seeking Torah instruction.

I feel that it is crucial for Judah to understand that the religion of most of the returning Ten Tribes is not the Christianity that said, "Kiss the Cross, or kiss the sword", but a **religion in the process of returning, not only to Torah observance, but also to Halachic Judaism as per Rabbinic Oral Torah interpretation.** This will form a bridge of peace and truth straight back to the dawn of civilization and the Noahide Covenant which, practically speaking, they are all keeping, plus a willingness to be more and to do more for HaShem.

According to the interpretation of our Sages, it is not Judah's job to combat these professing returnees in their new-old Hebraic religious convictions. They are returning to the basic understanding of Biblical belief in a spirit of Messiah. This is all bound up with their newfound desire to return to the Jewish people and to the Land. The main aspect of the mandate of Messiah Ben Yosef, according to the insight of great Jewish sages (like the noted Gaon of Vilna), is to bring the Tribes back home (*The Voice of the Turtle Dove* – Ch. 1, par.1). This mandate may embrace various historical movements and utilize religious trends which are today clearly identifiable in masses of self-professing, Torah-restoring, non-Jewish individuals around the world.

This trend is even manifested among non-religious 'strangers' craving for a closer identification with Torah and Judaism. Numerous Jewish Orthodox sages have commented on the positive contribution that some forms of Christianity have made to the evolution of humankind towards Messiah, the Bible and One G-d, which also is the Jewish mandate. It behoves Judah to understand them and their beliefs. They are not our enemies – they are to be treated like guests at a Jewish Sukkah party, when estranged or even very secular relatives appear who should nevertheless be embraced. A better comparison would be in the spirit of our patriarch Avraham who was very open in his outreach and did not concentrate on negative possibilities.

Likewise, with the coming reunion of the Tribes, it remains Judah's Divine responsibility to welcome and embrace returning 10-Israelites as long-lost relatives.

Obviously, 10-Tribers should subject themselves to the way as defined by the giants of Torah and show respect for Jewish Halacha. This subjection was foretold by Zechariah the Prophet in chapter 8:23: "In those days, ten people from all languages and nations will take firm hold of one Jew by the hem of his robe and say, 'Let us go with you, because we have heard that G-d is with you.'" The term 'Ten' used here, no doubt refers to 10-Israel, not just anyone. The Talmud in Pesachim says, that G-d only scattered the nation of Israel for the purpose of gathering righteous converts.

Judah needs to express faith in G-d, Who is bringing the reunion to the forefront of history and is working out all the various doctrinal disputes that exist. Remember, **Judaism is a religion of deed, not creed.**

The beliefs and practices of the returning Tribes will be purified, just as Judah is being purified.

Biblical prescriptions for identifying the Lost House of 10-Israel

Let us establish the Biblical details which we have been given about the identity and whereabouts of the Ten Lost Tribes.

Please understand, that the Tribes were not going to end up as jungle primitives, according to Torah. As Yair Davidiy and many other scholars have repeatedly demonstrated, the Tribes ended up as being the dynamic, vital streams of dominant forces among the nations. "They were to be blessed; many millions would emerge from them; other people would be blessed by contact with them. They were to rule over other nations, become exceedingly prosperous and possess vast natural resources. Monarchs of several nations, ruling at one and the same time, were to emerge from them ... Each tribe had its distinctive qualities. ... These Israelites were to possess the 'gates of their enemies' and 'the gates of those who hate them' (Genesis 24:60). This means major strategic points giving them an edge over all potential adversaries. The USA and Britain (and related nations) have had this advantage and still do. Descendants of Joseph were to become the most powerful nations in the world, and to bring a blessing to all the peoples of the earth." (Yair Davidiy, "Biblical Truth, The Lost Ten Tribes of Israel in the

West according to the Book of Genesis." A Brit-Am Publication, Russell-Davis Pub., 5763-2002, Jerusalem, Israel).

A 3-point measure to recognize re-identifying 10 Tribers

A growing mass of 10-Tribers could feel comfortable with the following Oral Torah thought from Rabbi Shimon bar Yochai, citing an ancient Biblical explanation: "For they have not rejected you but, Me (G-d), that I should reign over them" (1 Samuel 8:7). Three things they were to do:

- To reject the Rule of Heaven,

- To reject the spirit of direction and rule of Judah (David's House) and

- To reject the building of the Temple.

When did this transpire?

- During the rule of Jeroboam (when defiant 10-Israel demanded) 'What portion do we have in David?' (1 Kings 12: 16). This is their rejection of the Rule of G-d (through their rebellion against the spiritual guidance of Judah – refer to chapter 16 on 'the Mechoqeck') and of the Kingdom of HaShem,

- 'Neither do we have an inheritance in the son of Jesse!' This is (their rejection of) the House of David.

- 'To your tents O Israel! ' This is their rejection of the Temple

When will we see the signs of Redemption? - Not until they repent and ask for all three,

- as the prophet Hosea says: 'Afterwards, the children of Israel shall return and seek HaShem their G-d' (Hosea 3:4). This refers to the Kingdom of Heaven ... '

- and to David their king'. This is the rulership of David's house. '

- And they shall come trembling to the Lord and his goodness in the end of days. This means the Temple" (Yalkut Shimoni 2 - 106).

Thus, Oral Torah presents us with a clear 3-pinned measure of identifying returning 10-Israel. The mature-spirited Returnees of 10-Israel today, even those who are not acquainted with this Prophetic phenomenon or with the fact that they may actually conform, certainly do qualify according to these three criteria.

Prophecy stands vindicated!

PART 5

CONCLUSION

CHAPTER 22

Conclusion

Hopefully, with the information, viewpoints and confirmations of this book, we have established the underlying Oral Interpretation foundations of the NT which have been so well hidden for most of its readers until these enlightening times.

We have also shown how the roots of anti-Judaism and anti-Rabbinism are really at the core of the obstruction of the Divine Redemption Plan for mankind.

If therefore, the NT confirms the Oral Torah and Halacha, then it would behoove 10-Israel, in their process of Return to Torah, to more fully acquaint themselves with:

- the Scriptural foundations of the Oral Torah;

- the confirmations borne out by Judah's guarding and execution of Oral Torah throughout the ages;

- the confirmation of the sound realities engendered by Oral Torah that science, law, justice and society internationally bear witness to.

Through this acknowledgement and realization, Judaism will stand vindicated as the embodiment of the Will of the Creator G-d for humanity and the world. And that Judah's Oral interpretation is simply the correct interpretation of the Written Word of G-d.

In this respect, the absolute WONDER involved in the modern Hebrew Roots Restoration Movement and their Return to Torah becomes evident. This Miracle also then serves as further proof to the world and to Judah, of the very reason why the Divine Purpose intended the Return of 10-Israel not only to Torah, but to Oral Torah according to the Divine Mandate entrusted to Judah, viz. to guard and protect His Torah, and ensure conformity to His Will.

This realization of the sound foundation of Oral Torah will no doubt stir the urge in many souls (not only of 10-Israel but also of Judah) to pursue a more conforming life style.

May this knowledge and realization inspire 10-Israel to, in this way share in establishing *Tikkun Olam* (universal healing) on earth for all nations. May the message of this book bring Peace, Joy and fulfillment to these seeking souls.

This Addendum, while further presenting general evidence of the firm Scriptural foundations of Oral Torah, in so doing will therefore strive to draw souls closer to the true Source of Blessings: The Torah - the Tree of Life. May they thereby be secured of citizenship in His Universal Kingdom, when He restores the re-united Kingdom of Israel.

CHAPTER 23

Why Jews need not be proselytized?

To answer this question, we will not quote from the vast sources of Jewish literature and wisdom, but from the NT itself, in line with the author's reasoning contained in this book. As mentioned in the Introduction, the author simply uses the hidden Jewish secrets in the NT itself to establish this witness of the Jewish Torah Faith to NT Christian interpreters, without his endorsing either the existence of the NT Messiah nor the validity of the NT.

Accordingly, here is the **NT position** which confirms that the Nazarene whom it proclaims as Messiah, never came for Judah (the Jews) but merely to restore 10-Israel and to reconcile them back into Covenant relationship. According to the NT itself, Judah therefore has no need of being reconciled to the Covenant from which they, unlike 10-Israel, had never been cut off.

We start our review of the NT position by quoting the Words of the Nazarene himself:

Matthew 15:24 "But he (the Nazarene) answered and said, 'I was sent only unto the lost sheep of the House of Israel.'"

Matthew 10:5 "These twelve (apostles) he sent out with the following instructions: 'Don't go into the territory of the Goyim (other nations) and don't enter any other town in Shomron, but go rather to the lost sheep of the House of Israel. As you go, proclaim 'the Kingdom of Heaven is near.'"

About Paul's mandate the Nazarene said: **Acts 9:15** "This man (Saul / Paul) is my chosen vessel to bring my Name before the nations and kings and before the **Sons of Israel.**"

Bear in mind, that in those days the exile of the lost 'House of Israel' was well known. The great historian, Josephus, who was appointed by the Roman Empire to record the history of the Jews, refer to multitudes of these 'lost Israelites' who were still identified and living 'across the Euphrates river' in his time. The later books of the Tanakh ('Old Testament'), make a clear distinction between 'Israel and Judah'. The Nazarene's reference and instructions quoted above, must therefore refer to this 'Lost House', not to the 'lost souls' within Judah as it is generally interpreted.

Chapter 11 from the book of Romans claims (**v.25**) that this whole matter was concealed by G-d in earlier times. It concludes that Judah's rejection of the Gospel was simply for the benefit of the other nations, who were then granted the opportunity to receive the Nazarene (Rom 11:11-15,28,29). The NT therefore confirms and approves the rejection by Judah. Why then should believers of the NT insist that Jews should accept 'their' Messiah?

> **Ephesians 3:5, 6** "In past generations it was not made known to mankind, as the Spirit is now revealing it ...that in union with (the Nazarene) and through the

Gospel, the Gentiles were to be joint heirs, a joint body and joint sharers with the Jews in what G-d has promised." (*Stern*). In this, the NT once again confirms that Judah would be in the Covenant without having to accept the NT Messiah.

With all the new evidence provided today, 2000 years later, and by way of the astonishing re-identification of 'Lost Israel' (prophesied for the 'End Times'), over the last decade, as well as the 'increase in Knowledge' predicted by the prophet Daniel for the End Time (Daniel 12:3,4), it seems clear that the apostles of the New Testament either did not fully grasp, or ignored this very instruction of the NT to NOT go to Judah but "go rather to the lost sheep of the House of Israel."

The author in this review from a Halachic Jewish platform, has thus far extracted from the NT Scriptures itself, massive and convincing evidence that the "Gospel of the NT is in fact based NOT on Christian fundamentals which had been accorded it, but on true, ancient Halachic Oral Torah principles.

It should be convincingly clear therefore, as more and more Hebraic Restorers are discovering and proclaiming:

- that the NT Gospel is NOT a Gospel which frees you from all obligations. It does NOT put the responsibility on G-d to save you by Grace only "because He understands and forgives your inability to comply with His stringent and impossible Laws";

- that the NT Gospel is NOT a Gospel which has done away with the Laws of G-d, 'nailing them to the Cross';

309

- that the NT Gospel is NOT a Gospel which "annulled the 'Old, Jewish' Covenant and replaced it with a 'New' Covenant of Love and Grace only";

- that the NT Gospel is NOT a Gospel which transplanted the "old and outdated, burdensome religion of Judaism with a new, revitalized religion of 'freedom in the spirit' "

But, according to these hidden Jewish Secrets in the NT it is a 'Hebraic Gospel' which is based on the Eternal Promises to Avraham and Israel and conditional upon compliance with the Torah Requirements of the Covenant.

The need to observe the Law according to Jewish teachings and the Mosaic Code has been well hidden under cover of alternative translations in the NT. Following is a perfect example of this:

The Greek word *paradosis* according to Strong's Concordance G3862 refers to: *transmission, that is, (concretely) a precept; specifically the Jewish traditionary law: - ordinance, tradition.* The word *paradosis* has been used in the following texts, translated as *doctrines* and *teachings;*

> **1 Corinthians 11:2,** "But I praise you, brothers, that in all things you have remembered me, and even as I delivered them to you, you hold fast the **doctrines.**"

> **2 Thimothy 2:15,** "So, then, brothers, stand firm and strongly hold the **teachings** you were taught, whether by word or by our letter."

> **2 Thimothy 3:6**, "...draw yourselves back from every brother walking in a disorderly \way, and not according to the **teaching** which you received from us."

Why on earth then should Jews be expected to accept this non-Hebraic Faith and Torah-rejecting 'Messiah' presented by Christianity?

G-d is perfect and He does not change. He does not change a Perfect System.

The Gospel of Salvation offers the *same* ultimate benefits to all mankind, whether you are physically part of His Covenant People (the Jews) or part of the other nations. The ultimate reward is "eternal life in the physical Kingdom of G-d". The compliance parameters are also the *same* for Jews as for non-Jews, i.e. observance of G-d's Laws and Customs.

The *qualifying* process for this Divine Reward though, is different for Jews and non-Jews.

- Jews are and have always been under the Covenant and simply have to comply with the terms of this Covenant, i.e. they have to repent and live by the Terms of the Covenant as specified in the Torah (first 5 Books of the Bible) and as interpreted comprehensively by the Rabbinic sages in the Halacha (Oral Tradition).

- Those who are part of the Lost Ten Tribes of Israel, have to RETURN to the Torah Covenant. They, like the Jews, have to live by the Terms of the Covenant as specified in the Torah (first 5 Books of the Bible) and as interpreted comprehensively by the Rabbinic sages in the Halacha (Oral Tradition - refer to NT for its Injunction to this effect in Matthew 23:2; 5:17-20).

The authentic Hebrew Gospel has been contorted and replaced by a watered-down version of a 'Grace-only' and 'Holy Spirit inspired' licentious anti-Torah 'Gospel', to deceive and mislead the personal believer.

May this study serve to provide NT believers with the correct guidelines, as concealed in and underwritten by the NT itself, to return to the Torah Covenant and to the Eternal Kingdom of Peace, soon to be established in Jerusalem.

PART 6

ADDENDUM

CHAPTER 24

Historic Chain of Torah Transmission down to current Rabbinic age

Maimonides (Rambam) carefully records the generations since the Giving of Torah at Sinai until his own time 900 years ago. There had passed only 120 generations. We can even list them exactly. To be part of the golden chain of the transmission of Torah, all it takes is a lifetime of dedicated and devoted Torah living and learning. The crown of kingship is open to the Davidic dynasty. The crown of priesthood necessitates being of the seed of Aaron, the first High Priest. But when it comes to Torah the scenario changes completely. The family pedigree assures one of nothing and family history guarantees no one a place in Torah hierarchy. The only thing that counts is the individual's personal self-sacrifice over many years coupled with an ethical lifestyle, integrity and piety. All you need to do is look in the book of Exodus to see the requirements for being part of the Judicial system of Torah, the Judges. This biblical system provided the custodial, maintenance and managerial dimension of the historic covenantal faith community.

UNBROKEN CHAIN OF TRANSMISSION

Spiritual Leadership

1. Moses

2. Joshua 1312 BCE

The Elders 1260-860 BCE

3. Pinchas and the 70 Elders

4. Eli the Kohen

5. Samuel the Prophet

6. King David

The Prophets 860-360 BCE

7. Achiya

8. Elijah the Prophet

9. Elisha

10. Yehoyda the Priest

11. Zachariah ben Yehoyda

12. Hosea

13. Amos

14. Isaiah

15. Micah

16. Joel

17. Nachum

18. Habakkuk

19. Zephaniah

20. Jeremiah

21. Baruch ben Neriah

The Great Assembly 360-260 BCE

22. The Great Assembly consisted of 120 Elders, including Ezra, Zechariah, Daniel, and Mordechai

23. Shimon the Tzaddik

Tana'im Mishnaic Era 260 BCE - 200 CE

24. Antigonos of Socho

25. Yose ben Yoezer, Yose ben Yochanan

26. Yehoshua ben Perachiah, Nittai of Arbel

27. Yehuda ben Tabbai, Shimon ben Shatach

28. Shemaya and Avtalyon

29. Hillel and Shammai

30. R'Shimon ben Hillel, R'Yochanan ben Zakkai

31. Rabban Gamaliel the Elder, R'Eliezer ben Hyrcanus, R'Yehoshua ben Chananiah, R'Shimon ben Netanel, R'Elazer ben Arakh.

32. Rabban Shimon ben Gamaliel I, Rebbe Akiva, Rebbe Tarfon, R'Shimon ben Elazar, R'Yochanan ben Nuri.

33. Rabban Gamaliel II, Rabbe Meir, Rabbe Yishmael, Rebbe Yehuda, Rebbe Yose, R'Shimon bar Yochai

34. Rabbi Shimon ben Gamaliel II

35. Rabbi Yehuda the Prince* (*Codifier of the Mishnah in 190 C.E.)

Amora'im Talmudic Era 200-500 CE

36. Rav Shmuel, Rabbi Yochanan* (*Compiler of the Jerusalem Talmud)

37. Rav Huna, Rav Yehuda, Rav Nachman, Rav Kahana, Rabba bar bar Channa, Rav Ami, Rav Asi

38. Rabbah Rav Yosef, Rav Chisda, Rabba bar Huna.

39. Abaya, Rava

40. Rav Ashi, Ravina*
    (*Compilers of the Babylonian Talmud in 500 C.E.)

And onwards -120 generations of unbroken transmission up until Maimonides 900 years ago.

(Thanks to the Discovery booklet of Aish HaTorah.)

From Maimonides onwards, we can trace exactly with all the principle players, the next 35 generations until this very day.

CHAPTER 25

Scriptures that foretold the Restoration of the House of Israel

After the exile of the Northern Ten Tribes of Israel in the 8th century BCE, the Scriptures generally differentiate between "Judah" and "Israel", as between "the House of Judah" and "the House of Israel". The latter is also commonly referred to as "the House of Ephraim" or "the House of Joseph". The "House of Jacob" refers to all the Tribes of Israel. The "House of Israel", in some instances, when it appears not paired with a reference to Judah could also refer to all Twelve Tribes. The context should confirm which is meant.

Yermiyahu (Jeremiah) 3:14-18 "'Return, faithless people,' declares HaShem, 'for I am your Husband. I will choose you—one from a town and two from a clan—and bring you to Zion. Then I will give you shepherds after My own Heart, who will lead you with knowledge and understanding. In those days, when your numbers have increased greatly in the land,' declares HaShem, 'men will no longer say, 'The Ark of the Covenant of HaShem.'"

"It will never enter their minds or be remembered; it will not be missed, nor will another one be made. At that time they will call Jerusalem the Throne of HaShem, and all nations will gather in Jerusalem to honor the name of HaShem. No longer will they follow the stubbornness of their evil hearts. **In those days the House of Judah will join the House of Israel, and together they will come from a northern land to the land I gave your forefathers as an inheritance.**"

Yechezkiel (Ezekiel) 37:15-19 "And the Word of HaShem came to me saying, 'And you, son of man, take one stick to yourself and write on it, For Judah, and for his companions, the sons of Israel. And take another stick and write on it, For Joseph, the stick of Ephraim and all the house of Israel, his companions. And draw them one to one for yourself, into one stick. And they shall become one in your hand. And when the sons of your people shall speak to you, saying, 'Will you not declare to us what these mean to you?' Say to them, 'So says HaShem: Behold, I will take the stick of Joseph which is in the hand of Ephraim, and the tribes of Israel, his companions. **And I will put them with him, with the stick of Judah, and I will make them one stick, and they shall be one in My hand.**'"

Yechezkiel (Ezekiel) 37:20-28 "And the sticks shall be in your hand, the ones on which you write before their eyes. And say to them, 'So says HaShem: **Behold, I will take the sons of Israel from among the nations, there where they have gone, and will gather them from all around, and will bring them into their own land. And I will make them one nation in the land**, on the mountains of Israel, and one King shall be for a king to all of them. And they shall not be two nations still. And they will not be split into two kingdoms any more. And they will not still be defiled with their idols, even with their filthy idols, nor with all of their transgressions. But I will save them out of all their dwelling places where they have sinned in them, and I will cleanse them. So they shall be for a people to Me and I will be their G-d. And My Servant, David, shall be King over them. And there shall be one Shepherd to all of them. And they shall walk in My judgments and keep My statutes, and do them. And they shall dwell on the land that I have given to my servant, to Jacob, there where your fathers dwelt in it. And they shall dwell on it, they and their sons, and the sons of their sons, forever. And My Servant David shall be a ruler to them forever. And I will cut a covenant of peace with them, an everlasting covenant it shall be with them, and I will place them and multiply them, and I will put My sanctuary in their midst forever. And My tabernacle shall be with them, and I will be their G-d, and they shall be My people. And when My sanctuary shall be in their midst forever, the nations shall know that I, HaShem, sanctify Israel.'"

Yechezkiel (Ezekiel) 39:23-29 "And the nations will know that the people of Israel went into exile for their sin, because they were unfaithful to Me. So I hid My Face from them and handed them over to their enemies, and they all fell by the sword. I dealt with them according to their uncleanness and their offenses, and I hid My Face from them." **25-29** "Therefore this is what the Sovereign HaShem says: I will now bring Jacob back from captivity and will have compassion upon the whole House of Israel, and I will be zealous for My Holy Name. They will forget their shame and all the unfaithfulness they showed toward Me when they lived in safety in their land with no one to make them afraid. When I have brought them back from the nations and have gathered them from the countries of their enemies, I will show Myself holy through them in the sight of many nations. Then they will know that I am HaShem their G-d, for though I sent them into exile among the nations, I will gather them to their own land, not leaving any behind. I will no longer hide My Face from them, for I will pour out My Spirit on the house of Israel, declares the Sovereign HaShem."

Yechezkiel (Ezekiel) 36:1 "Son of man, prophesy to the mountains of Israel and say, 'O mountains of Israel, hear the word of HaShem. 2 This is what the Sovereign HaShem says: The enemy said of you, 'Aha! The ancient heights have become our possession.' 3 Therefore prophesy and say, 'This is what the Sovereign HaShem says: Because they ravaged and hounded you from every side so that you became the possession of the rest of the nations and the object of people's malicious talk and slander, 4 therefore, O mountains of Israel, hear the word of the Sovereign HaShem: This is what the Sovereign HaShem says to the mountains and hills, to the ravines and valleys, to the desolate ruins and the deserted towns that have been plundered and ridiculed by the rest of the nations around you- 5 this is what the Sovereign HaShem says: In my burning zeal I have spoken against the rest of the nations, and against all Edom, for with glee and with malice in their hearts they made my land their own possession so that they might plunder its pastureland.' 6 Therefore prophesy concerning the land of Israel and say to the mountains and hills, to the ravines and valleys: 'This is what the Sovereign HaShem says: I speak in my jealous wrath because you have suffered the scorn of the nations. 7 Therefore this is what the Sovereign HaShem says: I swear with uplifted hand that the nations around you will also suffer scorn. 8 But you, O mountains of Israel, will produce branches and fruit for my people Israel, for **they will soon come home.** 9 I am concerned for you and will look on you with favor; you will be plowed and sown, 10 and I will multiply the number of people upon you, even the whole house of Israel. The towns will be inhabited and the ruins rebuilt. 11 I will increase the number of men and animals upon you, and they will be fruitful and become numerous. I will settle people on you as in the past and will make you prosper more than before. Then you will know that I am HaShem. 12 I will cause people, my people Israel, to walk upon you. They will possess you, and you will be their inheritance; you will never again deprive them of their children. 13 " 'This is what the Sovereign HaShem says: Because people say to you, "You [Mountains of Israel] devour men and deprive your nation of its children," 14 therefore you will no longer devour men or make your nation childless, declares the Sovereign HaShem. 15 No longer will I make you hear the taunts of the nations, and no longer will you suffer the scorn of the peoples or cause your nation to fall, declares the Sovereign HaShem.' "

16 Again the word of HaShem came to me: 17 "Son of man, when the people of Israel were living in their own land, they defiled it by their conduct and their actions. Their conduct was like a woman's monthly uncleanness in my sight. 18 So I poured out my wrath on them because they had shed blood in the land and because they had defiled it with their idols. 19 I dispersed them among the nations, and they were scattered through the countries; I judged them according to their conduct and their actions. 20 And wherever they went among the nations they profaned My Holy Name, for it was said of them, 'These are HaShem's people, and yet they had to leave His land.' 21 I had concern for My Holy Name, which the House of Israel profaned among the nations where they had gone. 22 "Therefore say to the House of

Israel, 'This is what the Sovereign HaShem says: It is not for your sake, O House of Israel, that I am going to do these things, but for the sake of My Holy Name, which you have profaned among the nations where you have gone. 23 I will show the holiness of My Great Name, which has been profaned among the nations, the Name you have profaned among them. Then the nations will know that I am HaShem, declares the Sovereign HaShem, when I show myself Holy through you before their eyes. 24 " 'For I will take you out of the nations; I will gather you from all the countries and bring you back into your own land. 25 I will sprinkle clean water on you, and you will be clean; I will cleanse you from all your impurities and from all your idols. 26 I will give you a new heart and put a new spirit in you; I will remove from you your heart of stone and give you a heart of flesh. 27 And I will put My Spirit in you and move you to follow My Decrees and be careful to keep My Laws. 28 You will live in the land I gave your forefathers; you will be My People, and I will be your G-d. 29 I will save you from all your uncleanness. I will call for the grain and make it plentiful and will not bring famine upon you. 30 I will increase the fruit of the trees and the crops of the field, so that you will no longer suffer disgrace among the nations because of famine. 31 Then you will remember your evil ways and wicked deeds, and you will loathe yourselves for your sins and detestable practices. 32 I want you to know that I am not doing this for your sake, declares the Sovereign HaShem. Be ashamed and disgraced for your conduct, O House of Israel! 33 " 'This is what the Sovereign HaShem says: On the day I cleanse you from all your sins, I will resettle your towns, and the ruins will be rebuilt. 34 The desolate land will be cultivated instead of lying desolate in the sight of all who pass through it. 35 They will say, "This land that was laid waste has become like the Garden of Eden; the cities that were lying in ruins, desolate and destroyed, are now fortified and inhabited." 36 Then the nations around you that remain will know that I, HaShem have rebuilt what was destroyed and have replanted what was desolate. I, HaShem have spoken, and I will do it.' 37 "This is what the Sovereign HaShem says: Once again I will yield to the plea of the House of Israel and do this for them: I will make their people as numerous as sheep, 38 as numerous as the flocks for offerings at Jerusalem during her appointed Feasts. So will the ruined cities be filled with flocks of people. Then they will know that I am HaShem."

B'reisheet (Genesis) 17:1-8 "And when Abram was ninety years old and nine, HaShem appeared to Abram, and said unto him ...' I will make my covenant between Me and thee, and will multiply thee exceedingly ... As for Me, behold, My Covenant is with thee, and thou shalt be a father of many nations ... And I will establish My Covenant between Me and thee and thy seed after thee in their generations for an everlasting Covenant, to be a G-d unto thee, and to thy seed after thee. And I will give unto thee, and to thy seed after thee, the land wherein thou art a stranger, all the land of Canaan, for an everlasting Possession; and I will be their G-d.'"

B'reisheet (Genesis) 28:14 "Your descendants will be like the dust of the earth, **and you will spread out to the West and to the East, to the North and to the South. All peoples on earth will be blessed through you and your offspring.**"

D'varim (Deuteronomy) 4:27, 29-31 "And HaShem **shall scatter you among the peoples,** and you shall be left few in number among the gentiles where HaShem drives you." 29 "**But from there you shall seek HaShem your G-d, and shall find, when you search for Him with all your heart and with all your being.** 30 **In all your distress, when all these words shall come upon you in the latter days, then you shall return to HaShem your G-d and shall obey His voice.** 31 For HaShem your G-d is a compassionate G-d, He does not forsake you, nor destroy you, nor forget the covenant of your fathers which He swore to them."

D'varim (Deuteronomy) 30:1-5 "When all these blessings and curses I have set before you come upon you and you take them to heart wherever HaShem your G-d disperses you among the nations, and when you and your children return to HaShem your G-d and obey him with all your heart and with all your soul according to everything I command you today, then HaShem your G-d will restore your fortunes and have compassion on you and gather you again from all the nations where He scattered you. *Even if you have been banished to the most distant land under the heavens, from there HaShem your G-d will gather you and bring you back.* He will bring you to the land that belonged to your fathers, and you will take possession of it. He will make you more prosperous and numerous than your fathers."

Yesha'yahu (Isaiah) 10:20-22 "In that day the remnant of Israel, the survivors of the house of Jacob, will no longer rely on him who struck them down but will truly rely on HaShem, the Holy One of Israel. 21 **A remnant will return, a remnant**

SCRIPTURES THAT FORETOLD THE RESTORATION OF THE HOUSE OF ISRAEL

of Jacob will return to the Mighty G-d. 22 Though your people, O Israel, be like the sand by the sea, **only a remnant will return.** A Destruction has been decreed, that will bring inexhaustible integrity"

(*Jerusalem Bible*) (alt. righteousness) (a decisive end, overflowing with righteousness – *The Scriptures ISR*) (Holocaust?)

Yesha'yahu (Isaiah) 11:10-16 "And in that day there shall be a root of Jesse, which shall stand for an ensign of the people; to it shall the Gentiles seek: and his rest shall be glorious. 11 And it shall come to pass in that day, that HaShem shall set His Hand again the second time to recover the remnant of His people, which shall be left, from Assyria, and from Egypt, and from Pathros, and from Cush, and from Elam, and from Shinar, and from Hamath, and from the islands of the sea. 12 And He shall set up an ensign (signal) for the nations, **and shall assemble the outcasts of Israel and gather together the dispersed of Judah from the four corners of the earth. Then Ephraim's jealousy will come to an end, and the adversaries of Judah shall be cut off, Ephraim shall not envy Judah, and Judah shall not harass Ephraim** ... 16 There will be a highway for the remnant of his people that is left from Assyria, as there was for Israel when they came up from Egypt."

Yesha'yahu (Isaiah) 14:1 "HaShem will have pity on Jacob, he will choose Israel once more **and resettle them on their native soil. Foreigners will join them, attaching themselves to the House of Ya'akov.** Nations will take them and escort them to their homeland and the House of Israel will adopt them in the land of HaShem as male and female slaves"

(New Jerusalem Bible, David Stern)

Yesha'yahu (Isaiah) 25:6-8 "Then the great HaShem will make for all Tribes on this Hill, a feast rich with marrow and well-prepared dainties, and grape juice well thickened by age; And **remove on this Hill the Veil veiling the Tribesmen, and the covering that covers it from all the Heathen;** and HaShem Ever-Living destroy death for ever; and wipe tears from each face; and turn from the earth the reproach of His people; So the Living Life says!"

(*Ferrar Fenton translation*).

Yesha'yahu (Isaiah) 27:2 "That day, sing of the splendid vineyard! I, HaShem, am its Guardian, from time to time I water it; so that no harm befall it, I guard it night and day."

(*New Jerusalem Bible*)

Yesha'yahu (Isaiah) 27:6, 12, 13 "In days to come, Jacob will take root, Israel will bud and blossom and the surface of the world be one vast harvest." 12 "When that day comes, HaShem will start his threshing from the course of the River to the Torrent of Egypt, **and you will be gathered one by one, O children of Israel!**" 13 "When that day comes, the great ram's-horn will be sounded, and those lost in Assyria will come, and those banished to Egypt, **and they will worship HaShem on the holy mountain, in Jerusalem."**

Yesha'yahu (Isaiah) 37:31,32 "The surviving remnant of the House of Judah shall bring forth new roots below and fruits above. For out of Jerusalem will **come a remnant, and out of Mount Zion a band of survivors.** The zeal of HaShem Almighty will accomplish this."

Yesha'yahu (Isaiah) 43:1-21 "But now, this is what HaShem says - He Who created you, O Jacob, He Who formed you, O Israel: "Fear not, for I have redeemed you; I have summoned you by name; you are Mine. 2 When you pass through the waters, I will be with you; and when you pass through the rivers, they will not sweep over you. When you walk through the fire, you will not be burned; the flames will not set you ablaze. 3 For I am HaShem, your G-d, the Holy One of Israel, your Savior; .... 4 Since you are precious and honored in My sight, and because I love you, I will give men in exchange for you, and people in exchange for your life. 5 Do not be afraid, for I am with you; **I will bring your children from the East and gather you from the West. 6 I will say to the North, 'Give them up!' and to the South, 'Do not hold them back.' Bring my sons from afar and my daughters from the ends of the earth - 7 everyone who is called by My Name, whom I created for My Glory, whom I formed and made."**

9 All the nations gather together and the peoples assemble. Which of them foretold this and proclaimed to us the former

things? Let them bring in their witnesses to prove they were right, so that others may hear and say, "It is true." 10 "You are my witnesses," declares HaShem, "and My servant whom I have chosen, so that you may know and believe Me and understand that I Am He. Before Me no god was formed, nor will there be one after Me. 11 I, even I, am HaShem and apart from Me there is no Savior"....18 "Forget the former things; do not dwell on the past. 19 See, **I am doing a new thing!** Now it springs up; do you not perceive it? I am making a way in the desert and streams in the wasteland. 20 The wild animals honor Me, ... the jackals and the owls, because I provide water in the desert and streams in the wasteland, to give drink to My people, My Chosen, 21 the people I formed for Myself **that they may proclaim My Praise.**"

(Refer overall context as also in Yechezkiel (Ezek.) 20)

Yesha'yahu (Isaiah) 44:1-5 "Yet now hear, O Ya'akov (Jacob) My servant; and Yisra'el, whom I have chosen: This says HaShem that made you, and formed you from the womb, 'Who will help you? Fear not, O Ya'akov, My servant and you Yeshurun (meaning: 'straight and upright one'), whom I have chosen. 3 For I will pour water upon him that is thirsty, and floods upon the dry ground: I will pour My Spirit upon your seed (descendants), and My Blessings upon your offspring.' 4 And they shall spring up as among the grass, as willows by the water streams. 5 One shall say, 'I belong to HaShem; and another shall call himself by the Name of HaShem, another will call himself by Ya'akov's name, on his hand another shall write HaShem's Name and be surnamed 'Israel.'" (*Jerusalem Bible*)

Yesha'yahu (Isaiah) 45: 17-25 "**Yisra'el shall be saved by HaShem with an everlasting deliverance.** You are not to be ashamed nor hurt, forever and ever. 18 'Yes, thus', says HaShem, Creator of the Heavens, Who is G-d, Who formed the earth and made it ... 19 I am HaShem unrivalled. I have not spoken in secret. .... I HaShem, speak with directness. I express Myself with clarity." 20 "Gather yourselves and come; draw near together, you who have escaped from the Gentiles. 21 Speak up, present your case .... Who foretold this and revealed it in the past? Am I not HaShem? There is no other god besides Me - a G-d of integrity and a Saviour. There is none apart from Me. 22 "Turn to Me and be saved, all you ends of the earth! For I am G-d, and there is none else.' 25 .... To Him shall come ashamed, all who raged against Him. **Victorious and glorious through HaShem shall be all the descendants of Yisra'el.**"

Yesha'yahu (Isaiah) 46: 3-13 "Listen to me, **O house of Jacob, all you who remain of the house of Israel,** you whom I have upheld since you were conceived, and have carried since your birth." 9 Remember the former things, those of long ago; I am G-d, and there is no other; I am G-d, and there is none like me. 10 **I make known the end from the beginning, from ancient times, what is still to come. I say: My purpose will stand, and I will do all that I please.**

11 ...What I have said, that will I bring about; what I have planned, that will I do. 12 Listen to Me, you stubborn-hearted, you who are far from righteousness. 13 **I am bringing My Righteousness near, it is not far away; and My Salvation will not be delayed. I will grant salvation to Zion, My splendor to Israel."**

Yesha'yahu (Isaiah) 49:3-26 He said to me, "You are My servant, Israel, in whom I will display My splendor." ....5 And now HaShem says - He who formed me in the womb to be His servant, to bring Jacob back to Him and gather Israel to Himself, for I am honored in the eyes of HaShem and my G-d has been my strength. 6 He says: 'It is too small a thing for you to be my servant to restore the tribes of Jacob and bring back those of Israel I have kept. I will also make you a light for the Gentiles, that you may bring my salvation to the ends of the earth." 7 This is what HaShem says - the Redeemer and Holy One of Israel - to him who was despised and abhorred by the nations, to the servant of rulers: "Kings will see you and rise up, princes will see and bow down, because of HaShem, who is faithful, the Holy One of Israel, who has chosen you." 8 This is what HaShem says: "In the time of My Favor I will answer you, and in the day of salvation I will help you; I will keep you and will make you to be a covenant for the people, to restore the land and to reassign its desolate inheritances, 9 to say to the captives, 'Come out,' and to those in darkness, 'Be free!' "They will feed beside the roads and find pasture on every barren hill. 10 They will neither hunger nor thirst, nor will the desert heat or the sun beat upon them. He who has compassion on them will guide them and lead them beside springs of water. 11 I will turn all my mountains into roads, and My highways will be raised up. 12 See, they will come from afar - some from the north, some from the west, some from the region of Aswan." 13 Shout for joy, O heavens; rejoice, O earth; burst into song, O mountains! For HaShem comforts His people and will have compassion on His afflicted ones. 14 But Zion said, "HaShem has forsaken me, HaShem has forgotten me." 15 "Can a mother forget the baby at her breast and have no compassion on the child she has borne? Though she may forget, I will not forget you! 16 See, I have engraved you on the palms of My Hands; your walls are ever before Me. 17 Your sons hasten back, and those who laid you waste depart from you. 18 Lift up your eyes and look around; all your sons gather and come to you. As surely as I live," declares HaShem, "you will wear them all as ornaments; you will put them on, like a bride. 19 "Though you were ruined and made desolate and your land laid waste, **now you will be too small for your people,** and those who devoured you will be far away. 20 The children born during your bereavement will yet say in your hearing, '**This place is too small for us; give us more space to live in.**' 21 Then you will say in your heart, 'Who bore me these? I was bereaved and barren; I was exiled and rejected. Who brought these up? I was left all alone, but these - where have they come from?' " 22 This is what the Sovereign HaShem says: "See, I will beckon to the Gentiles, I will lift up My banner to the peoples; they will bring your sons in their arms and carry your daughters on their shoulders. 23 Kings will be your foster fathers, and their queens your nursing mothers. They will bow down before you with their faces to the ground; they will lick the dust at your feet. Then you will know that I am HaShem; those who hope in me will not be disappointed." 24 Can plunder be taken from warriors, or captives rescued from the fierce? 25 But this is what HaShem says: "Yes, captives will be taken from warriors, and plunder retrieved from the fierce; I will contend with those who contend with you, and your children I will save. 26 I will make your oppressors eat their own flesh; they will be drunk on their own blood, as with wine. Then all mankind will know that I, HaShem, am your Savior, your Redeemer, the Mighty One of Jacob."

Yesha'yahu (Isaiah) 51:9-11 Awake, awake, put on strength, O arm of G-d. Awake as in the days of old, in the ancient generations. Then the redeemed of HaShem shall return and come to Zion with singing, and everlasting joy on their heads; They shall obtain joy and gladness, sorrow and sadness shall flee.

Yesha'yahu (Isaiah) 60:8 "Who are these?"

(see connection to Bereshith (Genesis 48:8)

B'reisheet (Genesis) 48:8 "And Israel saw Joseph's sons, and said, "Who are these?" that fly along like doves to their nests?

(doves- see connection to Hoshea 7:11)

Hoshea (Hosea) 7:11 "Ephraim is like a dove, easily deceived and senseless—now calling to Egypt, now turning to Assyria."

Kol HaTor - 'Voice of the Dove' - a Biblical term for the Return (Refer to website menu)

Yesha'yahu (Isaiah) 60:9-10 Surely the islands look to Me; in the lead are the ships of Tarshish, bringing your sons from

afar, with their silver and gold, to the honor of HaShem your G-d, the Holy One of Israel, for He has endowed you with splendor. 10 "**Foreigners** will rebuild your walls, and their kings will serve you. Though in anger I struck you, in favor I will show you compassion."

Yesha'yahu (Isaiah) 60:21-22 "Then will **all your people** be righteous and **they will possess the land forever. They are the shoot I have planted, the work of My Hands, for the display of My Splendor.** 22 The least of you will become a thousand, the smallest a mighty nation. I am HaShem; **in its time I will do this swiftly.**"

Yesha'yahu (Isaiah) 61:7-9 "Instead of your shame and reproach, they rejoice **a second time in their portion. Therefore they take possession a second time in their land,** everlasting joy is theirs. For I, HaShem, love right-ruling; I hate robbery for burnt offering. And I shall give their reward in truth, and make an everlasting Covenant with them. **And their seed shall be known among the gentiles, and their offspring in the midst of the peoples. All who see them shall acknowledge them, that they are the seed HaShem has blessed.**"

Yesha'yahu (Isaiah) 62:4 "No longer will they call you **Deserted,** or name your land **Desolate**. But you will be called

Hephzibah, and your land Beulah; for HaShem will take delight in you, **and your land will be married."**

Yesha'yahu (Isaiah) **63:16-17** "For You are our Father, though Avraham does not know us, and Yisra'el does not recognize us. You, O HaShem, are our Father, our Redeemer – Your Name is from of old. O HaShem, why do You make us stray from Your Ways, and harden our heart from Your Fear? **Turn back, for the sake of Your servants, the Tribes of Your inheritance."**

Yesha'yahu (Isaiah) **66:19-22** "And I will set a sign among them, and I will send those that escape of them unto the nations, to Tarshish, Pul, and Lud, that draw the bow, to Tubal, and Javan, to the isles afar off, that have not heard My Fame, neither have seen My Glory; and they shall declare My Glory among the Gentiles. 20 'And they shall bring all your brethren for an offering unto HaShem out of all nations upon horses, and in chariots, and in litters, and upon mules, and upon swift beasts, to My Holy Mountain Jerusalem,' saith HaShem, as the children of Israel bring an offering in a clean vessel into the House of HaShem. 21 And I will also take of them for priests and for Levites, saith HaShem. For as the new heavens and the new earth, which I will make, shall remain before Me,' saith HaShem, 'so shall your seed and your name remain.'"

Yermiyahu (Jeremiah) **6:9** "This is what HaShem Almighty says: "**Let them glean the remnant of Israel as thoroughly as**

a vine; pass your hand over the branches again, like one gathering grapes."

Yermiyahu (Jeremiah) 16:14-21 "However, the days are coming," declares HaShem, "when men will no longer say, 'As surely as HaShem lives, who brought the Israelites up out of Egypt,' 15 but they will say, 'As surely as HaShem lives, **who brought the Israelites up out of the land of the north and out of all the countries where He had banished them.' For I will restore them to the land I gave their forefathers.** 16 "But now I will send for many fishermen," declares HaShem, "and they will catch them. After that I will send for many hunters, and they will hunt them down on every mountain and hill and from the crevices of the rocks. 17 My eyes are on all their ways; they are not hidden from me, nor is their sin concealed from My eyes. 18 I will repay them double for their wickedness and their sin, because they have defiled My Land with the lifeless forms of their vile images and have filled My Inheritance with their detestable idols." 19 O HaShem, my strength and my fortress, my refuge in time of distress, **to you the nations will come from the ends of the earth and say, "Our fathers possessed nothing but false gods, worthless idols that did them no good."**

Yermiyahu (Jeremiah) 23:3-6 "Therefore **I shall gather the remnant of My flock out of all the lands where I have driven them, and shall bring them back to their fold.** And they shall bear and increase. And I shall raise up shepherds over them, and they shall feed them. And they shall fear no more, nor be discouraged, nor shall they be lacking," declares HaShem." See, the days are coming," declares HaShem, when I shall raise for David a Branch of Righteousness, and a Sovereign shall reign and act wisely, and shall do right-ruling and righteousness in the earth. In His days **Yehudah shall be saved, and Israel dwell safely."**

Yermiyahu (Jeremiah) 23:7,8 "So, then the days are coming - it is HaShem Who speaks - when people will no longer say, "As HaShem lives Who brought the sons of Israel out of the Land of Egypt," but, "As HaShem lives, Who led back and brought home the descendants of the House of Israel out of the land of the North and from all the countries to which He had dispersed them, to live on their own soil."

Yermiyahu (Jeremiah) 16:14,15 " .... I will bring them back to the very soil I gave their ancestors." *rest of the text is identical*)

Yermiyahu (Jeremiah) 24:5-7 "This is what HaShem, the G-d of Israel, says: 'Like these good figs, I regard as good **the exiles from Judah** whom I sent away from this place to the land of the Babylonians. 6 My eyes will watch over them for their good, **and I will bring them back to this land. I will build them up and not tear them down; I will plant them and not uproot them. 7 I will give them a heart to know Me, that I am HaShem. They will be My People, and I will be their G-d, for they will return to Me with all their heart."**

Yermiyahu (Jeremiah) 29:13-14 "And you shall seek Me, and shall find Me, when you search for Me with all your heart.

And I shall be found by you,' declares HaShem, "and **I shall turn back your captivity (return you from exile), and shall gather you from all the Gentiles and from all the places where I have driven you,** declares HaShem. **And I shall bring you back to the place from which I have exiled you.**"

Yermiyahu (Jeremiah) 30:7-10 "The days are coming,' declares HaShem, 'when **I will bring my people Israel and Judah back from captivity and restore them to the land** I gave their forefathers to possess,' These are the words HaShem spoke concerning Israel and Judah." 9 "'On that Day' - it is HaShem Tzva'ot Who speaks, 'they will serve their G-d and David their King whom I will raise up for them. So do not be afraid My servant Jacob' - it is HaShem Who speaks - 'Israel do not be alarmed. Look, **I will rescue you from distant countries** and your descendants from the country where they are captive. Jacob will have quiet again and live at ease with no one to trouble him. For I am with you to save you. I will make an end of all the nations where I have scattered you; **I will not make an end of you**, only discipline you in moderation so as not to let you go unpunished. 10 "And you, do not fear, O Ya'akov My servant,' declares HaShem, 'nor be discouraged, O Israel. For look, I am saving you from afar, and **your seed from the land of their captivity. And Ya'akov shall return,** and have rest and be at ease, with no one to trouble him.'"

Yermiyahu (Jeremiah) 30:17-24

17 "But I will restore you to health and heal your wounds,' declares HaShem, 'because you are called an outcast, Zion for

whom no one cares.' 18 "This is what HaShem says: " '**I will return back the captivity (exile) of Jacob's tents** and have compassion on his dwellings; the city will be rebuilt on her ruins, and the palace will stand in its proper place.' 19 From them will come songs of thanksgiving and the sound of rejoicing. I will add to their numbers, and they will not be decreased; I will bring them honor, and they will not be disdained. 20 Their children will be **as in days of old**, and their community will be established before me; I will punish all who oppress them. 21 Their leader will be one of their own; their ruler will arise from among them. I will bring him near and he will come close to me, for who is he who will devote himself to be close to me?' declares HaShem. 22 " 'So you will be My People, and I will be your G-d.' " ......

24 The fierce anger of HaShem will not turn back **until He fully accomplishes the purposes of His heart. In the latter days you shall understand it.**"

Yermiyahu (Jeremiah) 31:1-14 "At that time," declares HaShem "I will be the G-d of all the clans of Israel, and they will be my people." 2 This is what HaShem says: "The people who survive the sword (in exile) will find favor in the desert; I will come to give rest to Israel." 4 I will build you up again and you will be rebuilt, O Virgin Israel. Again you will take up your tambourines and go out to dance with the joyful. 5 Again you will plant vineyards on the hills of Samaria; the farmers will plant them and enjoy their fruit. 6 There will be a day when watchmen cry out on the hills of Ephraim, 'Come, let us go up to Zion, to HaShem our G-d.' " 7 This is what HaShem says: "Sing with joy for Ya'akov; shout for the foremost of the nations. Make your praises heard, and say, HaShem, save your people, the remnant of Israel.' 8 See, **I will bring them from the land of the North and gather them from the ends of the earth.** Among them will be the blind and the lame, expectant mothers and women in labor; a great throng will return. 9 They will come with weeping; they will pray as I bring them back. I will lead them beside streams of water on a level path where they will not stumble, because I am Israel's father, and Ephraim is my firstborn son. 10 "Hear the word of HaShem, O nations; proclaim it in distant coastlands: '**He who scattered Israel will gather them** and will watch over his flock like a shepherd.' 11 For HaShem will ransom Ya'akov and redeem them from the hand of those stronger than they. 12 They will come and shout for joy on the heights of Zion; they will rejoice in the bounty of HaShem - the grain, the new wine and the oil, the young of the flocks and herds. They will be like a well-watered garden, and they will sorrow no more. 13 Then maidens will dance and be glad, young men and old as well. I will turn their mourning into gladness; I will give them comfort and joy instead of sorrow. 14 I will satisfy the priests with abundance, and my people will be filled with my bounty," declares HaShem.

---

16 ... "**They will return from the land of the enemy.** 17 So there is hope for your future," declares HaShem. "**Your children will return to their own land.** ...... 20 Is not Ephraim My dear son, the child in whom I delight? Though I often speak against him, I still remember him. Therefore My Heart yearns for him; I have great compassion for him," declares HaShem. 21 Return, O Virgin Israel, return to your towns. .... 22 How long will you wander, O unfaithful daughter? HaShem will create a new thing on earth - the Woman sets out to find

her Husband again." 23 This is what HaShem Almighty, the G-d of Israel, says: "**When I bring them back from captivity,** the people in the land of Judah and in its towns will once again use these words: 'HaShem bless you, O righteous dwelling, O sacred mountain.' 24 **People will live together in Judah and all its towns** - farmers and those who move about with their flocks. 25 I will refresh the weary and satisfy the faint."

27 "The days are coming," declares HaShem, "when I will plant **the House of Israel and the House of Judah** with the offspring of men and of animals. 28 Just as I watched over them to uproot and tear down, and to overthrow, destroy and bring disaster, so I will watch over them to build and to plant," declares HaShem.

35 This is what HaShem says, He who appoints the sun to shine by day, Who decrees the moon and stars to shine by night, Who stirs up the sea so that its waves roar - HaShem Almighty is his name: 36 "Only if these decrees vanish from my sight," declares HaShem, "will the descendants of Israel ever cease to be a nation before me." 37 This is what HaShem says: "Only if the heavens above can be measured and the foundations of the earth below be searched out will I reject all the descendants of Israel because of all they have done," declares HaShem. 38 "The days are coming," declares HaShem, "when this city will be rebuilt for me from the Tower of Hananel to the Corner Gate. 40 ..... **The city will never again be uprooted or demolished.**"

Yermiyahu (Jeremiah) 32:37-44   "See, **I am gathering them out of all the lands where I have driven them** in My displeasure, and in My wrath, and in great rage. And **I shall**

bring them back to this place, and shall let them dwell in safety. And they shall be My people, and I shall be their G-d. And I shall give them one heart and one way, to fear Me all the days, for the good of them and of their children after them. And I shall make an everlasting covenant with them, that I do not turn back from doing good to them. And I shall put My fear in their hearts so as not to turn aside from Me. And I shall rejoice over them to do good to them, and shall plant them in this land in truth, with all My heart and with all My being. For thus said HaShem, 'As I have brought all this great evil on this people, so I am bringing on them all the good that I am speaking to them. And fields shall be bought in this land of which you are saying, "It is a wasteland, without man or beast. It has been given into the hand of the Chaldeans." '**Fields shall be bought for silver, and deeds signed and sealed,** and witnesses be called, in the land of Binyamin, and in the **places around Yerushalayim, and in the cities of Yehudah, and in the cities of the mountains, and in the cities of the low country, and in the cities of the South.** For I shall turn back their captivity (return them from exile),' declares HaShem."

Yermiyahu (Jeremiah) 33:6-9 "... I will heal My people and will let them enjoy abundant peace and security. 7 **I will bring Judah and Israel back from captivity (return them from exile) and will rebuild them as they were before.** 8 I will cleanse them from all the sin they have committed against Me and will forgive all their sins of rebellion against Me. 9 Then this city (Jerusalem) will bring Me renown, joy, praise and honor before all nations on earth that hear of all the good things I do for it; and they will be in awe and will tremble at the abundant prosperity and peace I provide for it.."

Yermiyahu (Jeremiah) 33:10-13 "This is what HaShem says: 'You say about this place, "It is a desolate waste, without men or animals." Yet in the towns of Judah and the streets of Jerusalem that are deserted, inhabited by neither men nor animals, there will be heard once more 11 the sounds of joy and gladness, the voices of bride and bridegroom, and the voices of those who bring thank offerings to the house of HaShem, ... **'For I will restore the fortunes of the land as they were before,'** says HaShem. 12 This is what HaShem Almighty says: 'In this place, desolate and without men or animals—in all its towns there will again be pastures for shepherds to rest their flocks. 13 In the towns of the hill country, of the western foothills and of the Negev, in the territory of Benjamin, in the villages around Jerusalem and in the towns of Judah, flocks will again pass under the hand of the One who counts them,' says HaShem.

Yermiyahu (Jeremiah) 33:14-16 "See, the days are coming,' declares HaShem, 'when I shall establish the good word which I have promised to **the House of Israel and to the House of Yehudah:** In those days and at that time I cause a Branch of Righteousness to spring forth for David. And He shall do right-ruling and righteousness in the earth. In those days Yehudah shall be saved, and Jerusalem dwell in safety.

And this is that which shall be proclaimed to her: HaShem our Righteousness."

Yermiyahu (Jeremiah) 33:23-26 "The word of HaShem came to Jeremiah: 24 "Have you not noticed that these people are saying, 'HaShem has rejected the two kingdoms He chose'? So they despise My people and no longer regard them as a nation. 25 This is what HaShem says: 'If I have not established My Covenant with day and night and the fixed laws of heaven and earth, 26 then I will reject the descendants of Jacob and David My servant and will not choose one of his sons to rule over the descendants of Avraham, Isaac and Jacob. For **I will restore their fortunes and have compassion on them.'** "

Yermiyahu (Jeremiah) 46:27-28 "But as for you, do not fear, O My servant Ya'akov, and do not be discouraged, O Israel! For look, I am saving you from afar, and your descendants from the land of their captivity. And Ya'akov shall return, and shall have rest and be at ease, with no one disturbing. Do not fear, O Ya'akov My servant," declares HaShem, "for I am with you. Though I make a complete end of all the gentiles to which I have driven you, yet I do not make a complete end of you. But I shall reprove you in right-ruling, and by no means leave you unpunished."

Yermiyahu (Jeremiah) 50:4-5 "In those days and at that time," declares HaShem, **"the children of Israel shall**

come, they and the children of Judah together, weeping as they come, and seek HaShem their G-d. They shall ask the way to Zion, their faces toward it, 'Come and let us join ourselves to HaShem in an everlasting covenant, never to be forgotten.

Yermiyahu (Jeremiah) 50:19-20 "And I shall bring back Israel to his pasture, and he shall feed on Karmel and Bashan. And his being shall be satisfied on Mount Ephraim and Gilead. In those days and at that time," declares HaShem, "the crookedness of Israel shall be searched for, but there shall be none; and the sin of Judah, but none shall be found. For I shall pardon those whom I leave as a remnant."

Yermiyahu (Jeremiah) 51:5 "For neither Israel nor Judah is widowed by his G-d, HaShem Sabaoth Tzav'ot, though their land has been filled with sin against the Holy One of Israel."

Yechezkiel (Ezekiel) 11:16-20 "Therefore say: 'This is what the Sovereign HaShem says: Although I sent them far away among the nations and scattered them among the countries, yet for a little while I have been a Sanctuary for them in the countries where they have gone.' 17 "Therefore say: 'This is what the Sovereign HaShem says: scattered I will gather you from the nations and bring you back from the countries where you have been, and I will give you back the land of

SCRIPTURES THAT FORETOLD THE RESTORATION OF THE HOUSE OF ISRAEL

Israel again.' 18 "They will return to it and remove all its vile images and detestable idols. 19 I will give them an undivided heart and put a new spirit in them; I will remove from them their heart of stone and give them a heart of flesh. 20 so that they can keep My Laws and respect My Judgments and put them into practice. Then they will be My People and I shall be their G-d."

Yechezkiel (Ezekiel) 14:6-8 "So say to the House of Israel, "The Sovereign HaShem says this: **Come back**, turn away from your foul idols, turn your backs on all your loathsome practices; for if any member of the House of Israel – or any foreigner living in Israel – deserts Me to enshrine his foul idols in his heart and places the cause of his sinning right before his eyes and then approaches a prophet to consult Me through him, he will get his answer from Me, HaShem. I shall set my face against that person; I shall make him an example and a byword; I shall rid My People of him, and you will know that I am HaShem.

21-23 "The Sovereign HaShem says this, "Even if I send my four dreadful scourges on Jerusalem – sword, famine, wild beasts and plague – to denude it of human and animal, even so, there will be a remnant left, a few men and women who come through; when they come to you and you see their conduct and actions, you will take comfort in spite of the disaster which I have brought on Jerusalem, in spite of all I have brought on her, They will comfort you, when you see their conduct and actions, and so you will know that I have not done in vain all I have done to her – declares the Sovereign HaShem."

(*New Jerusalem Bible*)

Yechezkiel (Ezekiel) 20:34-44 "**I will bring you from the nations and gather you from the countries where you have been scattered**—with a mighty hand and an outstretched arm and with outpoured wrath. 35 I will bring you into the desert of the nations and there, face to face, I will execute judgment upon you. 36 As I judged your fathers in the desert of the land of Egypt, so I will judge you, declares the Sovereign HaShem. 37 I will take note of you as you pass under my rod, and I will bring you into the bond of the Covenant. 38 I will purge you of those who revolt and rebel against Me. Although I will bring them out of the land where they are living, yet they will not enter the land of Israel. Then you will know that I am HaShem. 39 " 'As for you, **O house of Israel**, this is what the Sovereign HaShem says: Go and serve your idols, every one of you! But afterward you will surely listen to me and no longer profane my holy name with your gifts and idols. 40 For on my holy mountain, the high mountain of Israel, declares the Sovereign HaShem, there in the land **the entire house of Israel will serve me, and there I will accept them**. There I will require your offerings and your choice gifts (gifts of your firstfruits), along with all your holy sacrifices. 41 I will accept you as fragrant incense when I bring you out from the nations and gather you from the countries where you have been scattered, and I will show myself holy among you in the sight of the nations. 42 **Then you will know that I am HaShem, when I bring you into the land of Israel, the land I had sworn with uplifted hand to give to your fathers.** 43 There you will remember your conduct and all the actions by which you have defiled yourselves, and you will loathe yourselves for all the evil you have done. 44 You will know that I am HaShem, when I deal with you for My Name's sake and not according to your evil ways and your corrupt practices, **O house of Israel**, declares the Sovereign HaShem.' "

Yechezkiel (Ezekiel) 28:25-26 25 " 'This is what the Sovereign HaShem says: **When I gather the people of Israel from the nations where they have been scattered, I will show Myself Holy among them in the sight of the nations. Then they will live in their own land, which I gave to My servant Ya'akov.** 26 They will live there in safety and **will build houses and plant vineyards;** they will live in safety when I inflict punishment on all their neighbors who maligned them. Then they will know that I am HaShem their G-d.' "

Yechezkiel (Ezekiel) 34:11-30 " 'For this is what the Sovereign HaShem says: **I Myself will search for My sheep and look after them.** 12 As a shepherd looks after his scattered flock when he is with them, so will I look after My sheep. I will rescue them from all the places where they were scattered on a day of clouds and darkness. 13 **I will bring them out from the nations and gather them from the countries, and I will bring them into their own land.** I will pasture them on the mountains of Israel, in the ravines and in all the settlements in the land. 14 I will tend them in a good pasture, and the mountain heights of Israel will be their grazing land. There they will lie down in good grazing land, and there they will feed in a rich pasture on the mountains of Israel. 15 **I Myself will tend My sheep and have them lie down, declares the**

Sovereign HaShem. 16 I will search for the lost and bring back the strays. I will bind up the injured and strengthen the weak, but the sleek and the strong I will destroy. I will shepherd the flock with justice. 17 " 'As for you, My flock, this is what the Sovereign HaShem says: I will judge between one sheep and another, and between rams and goats. 18 Is it not enough for you to feed on the good pasture? Must you also trample the rest of your pasture with your feet? Is it not enough for you to drink clear water? Must you also muddy the rest with your feet? 19 Must My flock feed on what you have trampled and drink what you have muddied with your feet? 20 " 'Therefore this is what the Sovereign HaShem says to them: See, I Myself will judge between the fat sheep and the lean sheep. 21 Because you shove with flank and shoulder, butting all the weak sheep with your horns until you have driven them away, 22 I will save My flock, and they will no longer be plundered. I will judge between one sheep and another. 23 I will place over them one shepherd, My servant David, and he will tend them; he will tend them and be their shepherd. 24 I HaShem will be their G-d, and My servant David will be prince among them. I HaShem have spoken. 25 " 'I will make a Covenant of peace with them and rid the land of wild beasts so that they may live in the desert and sleep in the forests in safety. 26 I will bless them and the places surrounding My hill. I will send down showers in season; there will be showers of blessing. 27 The trees of the field will yield their fruit and the ground will yield its crops; the people will be secure in their land. They will know that I am HaShem, when I break the bars of their yoke and rescue them from the hands of those who enslaved them. 28 They will no longer be plundered by the nations, nor will wild animals devour them. They will live in safety, and no one will make them afraid. 29 I will provide for them a land renowned for its crops, and they will no longer be victims of famine in the land or bear the scorn of the nations. 30 Then they will know that I, HaShem their G-d, am with them and that they, **the house of Israel, are My people,** declares the Sovereign HaShem"

Yechezkiel (Ezekiel) 35 1 "The Word of HaShem came to me: 2 "Son of man, set your face against Mount Seir; prophesy against it 3 and say: 'This is what the Sovereign HaShem says: I am against you, Mount Seir, and I will stretch out My hand against you and make you a desolate waste. 4 I will turn your towns into ruins and you will be desolate. Then you will know that I am HaShem .

5 " 'Because you harbored an ancient hostility and delivered the Israelites over to the sword at the time of their calamity, the time their punishment reached its climax, 6 therefore as surely as I live, declares the Sovereign HaShem, I will give you over to bloodshed and it will pursue you. Since you did not hate bloodshed, bloodshed will pursue you. 7 I will make Mount Seir a desolate waste and cut off from it all who come and go. 8 I will fill your mountains with the slain; those killed by the sword will fall on your hills and in your valleys and in all your ravines. 9 I will make you desolate forever; your towns will not be inhabited. Then you will know that I am HaShem. 10 " 'Because you have said, **"These two nations (Northern and Southern Kingdom) and these two lands will be ours and we will take possession of them,"** even though I HaShem was there, 11 therefore as surely as I live, declares the Sovereign HaShem, I will treat you in accordance with the anger and jealousy you showed in your hatred of them and I will make Myself known among them when I judge you. 12 Then you will know that I HaShem have heard all the contemptible things

you have said against **the mountains of Israel.** You said, "They have been laid waste and have been given over to us to devour." 13 You boasted against Me and spoke against Me without restraint, and I heard it. 14 This is what the Sovereign HaShem says: While the whole earth rejoices, I will make you desolate. 15 Because you rejoiced when the inheritance of the house of Israel became desolate, that is how I will treat you. You will be desolate, O Mount Seir, you and all of Edom. Then they will know that I am HaShem.' "

Yechezkiel 47 : 1-12 has a vision of the New Temple with living waters flowing from it towards the Dead Sea and the Mediterranean.

13 "This is what the Sovereign HaShem says: "**These are the boundaries by which you are to divide the land for an inheritance among the twelve tribes of Israel, with two portions for Joseph. 14 You are to divide it equally among them. Because I swore with uplifted hand to give it to your forefathers. This land will become your inheritance.** 15 "This is to be the boundary of the Land: "On the North side it will run **from the Great Sea** by the Hethlon road past Lebo Hamath to Zedad, 16 Berothah and Sibraim (which lies on the border between Damascus and Hamath), as far as Hazer Hatticon, which is on the border of Hauran. 17 The boundary will extend from the sea to Hazar Enan, along the northern border of **Damascus,** with the border of Hamath to the North. This will be **the North boundary.** 18 "On the East side the boundary will run between Hauran and **Damascus,** along the Jordan between Gilead and the land of Israel, to the Eastern sea and as far as Tamar. This will be the

East boundary. 19 "On the South side it will run from Tamar as far as the waters of Meribah Kadesh, then along the **Wadi of Egypt to the Great Sea**. This will be **the South boundary**. 20 "On the West side, the Great Sea will be the boundary to a point opposite Lebo Hamath. This will be **the West boundary**. 21 **"You are to distribute this land among yourselves according to the Tribes of Israel. 22 You are to allot it as an inheritance for yourselves and for the aliens who have settled among you and who have children. You are to consider them as native-born Israelites; along with you they are to be allotted an inheritance among the Tribes of Israel. 23 In whatever Tribe the alien settles, there you are to give him his inheritance,"** declares the Sovereign HaShem."

Yechezkiel (Ezekiel) 48 Verses 1 - 28 deal with the apportionment of the Land (between the borders determined in ch. 47) amongst the Twelve Tribes. 29 **"This is the Land you are to allot as an inheritance to the tribes of Israel, and these will be their portions,"** declares the Sovereign HaShem. 30 "These will be the exits of the city: Beginning on the North side, which is 4,500 cubits long, 31 **the gates of the city will be named after the Tribes of Israel**. The three gates on the North side will be the gate of Reuben, the gate of Judah and the gate of Levi. 32 On the East side, which is 4,500 cubits long, will be three gates: the gate of Joseph, the gate of Benjamin and the gate of Dan. 33 On the South side, which measures 4,500 cubits, will be three gates: the gate of Simeon, the gate of Issachar and the gate of Zebulun. 34 On the West side, which is 4,500 cubits long, will be three gates: the gate of Gad, the gate of Asher and the gate of Naphtali. 35 "The distance all around will be 18,000 cubits. "And the name of the city from that time on will be: **HaShem is there** ."

Daniel 12 1 "At that time Michael, the great prince who protects your people, will arise. There will be a time of distress such as has not happened from the beginning of nations until then. **But at that time your people—everyone whose name is found written in the book—will be delivered.** 2 Multitudes who sleep in the dust of the earth will awake: some to everlasting life, others to shame and everlasting contempt. 3 Those who are wise will shine like the brightness of the heavens, and those who lead many to righteousness, like the stars for ever and ever. 4 But you, Daniel, close up and seal the words of the scroll until the time of the end. Many will go here and there to increase knowledge." 5 Then I, Daniel, looked, and there before me stood two others, one on this bank of the river and one on the opposite bank. 6 One of them said to the man clothed in linen, who was above the waters of the river, "How long will it be before these astonishing things are fulfilled?" 7 The man clothed in linen, who was above the waters of the river, lifted his right hand and his left hand toward heaven, and I heard him swear by him who lives forever, saying, "It will be for a time, times and half a time. When the power of the holy people has been finally broken, all these things will be completed." 8 I heard, but I did not understand. So I asked, "My Lord, what will the outcome of all this be?" 9 He replied, "Go your way, Daniel, because the words are closed up and sealed until the time of the end ..... 13 As for you, go your way till the end. You will rest, and then at the end of the days you will rise to receive your allotted inheritance."

Amos 5:1 " Listen to this Oracle spoken against you, O House of Israel, this lament I take up concerning you: "The Virgin of Israel fell, and will never get up" .... 4 For HaShem says this to the House of Israel: 'Seek Me, and you shall live'.

Rabbi Eliezer explains the words "It will never get up?" as follows: "A possible explanation is that the House of Israel will not "get up" as an independent entity, but it will get up as an entity totally incumbent to the kingdom of Judah."

Amos 9:8 - "Now My eyes are turned on the sinful Kingdom ('the sons of Israel, verse 7) to wipe it off the face of the earth. Yet I am not going to destroy the House of Ya'akov completely", it is HaShem Who speaks. 9 "For now I will issue orders and shake the House of Israel amongst all the nations, as you shake a sieve, so that not one pebble can fall on the ground. 10 All the sinners of My People are going to perish by the sword, all those who say 'No misfortune will ever touch us, nor even come anywhere near us.' 11 That Day **I will re-erect the Fallen Succah (Tabernacle) of David**, make good the gaps in it, restore its ruins and rebuild it as it was in the days of old, 12 **so that they can conquer the remnant of Edom and all the nations bearing My Name.** It is HaShem Who speaks, and He will carry this out .... 14 **I mean to restore the fortunes of My People**

Israel. They will rebuild the ruined cities and live in them, plant vineyards and drink their wine, dig gardens and eat their produce. **15 I will plant them in their own country, never to be rooted up again out of the Land I have given them**', says HaShem your G-d."

Tzefanyah 2:1-11 "**Gather together, gather together,** O shameful nation, 2 before the appointed time arrives and that day sweeps on like chaff, before the fierce anger of HaShem comes upon you, before the day of HaShem's wrath comes upon you. 3 Seek HaShem, all you humble of the land, you who do what he commands. Seek righteousness, seek humility; perhaps you will be sheltered on the day of HaShem's anger. 4 Gaza will be abandoned and Ashkelon left in ruins. At midday Ashdod will be emptied and Ekron uprooted. 5 Woe to you who live by the sea, O Kerethite (Philistine tribe) people; the word of HaShem is against you, O Canaan, land of the Philistines. "I will destroy you, and none will be left." 6 The land by the sea, where the Kerethites dwell, will be a place for shepherds and sheep pens. 7 "**And the coast shall be for the remnant of the house of Judah**; there they will find pasture. In the evening they will lie down in the houses of Ashkelon. **HaShem their G-d will care for them; he will bring back their captives (the exiled ones)** 8 "I have heard the insults of Moab and the taunts of the Ammonites, who insulted my people and made threats against their land. 9 Therefore, as surely as I live," declares HaShem Almighty, the G-d of Israel, "surely Moab will become like Sodom, the Ammonites like Gomorrah— a place of weeds and salt pits, a wasteland forever. **The remnant of my people** will plunder them; **the survivors of my nation will inherit their**

land." 10 This is what they will get in return for their pride, for insulting and mocking the people of HaShem Almighty. 11 HaShem will be awesome to them when he destroys all the gods of the land. The nations on every shore will worship him, every one in its own land."

Tzefanyah (Zephaniah) 3:12 - 20 "In your midst, I will leave a lowly and humble People. And those who are left in Israel, will seek refuge in the Name of HaShem. 13 The remnant of Israel will do no wrong; they will speak no lies, nor will deceit be found in their mouths. They will eat and lie down and no one will make them afraid." 14 "Sing, O daughter of Zion; shout, O Israel; be glad and rejoice with all the heart, O daughter of Jerusalem. **HaShem has taken away your judgments, He has cast out your enemy: HaShem, the King of Israel, is in the midst of you:** you shall not see evil any more. In that day it shall be said to Jerusalem, 'Fear not,' and to Zion, 'Let not your hands be slack. HaShem your G-d is in you midst, a victorious Warrior. He will rejoice over you with joy; He will renew you by His Love; He will dance with shouts of Joy for you.' 18 I will gather those of yours who grieve over the appointed feasts and bear the burden of reproach (because they can not keep them). 19 When that time comes, I will deal with all those who oppress you. I will save her who is lame, gather her who was driven away and make them whose shame spread over the earth the object of praise and renown. 20 **At that time will I bring you again,** even in the time that I gather you: for **I will make you a name and a praise among all people of the earth, when I turn back your captivity before your eyes,'** says HaShem."

(David Stern translation)

Zecharyah (Zechariah) 2:7-12   "Come, O Zion! Escape, you who live in the Daughter of Babylon!" 8 For this is what HaShem Almighty says: "After he has honored me and has sent me against the nations that have plundered you—for whoever touches you touches the apple of His eye. 9 I will surely raise my hand against them so that their slaves will plunder them. Then you will know that HaShem Almighty has sent me. 10 "Shout and be glad, O Daughter of Zion. For I am coming, and I will live among you," declares HaShem. 11 **"Many nations will be joined with HaShem in that day and will become My people. I will live among you and you will know that HaShem Almighty has sent me to you. 12   HaShem will inherit Judah as his portion in the Holy Land and will again choose Jerusalem."**

Zecharyah (Zechariah) 8:2-14 "HaShem Tzav'ot *(of Hosts)* says this, 'I am extremely jealous for Zion, with great fury for her sake. 3 HaShem Tzva'ot says this, **'I am coming back to Zion and shall live in Jerusalem .....** 6 "Thus said HaShem Tzva'ot, 'If this *(His Return)* seems a Miracle in the eyes of the remnant of this people in those days, should it also be a Miracle in My eyes?' 7   Thus said HaShem Tzva'ot, **'See, I am saving My people from the countries of the East and from the countries of the West. And I shall bring them back, and they shall dwell in the midst of Jerusalem. And they shall be My people, and I shall be their G-d, in truth and in righteousness."** ..... *(Jerusalem Bible, David Stern)*. 11 "But from now on,

I will not treat the remnant of this People as I did before, ' says HaShem Tzva'ot. 13 'Now they will sow in Peace, the vine will give its fruit, the ground will produce its yield, the sky will give its yield - and I will cause the remnant of this People to possess all these things. 14 House of Judah and House of Israel, just as you were formerly a curse amongst the nations, now I will **save you, and you shall be a blessing.** Do not fear, but take courage."

Zecharyah (Zechariah) 8:23 "Thus says HaShem of Hosts: 'In those days it shall come to pass, that ten men *(referring to Ten Tribes?)* shall take hold, out of all the languages of the nations, they shall take hold of the skirt of him that is a Jew, saying, 'We will go with you, for we have heard that G-d is with you.'"

Zecharyah (Zechariah) 9:13-17 "**For I have bent Judah as My bow, and made Ephraim its arrow,** and I shall stir up your sons, O Zion, against your sons, O Greece, and I shall make you like the sword of a mighty man." .... 16 "And HaShem their G-d shall save them in that day, as the flock of His people, for the y will be like gems in a crown sparkling over His Land. 17 What wealth is theirs, what beauty?'"

Zecharyah (Zechariah) 10:6-12 "And I will strengthen **the House of Judah,** and I will save **the House of Joseph,** and **I will bring them back** in My Compassion for them: and they shall be as though I had not driven them out for I am HaShem their G-d, and I will hear them. **7-10** And they of Ephraim shall be like warriors, and their heart shall rejoice as through wine: yea, their children shall see it, and be glad; their heart shall rejoice in HaShem. I will whistle for them, and **gather them; for I have redeemed them: they shall be as numerous as they were before.** 9. And I will sow them among the people: and they shall remember Me in far countries; and they shall live with their children, and **then return. I will bring them again also out of the land of Egypt, and gather them out of Assyria; and I will bring them into the land of Gilead and Lebanon; until there is no more room for them.** 11 And he shall pass through the sea with affliction, and shall smite the waves in the sea, and all the deeps of the river shall dry up: and the pride of Assyria shall be brought down, and the sceptre of Egypt shall depart away. And I will strengthen them in HaShem; and they shall travel here and there in His Name, says HaShem."

Hoshea (Hosea) 2:1 (alt.1:10) "Nevertheless, the people of Israel will number as many as the grains of sand by the sea, which cannot be counted or measured, so that the time will come when, instead of being told, "You are not My People,' it will be said to them, "You are the children of the Living G-d". 2:2 (alt. 1:11) Then the people of **Judah** and the people of **Israel** will be **reunited,** and they will appoint one leader and will come up out of the land, for that will be a great day, the day of **Jezreel**." (the replanting of those who were scattered).

(David Stern)

Hoshea (Hosea) 2:13-23 I will punish her for the days she burned incense to the Baals; she decked herself with rings and jewelry, and went after her lovers, but me she forgot," declares HaShem. 14 "Therefore I am now going to allure her; I will lead her into the valley of Achor and speak tenderly to her. 15 **There I will give her back her vineyards, and will make the Valley of Achor a door of hope. There she will sing as in the days of her youth, as in the day she came up out of Egypt. 16 "In that day," declares HaShem, "you will call me 'my husband'; you will no longer call me 'my master.'** 17 I will remove the names of the Baals from her lips; no longer will their names be invoked. 18 In that day I will make a Covenant for them with the beasts of the field and the birds of the air and the creatures that move along the ground. Bow and sword and battle I will abolish from the land, so that all may lie down in safety. 19 **I will betroth you to me forever; I will betroth you in righteousness and justice, in love and compassion. 20 I will betroth you in faithfulness, and you will acknowledge HaShem** 21 "In that day I will respond," declares HaShem —"I will respond to the skies, and they will respond to the earth; 22 and the earth will respond to the grain, the new wine and oil, and they will respond to Jezreel. (HaShem plants) 23 I **will plant her for myself in the land; I will show my love to the one I called 'Not my loved one. I will say to those called 'Not my people,' 'You are my people'; and they will say, 'You are my G-d.' "**

Hoshea (Hosea) 3:1-5 "HaShem said to me, "Go a second time, show your love to your wife again, though she is loved by another and is an adulteress. Love her just as HaShem loves the people of Israel, though they turn to other gods and love the sacred raisin cakes (*offered to these gods*). 2. So I bought her back for myself for fifteen pieces of silver and eight bushels of barley. 3. Then I told her, "You are to remain in seclusion for a long time and be mine; you must not be a prostitute or be intimate with any man, and I will do the same for you."

4 For the sons of Israel will live many days without king or prince, without sacrifice or sacred stones, without standing stone, ritual vest or household gods. 5 Afterwards, the Israelites will repent and seek HaShem their G-d and David their king. **They will come trembling to HaShem and to his blessings in the last days."**

(D. Stern, Jerusalem Bible)

Hoshea (Hosea) 6:1-11 "Come, let us return to HaShem. He has torn us to pieces but He will heal us; He has injured us but He will bind up our wounds. 2 **After two days He will revive us; on the third day He will restore us, that we may live in His Presence.** 3 Let us acknowledge HaShem; let us press on to acknowledge Him. As surely as the sun rises, He will appear; He will come to us like the winter rains, like the spring rains that water the earth." 4 "**What can I do with you, Ephraim? What can I do with you, Judah?** Your love is like the morning mist, like the early dew that disappears. 5 Therefore I cut you in pieces with My prophets, I killed you with the words of My Mouth; My judgments flashed like lightning upon you. 6 For I desire mercy, not sacrifice, and acknowledgment of G-d rather than burnt offerings. 7 Like Adam, they have broken the Covenant— they were unfaithful to Me there. 8 Gilead is a city of wicked men, stained with footprints of blood. 9 As marauders lie in ambush for a man, so do bands of priests; they murder on the road to Shechem, committing shameful crimes. 10

I have seen a horrible thing in the House of Israel. There Ephraim is given to prostitution and Israel is defiled. 11 "Also for you, Judah, *(Note: Israel AND Judah)* a harvest is appointed. "Whenever I would restore the exile of my people."

Hoshea (Hosea) 11:7-10 "My people is unsure about returning to Me. It is summoned to the Most High One, but it does not rise in unity. Ephraim, how can I give you up, or surrender you Israel? .... My Heart recoils at the idea, as compassion warms within Me. I will not give vent to the fierceness of My Rage. I will not return to destroy Ephraim. For I am G-d, not a human being; the Holy One amongst you, so I will not come in fury. 10. They will follow HaShem [when He calls] like a roaring lion, for when He roars, the children **will hasten from the West.** They will hasten like a bird from Egypt and like a dove from Assyria; and I shall resettle them in their homes."

(Stone Chumash translation and David Stern translation) (Note: Ref to 'Dove' Kol HaTor = Voice of the Dove)

Hoshea (Hosea) 14 1 Return, O Israel, to HaShem your G-d. Your sins have been your downfall! 2 **Take words with you and return to HaShem.** Say to him: "Forgive all our sins and receive us graciously, that we may offer the fruit of our lips. 3 Assyria cannot save us; we will not mount warhorses. We will never again say 'Our g-ds' to what our own hands have made, for in you the fatherless find compassion." 4 "I will heal their waywardness and love them freely, for my anger has turned away from them. 5 **I will be like the dew to Israel; he will blossom like a lily.** Like a cedar of Lebanon he will send down his roots; 6 **his young shoots will grow.** His splendor will be like an olive tree, his fragrance like a cedar of Lebanon. 7 Men will dwell again in his shade. He will flourish like the grain. **He will blossom like a vine,** and his fame will be like the wine from Lebanon. 8 O Ephraim, what more have I to do with idols? I will answer him and care for him. I am like a green pine tree; your fruitfulness comes from me." 9 Who is wise? He will realize these things. Who is discerning? He will understand them. The ways of HaShem are right; the righteous walk in them, but the rebellious stumble in them."

Michah (Micah) 2:12 "I shall certainly gather all of you, O Ya'akov (Jacob), I shall gather the remnant of Yisra'el (Israel), bring them together like sheep in the fold, like a flock in the midst of their pasture, it will be noisy with the sounds of people. 13 .... their King will go out in front of them - HaShem at their head".

Michah (Micah) 4:1-7 "In the last days the mountain of HaShem's Temple will be established as chief among the mountains; it will be raised above the hills, and nations will stream to it. 2 Many nations will come and say, "Come, let us go up to the mountain of HaShem, to the house of the G-d of Jacob. He will teach us his ways, so that we may walk in His paths." The Law will go out from Zion, the Word of HaShem from Jerusalem. 3 He will judge between many peoples and will settle disputes for strong nations far and wide. They will beat their swords into plowshares and their spears into pruning hooks. Nation will not take up sword against nation, nor will they train for war anymore. 4 Every man will sit under his own vine and under his own fig tree, and no one will make them afraid, for HaShem Almighty has spoken. 5 All the nations may walk in the name of their gods; we will walk in the Name of HaShem our G-d for ever and ever. **6 "In that day," declares HaShem "I will gather the lame; I will assemble the exiles and those I have afflicted. 7 I will make t9he lame a remnant, those driven away a strong nation. HaShem will rule over them in Mount Zion from that day and forever."**

Michah (Micah) 5:3-15 "Therefore Israel will be abandoned until the time when she who is in labor gives birth **and the rest of his brothers return to join the Israelites.** He will stand and shepherd his flock in the strength of HaShem, in the majesty of the name of HaShem his G-d. And they will live securely, for then his greatness will reach to the ends of the earth. .....7 **The remnant of Jacob will be in the midst of many nations** like dew from HaShem, like showers on the grass, which do not wait for man or linger for mankind. 8 **The remnant of Jacob will be among the nations, in the midst of many peoples,** like a lion among the beasts of the forest, like a young lion among flocks of sheep, which mauls and mangles as it goes, and no one can rescue. 9 Your hand will be lifted up in triumph over your enemies, and all your foes will be destroyed. 10 "In that day," declares HaShem "I will destroy your horses from among you and demolish your chariots. 11 I will destroy the cities of your land and tear down all your strongholds. 12 I will destroy your witchcraft and you will no longer cast spells. 13 I will destroy your carved images and your sacred stones from among you;

you will no longer bow down to the work of your hands. 14 I will uproot from among you your Asherah poles and demolish your cities. 15 **I will take vengeance in anger and wrath upon the nations that have not obeyed me.**"

Yoel 2:11-32 HaShem thunders at the head of His army; His forces are beyond number, and mighty are those who obey His Command. The day of HaShem is great; it is dreadful. Who can endure it? 12 "Even now," declares HaShem, "**return to me with all your heart, with fasting and weeping and mourning.**" 13 Rend your heart and not your garments. **Return to HaShem your G-d,** for He is gracious and compassionate, slow to anger and abounding in love, and He relents from sending calamity. ,......15 Blow the trumpet in Zion, declare a holy fast, call a sacred assembly. 16 Gather the people, consecrate the assembly; bring together the elders, gather the children, those nursing at the breast. Let the bridegroom leave his room and the bride her chamber. 17 Let the priests, who minister before HaShem weep between the Temple porch and the altar. Let them say, "**Spare your people**, O HaShem, do not make **Your inheritance** an object of scorn, a byword among the nations. Why should they say among the peoples, 'Where is their G-d?' " 18 **Then HaShem will be jealous for His Land and take pity on His people.** 19 HaShem will reply to them: "I am sending you grain, new wine and oil, enough to satisfy you fully; **never again will I make you an object of scorn to the nations.** 20 "I will drive the northern army far from you, pushing it into a parched and barren land, with its front columns going into the eastern sea (Dead Sea)and those in the rear into the western sea. (The Mediterranean)And its stench will go up; its smell will rise." Surely H e has done great things. 21 Be not afraid,

O land; be glad and rejoice. Surely HaShem has done great things....... 23 Be glad, O people of Zion, rejoice in HaShem your G-d, for He has given you the autumn rains in righteousness. He sends you abundant showers, both autumn and spring rains, as before. 24 The threshing floors will be filled with grain; the vats will overflow with new wine and oil. 25 " I will repay you for the years the locusts have eaten— the great locust and the young locust, the other locusts and the locust swarm, My great army that I sent among you. 26 You will have plenty to eat, until you are full, and you will praise the name of HaShem your G-d, who has worked wonders for you; **never again will My people be shamed.** 27 **Then you will know that I am in Israel,** that I am HaShem your G-d, and that there is no other; **never again will My people be shamed.** 28 "And afterward, I will pour out My Spirit on all people. Your sons and daughters will prophesy, your old men will dream dreams, your young men will see visions. 29 Even on My servants, both men and women, I will pour out My Spirit in those days. 30 I will show wonders in the heavens and on the earth, blood and fire and billows of smoke. 31 The sun will be turned to darkness and the moon to blood before the coming of the great and dreadful day of HaShem. 32 **And everyone who calls on the Name of HaShem will be saved; for on Mount Zion and in Jerusalem there will be deliverance, as HaShem has said, among the survivors whom HaShem calls.**"

Yoel 4 (3 in some versions) "For then, at that time, when **I restore the fortunes of Judah and Jerusalem,** 2 I will gather all nations and bring them down to the Valley of Yahu'shaphat. (*HaShem judges*)There I will enter into judgment against them concerning **My Inheritance, My people Israel, for they**

scattered My people among the nations and divided up My Land."

Yoel 3:16-17 "HaShem will roar from Zion and thunder from Jerusalem; the earth and the sky will tremble. **But HaShem will be a Refuge for His people, a stronghold for the people of Israel.**

17 "Then you will know that I, HaShem your G-d, dwell in Zion, My holy hill. Jerusalem will be holy; never again will foreigners invade her."

Ovadyah (Obadiah) : 1:17-21 "But on Mount Zion there will be a holy remnant who will escape, and the House of Ya'akov will repossess their rightful Inheritance. *(David Stern translation)* it will be holy, **and the house of Jacob will possess its inheritance. 18 The house of Jacob will be a fire and the house of Joseph a flame;** the house of Esau will be stubble, and they will set it on fire and consume it. There will be no survivors from the house of Esau." HaShem has spoken. 19 People from the Negev will occupy the mountains of Esau, and people from the foothills will possess the land of the Philistines. **They will occupy the fields of Ephraim and Samaria, and Benjamin will possess Gilead.** 20 This company of Israelite exiles who are in Canaan will possess the land as far as Zarephath (France and UK) the exiles from Jerusalem who are in Sepharad (Spain) will possess the towns of the Negev. 21 Deliverers will go up on Mount Zion to govern the mountains of Esau. **And the Kingdom will be HaShem's."**

Malachi 3:1-6 "See, I will send My Messenger, who will prepare the way before Me. Then suddenly HaShem you are seeking, will come to His Temple; the Messenger of the Covenant, Whom you desire, will come," says HaShem Almighty. 2 But who can endure the day of His coming? Who can stand when He appears? For He will be like a refiner's fire or a launderer's soap. 3 He will sit as a Refiner and Purifier of silver; He will purify the Levites and refine them like gold and silver. Then HaShem will have men who will bring offerings in righteousness, 4 and the offerings of Judah and Jerusalem will be acceptable to HaShem, as in days gone by, as in former years. 5 "So I will come near to you for judgment. I will be quick to testify against sorcerers, adulterers and perjurers, against those who defraud laborers of their wages, who oppress the widows and the fatherless, and deprive aliens of justice, but and do not fear Me," says HaShem Almighty. 6 "I HaShem do not change. So you, **O descendants of Jacob, are not destroyed."**

Tehillim (Psalm) 2 "Why do the nations conspire and the peoples plot in vain? 2 The kings of the earth take their stand and the rulers gather together against HaShem and against his Anointed One. 3 "Let us break their chains," they say, "and throw off their fetters." 4 The One enthroned in heaven laughs; HaShem scoffs at them. 5 Then He rebukes them in His anger and terrifies them in His wrath, saying, 6 "I have installed my king King on Zion, My holy hill." .... 8 **Ask of me, and I will make the nations your inheritance, the ends of the earth your possession. 9 You will rule them with an iron sceptre; you will dash them to pieces like pottery."** 10 Therefore, you kings, be wise; be warned, you rulers of the earth. 11 Serve HaShem with fear and rejoice with trembling.

Tehillim (Psalm) 14:7 7"Oh, that salvation for Israel would come out of Zion! **When HaShem turns back the exile of his people,** *(alt. brings His people Home - Hebr; returns His people's fortunes - D. Stern)* **let Jacob rejoice and Israel be glad!"**

Tehillim (Psalm) 22:27-31 "Let all the ends of the earth remember and turn to HaShem, And all clans of the nations bow themselves before You. For the reign belongs to HaShem, and He is ruling over the nations. All the fat ones of the earth shall eat and bow themselves; all who go down to the dust bow before Him, even he who did not keep alive his own life. **A seed shall serve Him.** *(Seed of Jacob)* It is declared of HaShem to the coming generation. They shall come and declare His righteousness to a people yet to be born, For He shall do it!"

Tehillim (Psalm) 50:1-6 "The Mighty One, G-d, HaShem, speaks and **summons the earth from the rising of the sun to the place where it sets.** 2 From Zion, perfect in beauty, G-d shines forth. 3 Our G-d comes and will not be silent; a fire devours before Him, and around Him a tempest rages. 4

He summons the heavens above, and the earth, **that he may judge his people**: 5 **"Gather to me my consecrated ones, who made a Covenant with Me by sacrifice."** 6 And the heavens proclaim His righteousness, for G-d Himself is judge. Selah"

Tehillim (Psalm) 53:6 Oh, that salvation for Israel would come out of Zion! When G-d returns the exiles of His people, let Jacob rejoice and Israel be glad!

Tehillim (Psalm) 60:6-12 "G-d has spoken from His Sanctuary: **"In triumph I will portion out Shechem and measure off the Valley of Succoth.** 7 Gilead *(part of Jordan)* is Mine, and Manasseh is Mine; Ephraim is My Helmet, **Judah My Scepter.** 8 Moab is My Washbasin, upon Edom I toss My Sandal; over Philistia I shout in triumph." 9 Who will bring Me to the fortified city? Who will lead Me to Edom? 10 Is it not you, O G-d, You Who have rejected us and no longer go out with our armies? 11 Give us aid against the enemy, for the help of man is worthless. 12 With G-d we will gain the victory, and He will trample down our enemies." (Same content in Tehillim 108:6-13).

Tehillim (Psalm) 68:21-35 "Surely G- d will crush the heads of His enemies, the hairy crowns of those who go on in their sins. 22 HaShem says, "I will bring them from Bashan; I will bring them from the depths of the sea, 23 that you may plunge your feet in the blood of your foes, while the tongues of your dogs have their share." 24 Your procession has come into view, O G-d, the procession of my G-d and King into the sanctuary. 25 In front are the singers, after them the musicians; with them are the maidens playing tambourines. 26 Praise G-d in the great congregation; **praise HaShem in the assembly of Israel. 27 There is the little tribe of Benjamin, leading them, there the great throng of Judah's princes, and there the princes of Zebulun and of Naphtali.** 28 Summon Your power, O G-d; show us Your strength, O G-d, as you have done before. 29 Because of Your Temple at Jerusalem kings will bring You gifts. 30 Rebuke the beast among the reeds, the herd of bulls among the calves of the nations. Humbled, may it bring bars of silver. Scatter the nations who delight in war. 31 Envoys will come from Egypt; Cush will submit herself to G-d. 32 Sing to G-d, O kingdoms of the earth, sing praise to HaShem 33 to Him Who rides the ancient skies above, Who thunders with mighty voice. 34 Proclaim the power of G-d, **whose majesty is over Israel,** whose power is in the skies. 35 You are awesome, O G-d, in Your sanctuary; **the G-d of Israel gives power and strength to His people.** Praise be to G-d!"

Tehillim (Psalm) 69:34-36 "Let heaven and earth praise Him, the seas and all that move in them, 35 for G-d will save Zion **and rebuild the cities of Judah. Then people will settle there and possess it; 36 the children of His servants will inherit it, and those who love His Name will dwell there."**

Tehillim (Psalm) 78:1-10 "O My people, hear My Teaching; listen to the Words of My Mouth. 2 I will open My Mouth in parables, **I will utter hidden things, things from of old-** 3 what we have heard and known, what our fathers have told us. 4 We will not hide them from their children; we will tell the next generation the praiseworthy deeds of HaShem, His Power, and the wonders He has done. 5 **He decreed Statutes for Jacob and established the Law in Israel, which He commanded our forefathers to teach their children,** 6 so the next generation would know them, even the children yet to be born, and they in turn would tell their children. 7 Then they would put their trust in G-d and would not forget His Deeds but would keep His Commands. 8 They would not be like their forefathers— a stubborn and rebellious generation, whose hearts were not loyal to G-d, whose spirits were not faithful to Him. 9 **The men of Ephraim,** though armed with bows, turned back on the day of battle; **10 they did not keep G-d's Covenant and refused to live by His Law.....** 67 Then He rejected the tents of Joseph, He did not choose the Tribe of Ephraim; **68 but He chose the Tribe of Judah,** Mount Zion, which He loved. 69 He built His Sanctuary like the heights, like the earth that He established forever. 70 He chose David His servant and took him from the sheep pens; 71 from tending the sheep He brought him **to be the shepherd of His people Jacob, of Israel His Inheritance.** 72 And David shepherded them with integrity of heart; with skillful hands he led them."

Tehillim (Psalm) 80 "Hear us, O Shepherd of Israel, You Who lead Joseph like a flock; You Who sit enthroned between the cherubim, shine forth 2 before Ephraim, Benjamin and Manasseh. Awaken Your Might; come and save us. 3 **Restore us,** O G-d; make Your Face shine upon us, that we may be saved. 4 O HaShem, G-d Almighty, how long will Your anger smolder against the prayers of Your people? 5   You have fed them with the bread of tears; You have made them drink tears by the bowlful. 6   You have made us a source of contention to our neighbors, and our enemies mock us. 7 **Restore us**, O G-d Almighty; make Your Face shine upon us, that we may be saved. 8 You brought a **vine (Israel) (See connection to Yesha'yahu (Isaiah) 5 and its symbolism)** out of Egypt; **You drove out the nations and planted it.** 9   You cleared the ground for it, and it took root and filled the land. 10 The mountains were covered with its shade, the mighty cedars with its branches. 11 It sent out its boughs to the Sea, its shoots as far as the River. 12   Why have You broken down its walls so that all who pass by pick its grapes? 13   Boars from the forest ravage it and the creatures of the field feed on it.

14 Return to us, O G-d Almighty! Look down from heaven and see! **Watch over this vine, (Israel)** 15   the root Your right Hand has planted, the son You have raised up for Yourself. 16   Your vine is cut down, it is burned with fire; at Your rebuke your people perish. 17   Let Your Hand rest on the man at Your right hand, the son of man You have raised up for Yourself. 18 Then we will not turn away from You; **revive us,** and we will call on Your Name. 19 **Restore us**, O HaShem G-d Almighty; make Your Face shine upon us, that we may be saved."

Tehillim (Psalm) 85:1-4 "You showed favor to your land, O HaShem, **You return back the exiles of Jacob.** 2 You forgave the iniquity of your people and covered all their sins. Selah 3

You set aside all your wrath and turned from your fierce anger. 4 **Restore us again**, O G-d our Savior, and put away Your displeasure toward us."

Tehillim (Psalm) 102:13-22 "**You will arise and have compassion on Zion, for it is time to show favor to her; the appointed time has come.** 14 For her stones are dear to our servants; her very dust moves them to pity. 15 The nations will fear the Name of HaShem, all the kings of the earth will revere Your Gory. 16 **For HaShem will rebuild Zion** and appear in His glory. 17 He will respond to the prayer of the destitute; He will not despise their plea. 18 **Let this be written for a future generation, that a people not yet created may praise HaShem.** 19 "HaShem looked down from His Sanctuary on high, from heaven he viewed the earth, 20 to hear the groans of the prisoners and release those condemned to death." 21 So the Name of HaShem will be declared in Zion and His praise in Jerusalem 22 when the peoples and the kingdoms assemble to worship HaShem."

Tehillim (Psalm) 126 "**When HaShem brought back the captives to Zion, we were like men who dreamed.** 2 Our mouths were filled with laughter, our tongues with songs of joy. Then it was said among the nations, "HaShem has done great things for them." 3 HaShem has done great things for us, and we are filled with joy. 4 **Return us back from exile O HaShem**, like streams in the Negev. 5 Those who sow in tears will reap with songs of joy. 6 He who goes out weeping, carrying seed to sow, will return with songs of joy, carrying sheaves with him." (Joy about the harvest of Israel in the Nations)

---

1 Divrei ha Yamim (1 Chronicles) 5:2 "and though Judah was the strongest of his brothers and a ruler came from him, the rights of the firstborn belonged to Joseph."

---

1 Shmuel 12:7,8 (1 Samuel 12:7,8) ".... This is what HaShem, the G-d of Israel, says: 'I anointed you king over Israel, and I delivered you from the hand of Saul. [8] ..... I gave you the house of Israel and Judah."

Source:

(*Special thanks to Agatha v d Merwe, South Africa, for extracting this compre*http://www.kolhator.org.il *hensive listing from the Scriptures*).

Consult this Web Page also for other authoritative sources of confirmation of the prophesied Reconciliation and Redemption of Israel.

CHAPTER 26

Glossary

10-Israel

The Ten Lost Tribes are referred to in the Bible as 'Ephraim' or 'Joseph'. Among commentators and spiritual leaders in the Hebraic Restoration Movement, which represent multitudes of sincere and serious non-Jewish Bible believers, many diverse references are used to refer to the Lost Ten Tribes of Israel, e.g. Joes (in contrast to Jews), Messianic Israel, Ephraimites, Yosephites to name a few. The term "10-Israel" has become a popular usage term to include all of these various references. The cryptic description '10-Israel' was originally coined by Ovadyah Avrahami, co-founder of the Kol HaTor Vision to promote knowledge about the Prophetic concept of a Reconciliation between the House of Judah and the House of Israel, as the culmination stage of the Redemption (*Geulah*).

Calendar – Biblical Calendar – Sacred Calendar – Jewish Calendar

Why does the Torah begin with the Genesis story? You would expect that the user manual of mankind for life should start with the first commandment addressed to the people of Israel

379

when they became free from Egyptian bondage. Their lives became their own; hence, time became their own – a seemingly appropriate place to receive the command to establish a calendar. The reason for starting with the Genesis story as the Psalms tell us, "the power of G-d's work He declared to them in order to give to Israel the inheritance of the nations." In other words, the entire Genesis story was important in order to establish G-d's absolute position and ownership of the world and everything in it and therefore His absolute right to give a portion of it to the people He chose to receive the holy land.

Exodus 12 "this month shall be for you the beginning of months…" This verse was directed at Moses and Aaron and by extension the elders/sages that would follow them. (Deut. 17). From here we see that those dealing with the calendar need to have a legal status similar to Moses and Aaron, giants of mind and soul leading the covenantal faith community. (Gemorrah, Rosh HaShanah 25B, 22A). The extremely important decisions of the calendar obviously would be in the hands of the judges and courts whose establishment was ordained throughout scripture. When the Psalm says "a statute for Israel is the judgment of the G-d of Jacob" we are being clearly being told that the decision of a new moon made by His Hebrew servants will be accepted by G-d Himself as the official and operative calendar for the purposes of the new year and the feasts.

Leviticus 23:4 "these are the appointed festivals of HaShem, which you shall designate in their appointed time." G-d has no other appointed times other than those designated by His people. Even if the leadership of G-d's chosen people makes mistakes they are the only Biblical designators and appointers of time to deal with the calendar, not some good-hearted Johnny-come-lately gentile from the Midwest of USA or

Buckingham Palace or from Toronto or Johannesburg. If you have a sports team and someone fumbles the ball it is their mandate to retrieve the ball and continue towards victory. The only one who can make a touchdown, a homerun or sink a goal on the official playing field is a legal member of that particular ball team under contract with the management. In no sport could someone jump out of the spectator bleachers and try to run away with the ball and make a point with it. Whatever advancement was made would *not* be considered or counted and security would escort the overly enthusiastic fan out of the stadium. The same metaphor applies for a beautiful symphony. If a musician strikes a wrong note, no orchestra would tolerate anyone from the audience jumping up and taking over the performer's instrument. Remember please, the fatal rebellion of Korach was of the same spirit against the Biblically placed and historically continuous chain of sages, the giants of mind and soul of the Oral Torah.

The calendar determinations for the Biblical holidays (as with the entire wider interpretation of the Word – ref. Addendum / Study on Mechoqeck) were entrusted to the Rabbis. Biblical law demands that the month of Nissan (Passover) must occur in the Spring and the month of Tishri, with the harvest festival of Succoth, must be in Fall, hence the necessity for a solar and lunar calendar. Deuteronomy 16:1 demands that Passover be in the Spring, 'For in the month of springtime the L-rd, you G-d took you out of Egypt.' Numbers 9:1-3 tells us that the Passover offering needs to be offered on the 14th day of the 1st month (Nissan). 'The children of Israel shall make the Pesach offering in its appointed time. On the 14th of this month, in the afternoon shall you make it, in its appointed time, according to all of its decrees and laws shall you make it." Not only the exact style and nature of the offering was dependent on oral explanation of 'decrees and laws', but the very fixing of the calendar was completely dependent on our Oral Tradition.

Chag / Chagim (Feast Day/s)

When G-d gave the laws of Booths (Succoth) to Moses (Leviticus 23), He said you should dwell in the Succah for seven days. In the Written Torah G-d did not explain what would comprise a valid Succah; the minimum measurements, what materials are suitable for the roof, and what are not, etc. Would G-d order you to sit in something, pray, eat, sleep in something and not define what that something is? Of course not. G-d explained the details **orally** to Moses. The details of what would compromise a valid Succah are provided in the Oral Torah. Further, the Oral Torah explains that the full legal obligation to be in the Succah, sleep there, etc., actually applies to men and not to women. Yet, women still receive reward for doing so. Also, the obligation to sleep in a Succah is not operative on someone in the middle of a journey (Rambam: Introduction to Zeraim).

Halacha

Halacha defines the 'Walk with G-d'. It implies a dynamic, vibrant, alive interface with G-d's wisdom that climaxes in a specific instruction and directive on a practical level for us in living our lives. Halacha is the user manual for life on this planet, according to G-d's love and will. Rabbi Levi Cooper of the Pardes Institute defines it as follows: "The term 'Halacha' comes from the same root as 'halicha'- walking, going or progressing. Plumbing the depths of the tradition should be an exercise in growth. Even if one begins studying the texts of our heritage for the wrong reasons, such as a desire for communal recognition or reward, the ultimate goal is to progress

G L O S S A R Y

from these initial incentives and to forsake them in due time. While Torah study may begin for the wrong intent, it should evolve towards the ideal goal. Yes, we believe there is great, even unimaginable reward for the sincere student and observer of Torah! However, all across history and the Torah world, people are striving to learn and guard HaShem's words for their own sake, because it is true, and the right path to be walking "from here (this world) to eternity."

HaShem (The Name)

Lit. in Hebrew, *The Name of G-d*, referring to the 4-letter Tetragrammaton which Judaism refrains from pronouncing and writing. In quoting Bible Scripture which reflects the 4-letter Name, it is customary therefore to use the phrase *HaShem* rather than the actual Name of G-d or *the LORD* as various translations of the Scriptures do.

Judaism – Torah Judaism

Bible-based, attempting to be commandment observing, as transmitted by our Prophets and Sages from Sinai in an unbroken transmission of teaching, and communication. All of this in the spirit of love and joy with sensitivity to our people and all people, trying to be at peace with nature, the animal Kingdom, striving for harmony within oneself, family, between man and woman and in relationship with the Creator (Who was, is and will be. Who is both a judge and a loving all-present, all-knowing all-powerful absolute unity. Who is beyond us, transcendent, yet very accessible and close to everyone (eminent). In brief, as the Mishnah directs, "Be as the disciples of Aaron, loving peace, loving your fellow creations and drawing them closer to Torah."

Kosher

Deuteronomy 12:25 "... you may slaughter from your cattle and your flocks that the L-ord has given you and I have commanded you, and you may eat in your cities according to your hearts entire desire." Let us paraphrase the Encyclopedia Britannica. Scientific opinion indicates that severance of the carotid arteries and the jugular vein (with the razor-sharp ritual knife) in one swift movement results in immediate loss of consciousness. The after-struggle is reflex muscular action alone. It is a very painless way to raise the animal up spiritually together with everything that ever went into the physical raising of that animal. This takes the animal to a higher plane. Thus, through its health-imbuing properties, the human being can live and better serve G-d and humankind. The ancient law stands on humanitarian high ground when compared to the head-crushing and strangulation inflicted on animals through non-kosher methods of slaughter. Many rabbinic Torah authorities feel that unless people serve G-d, thus using their food consumption for that higher purpose they do not really have an ethical or moral right to eat them. Judaism has led the world in legislation against animal cruelty and some of the modern societies for animal protection and been founded and supported through tradition-conscious Jews.

Where in the twenty-four books of Hebrew Scriptures did G-d explain how to perform this ritual slaughter? Deuteronomy 12:21 states   clearly, "You shall slaughter it as I have commanded you." Again and again, from any honest reading of the Scriptures, the answer to that question cannot be found. The answer, my friend, is flowing in the Oral Torah. The answer is in the Oral Torah.

Leviticus 11:1-8 "But this is what you shall not eat from among these that bring up their cud or thaty have split hooves. The camel, for it brings up its cud, but its hoof is not. The Shofan, for it brings up its cud but its hoof is not split. The Arnevet, for it brings up its cud but its hoof is not split. The pig, for its hoof is split, but it does not chew its cud...."

The identifying signs of permitted animals are those that have the true cloven hoof and the chewing of the cud (rumination). Also says the Oral Law, all ruminators have no incisor teeth in the upper jaw. Furthermore, all ruminators have a cloven hoof except for the camel and its family. All cloven hoofed animals ruminate, except for the pig. Therefore, says the Oral Tradition, if you find an animal whose species cannot be identified, check out its hooves. If the hooves are mutilated or missing, then check out the mouth. If no incisor teeth in its upper jaw are present, you can be sure it is a clean animal species as long as you can recognize a camel. If you find an animal whose mouth has been has been mutilated, check the hooves. If they are cloven, the animal is clean as long as you can recognize a pig. Zoologists have discovered over 5,000 different kinds of mammals. Why would the Bible and Oral tradition stick its neck out 3,300 years ago and make such absolute statements regarding the animal kingdom? Did the scribes and the Rabbis have access to the Discovery Channel and National Geographic to check out every hemisphere, to investigate every nook and cranny of forest, hill, jungle, or prairie? In other words, asks the Talmud (Chulin 60/b), "Was Moses a hunter or an archer" (a zoologist)? This refutes those who maintain that the Torah was not divinely revealed.

It was taught in the Academy of Rebbe Yishmael that the Torah states, "THE CAMEL SHALL BE UNCLEAN TO

YOU, ALTHOUGH IT CHEWS ITS CUD." The Ruler of the Universe knows that the camel chews its cud and yet, it's impure. Therefore, the verse specifies it. In other words, the redactor of the Bible - G-d Himself - knew all the species the zoologists would eventually discover throughout history. The same G-d of pure oneness, who can see the unity of history and nature, could have the oral and written tradition go out on a limb describing the wild kingdom without any fear of future contradictions.

What about fish? You know what kind of cigarettes a Rabbi smokes? A "gefilter" cigarette. Fish need fins and scales (microscopic ones are not included). Leviticus 11:9-10, Deuteronomy 14:9b, Mishnah in Talmud Niddah 6:9, all clearly say, "Every creature that has scales will have fins, but there are those which have fins but no scales." The Talmud Niddah 51/b goes on to say, if so, then why did G-d not write scales and there would be no need to mention fins? Rebbe Abbahu replied, and so it was also taught at the school of R. Ishmael: "To make the teaching great and glorious" (Isaiah 42:21).

More than 25,000 new species of fish have been discovered in the last one hundred years. How could the Talmud have been so sure of itself? Because the information given in the Talmud comes directly from the very Author of life, who knows oceanography and marine biology best.

Mezuzah

Deuteronomy 6:5-9 "And write them on the doorposts of your house and upon your gates ..." What are you to write? Who is authorized to write? How, what, and when should it be written on your gates? What if you are a renter and the doorposts and gates are not yours? Here, again, appropriate fulfillment of G-d's Command requires total reliance on the Oral Torah. The Jews never had a doubt as to the divine directive because the Oral Torah filled in the spaces. The mezuzah is a well-known feature in Jewish properties without debate, confusion, or subjectivity.

Mikvah

We clearly see the continuity of the Biblical Oral tradition - how carefully it was preserved and transmitted. Likewise, numerous mikvot (ritual baths) have been uncovered, dating from the First Temple era. Once again, they conform to the rigorous standards of any ultra-Orthodox Jew of today. The Bible cryptically says, "waters bring purity" and that recalls numerous religious precepts for layman, priests, men, and women that requires a ritual bath for purification. Complete reliance is again placed on the Oral Torah for the practical real time application of these crucially important biblical injunctions. Virtually no problems have crept into the Hebrew Bible. Even in the Hebrew Biblical Oral Torah we see an absence of problems that would halt or obstruct actual observance of the Biblical Commandments. These discoveries of ancient ritual baths and tefillin are truly amazing and mind boggling proof that the ancient Oral Biblical teachings are being faithfully kept.

Mishnah

The Compilation of the Oral Torah. Because of persecutions and in the aftermath of the Second Temple destruction, learning conditions deteriorated to such a dangerous state that some of the previously Oral Torah needed to be put into writing (Gitten 60b, Rashi, Berachos 54b - the received elucidation, application and explanation of the written Torah.

NOTE - As the scholar, teacher, activist, HaRav Zvi Friedman (Chabad.org) explains with clarity and simplicity, so as to be accessible to all humankind: "But the truth is, there is no text without context. Context is to text what water is to fish, roads are to cars and the internet is to web browsers. The text is still text without context, but it's totally meaningless and irrelevant. Context is the breath of life. Because context is what tells you the purpose of the text, how to read it and what to do with it.

"Political parodies, such as *Gulliver's Travels* and *Animal Farm*, are good examples of books that take on new meanings when you know their context. A personal diary or a biography written for family members, might be another example. The insider reads a totally different story than an outsider who just sneaks a peek.

Shabbat

Isaiah 45:19, and Exodus 16:29-30 "Let every man remain in his place on the Sabbath."

Isaiah 58:13-14 "If you restrain your foot because of the Sabbath from performing your affairs..." "...and if you do restrain your foot...then you shall find delight with the L-rd..."

What does it mean to not leave your place and to restrain your foot? The Sabbath laws carry the most severe penalties, but great reward. Therefore, it is very important to understand how to observe Shabbat exactly. It is defined in the Oral Torah.

Talmud

Another compilation of Oral Torah (specifically Gemarah, which explains the Mishnah) to protect the Oral Version from becoming lost, in conformity with the Divine caution: "And you should guard My Precepts' (Lev. 18:30). Accordingly the Sages and Elders were empowered to make protective legislative degrees (fences) around the Torah. Not a new Torah, but merely injunctions, laws, a hedge of roses to enhance the love, reverence and safety of Biblical instructions, values and directives. (Rambam *Commentary on Avos* 1:2, Gemarah Yevamos 21a, Moed Katan 5a, Torah Temimah, Leviticus 18:30, Sifra Rashi, ad. Loc., Rambam)

Tanach

Also known as 'The Old Testament' to Gentiles. For the historic people of the Jewish nation, Tanach is the 'Whole Testament'. 'Tanach' is an acronym "T-N-ch" where:

- ' T ' represents 'Torah' meaning the five books of Moses.

- ' N ' equals *Nevi'im* (Prophets) – the Prophetic books of the Bible which were all recognized and preserved by the Sages and Elders.

- The ' Ch ' of Tanach represents Ketuvim, the writings, like Psalms, Kings, the 5 megillos i.e. Ruth, Ester, Song of Songs, Koheles, Lamentations.

All together we have in our Tanakh 929 chapters, 23,101 verses, 304,901 words and 1,159,705 letters. We know this, because we were the ones given the job to save, guard, keep, transmit and pass on the Torah. Eventually its messages would reach the whole of humanity, which would lead to a redeemed world. The result of faithfully and earnestly trying to absorb and keep this Torah of life, will be a brotherhood of humankind and recognition of the one Creator and His sovereignty.

Tefillin

Two men, one Jewish and one Gentile, arrived late at night in the emergency room at a hospital. In the morning the Jewish man donned tefillin and prayed. The Gentile man was amazed and said to the visiting doctor, "These Jews are really something. He's here one night and already he's taking his own blood pressure."

These little boxes and straps have been uncovered by archaeologists dating from thousands of years ago, hundreds of years before a portion of the Oral Torah had to be put into writing.

The Torah says (Exodus 13:9) "And it shall be as a sign on your arm and a reminder between your eyes, so that the L-rd's Torah will be in your mouth. For with a strong hand the L-rd removed you from Egypt."

Look at (Exodus 13:16) - "It shall be a sign upon your arm and ornament (frontlets) between your eyes – for with a strong hand G-d took you out of Egypt." Deut. 6:8 makes it clear that this is a real time command. "Bind them as assign upon your arm and let them be frontlets between your eyes (Deut. 11:18) - "Place these words of mine" (which words?). The command says "these words" - quite specific - so, friend, which words?

The hundreds of details describing tefillin, who must wear them, how to make them, exactly how to wear them, etc. was faithfully transmitted for 3,300 years. The entire Jewish people accept these traditions until this day - 3,300 years after the Command was articulated - and still practice it in its original fashion. This archaeological revelation shows that the tefillin of yester-year are the same as the ones used today. The fact that the tefillin conforms exactly with those of thousands of years ago, is truly profound.

Again, because of the terrible persecution and dispersion, a danger arose of forgetting the Oral Law. Thus part of it was written down, the Mishnah, and later, the Gemorrah, was also committed to writing. The Mishnah and Gemorrah together comprise the Talmud.

Ten Triber

Popular reference to a person who believes in the Biblical Promises of the re-identification and return in the End Times, of the physical descendants of the Lost Ten Tribes of Israel. This descriptive term is used also for people who unknowingly conform to the identifying criteria of 10-Israel as defined above and who pursue reconciliation and return to Torah principles and to the Land of Israel.

Torah

The written record contained in the first five Books of the Bible. It is regarded by Judaism as a "Love Letter" given by G-d to the Hebrew nation at Sinai and throughout their forty years wandering in the Wilderness. The Torah is G-d's infinite Wisdom and Will constricted and contracted and brought down in a form which could be accessible to mankind. The Prophets and Writings are the continuation of Divine revelation through the prophets and sages. This entire dynamic package is called the Tanach and contains His "household rules" for His elect nation or family and by extension, for all of mankind.

Tzit-tzit

Tzit-tzit is another complex Commandment whose understanding was assigned to the Oral Torah. Numbers 15:37-40 "...HAVE MEN MAKE TASSELS ON THE CORNERS OF THEIR GARMENTS FOR ALL GENERATIONS..." What these are and how they are worn and what symbolism the details expound, etc., are clearly spelled out in the Oral Torah. Jews for 3,300 years have been wearing these fringes and know what they are. They have an unbroken Sinaitic tradition explaining the Torah's command to wear tassels on their garments. The Oral Torah brings color and life to the Biblical painting, making the Written Torah commands possible to fulfill in a practical manner.

CHAPTER 27

Bibliography

Avrahams, Israel. *Studies in Pharisaism and the Gospels*. Repr. New York: Ktav, 1967.

Albert Schweitzer Library: *The Mysticism of Paul the Apostle* (John Hopkins University Press: 1998).

Alon, Gedalyahu. *Studies in the Jewish History of the Second Commonwealth and the Mishnaic-Talmudic Period*. Tel Aviv: Hakibbutz Hameuchad, 1957-58. (Hebrew).

Appel, W. *Cults in America: Programmed for Paradise*. New York: Holt,

Winston, and Reinhart, 1983.

Aquinas, Thomas. *Basic Writings of St. Thomas Aquinas*. Edited by A. Pegis. Vol. 2. New York, 1945.

St. Bernard's Sermons for the Seasons and Principal Festivals of the Year. Translated by a priest of Mt. Melleray. Westminster, Maryland, 1950.

Babylonian Talmud, standard editions, supplemented by R. Rabbinovich. *Diqduqei Soferim.* Jerusalem, 1960, and by *Hesronot HaShas.* Tel Aviv, 1954.

Baer, Yitzhak. *"The Disputations of R. Yechiel of Paris and of Nachmanides"* (Hebrew). *Tarbiz* 2 (1931).

Bekhor Shor, Joseph. *Perush 'al Ha Torah.* Jerusalem, 1956/7.

Ben-Sasson, Hayyim H. *"Disputations and Polemics."* In *Encyclopedia Judaica.* Vol. 6 Jerusalem, 1971, cols. 79-103.

Berger, David. *The Jewish-Christian Debate in the High Middle Ages, A Critical Edition of the Nizzahon Vetus,* Jason Aronson Inc. Northvale, New Jersey London 1996

Bivin, David. *"Hebraic Idioms in the Gospels."* Jerusalem Perspective 22 (1989) 6-7.

Broshi, Magen. *"Hatred: An Essene Religious Principle and its Christian Consequences."* Antikes Judentum und Fruhes Christentum. Berlin: Walter de Gruyter (1999) 245-252.

Brothers, Richard. *A Revealed Knowledge of the Prophecies and Times wrote under the Direction of God by Man that will be Revealed to the Hebrews as their Prince.* (I) London: [s.n.], 1974; (II) Philadelphia:

Robert Campbell, 1795.

Crispin, Gilbert. *Gisleberti Crispini Disputatio Judaei et Christiani.* Edited by B. Blumenkranz. Utrecht, 1956.

Cross, F. L., ed. *Oxford Dictionary of the Christian Church.* London: Oxford University Press, 1958.

Da'at Zeqenim miBa'alei Ha Tosafot. In the standard editions of the Hebrew Pentateuch with commentaries.

Disseminating the Inner Dimension of the Torah, PO Box 1015, Kfar Chabad, 72915, Israel. Website: www.inner.org

Doherty, Earl - *"The Nazarene Puzzle,"*

Eidelberg, Joseph. *The Japanese and the Ten Lost Tribes.* Givatayim: Sycamore Press, 1985.

Eisenberg, Gary D. *Smashing The Idols A Jewish Inquiry into the Cult Phenomenon* Jason Aronson Inc. Northvale, New Jersey London, 1988.

Eisenstein, J. D., ed. *Ozar Vikkuhim.* New York, 1928.

Epstein, J. N. *Introduction to Tannaitic Literature: Mishnah, Tosephta and Halakhic Midrashim.* Jerusalem: Magnes Press; and Tel Aviv: Dvir, 1957. (Hebrew)

Fanning, W. "Baptism." In *Catholic Encyclopedia.* Vol. 2, New York, 1907, pp.258-74.

Flavius, Josephus. *The Jewish War.* Grand Rapids, Michigan: Zondervan Publishing House, 1982.

Ferm, Prof. Vergilius - *Encyclopaedia of Religion.*

Flusser, David. *"The Jewish-Christian Schism, Part 1."* Immanuel 16 (1983) 45. *Jewish Sources in Early Christianity.* New York: Adams Books, 1987.

Ginsburgh, Rabbi Yitzchak. *Living in Divine Space.* Gal Einai,

Godbey, Allen H. *The Lost Tribes, a Myth: Suggestions towards rewriting Hebrew History.* Durham, N.C.: Duke University Press, 1930.

Hulen, A. B. "The Dialogue with the Jews as Source for the Early Jewish Argument against Christianity." *Journal of Biblical Literature* 51 (1932)

Josephus. *Collected Works.* Translated by H. Thackeray, R. Marcus, A. Wilkgren, and L. Feldman. London, 1926-65.

Commentaries to the Prophets and Hagiographa. In the standard editions of the Hebrew Bible with commentaries.

Justin Martyr. *Dialogue avec Tryphon.* Edited and translated by G. Archambault. Paris, 1909.

Lachs, Samuel Tobias. *A Rabbinic Commentary on the New Testament: The Gospels of Matthew, Mark and Luke.* Hoboken: Ktav, 1987.

Liddell, Henry George, and Robert Scott. *A Greek-English Lexicon.* Revised and augmented by Henry Stuart Jones with Roderick McKenzie. Oxford: Clarendon Press, 1968.

Lindsey, Robert. *The Jesus Sources: Understanding the Gospels.* Tulsa: HaKesher, 1990.

Maimonides, Moses. *Guide for the Perplexed.* Translated by Shlomo Pines. Chicago, 1963.

Marcion - www.marcion.info/

Mechoulan, Henry & Gerard Nahon (eds.) *Manasseh Ben Israel-The Hope of Israel.* Oxford: Littman Library of Jewish Civilization, Oxford University Press, 1987.

Miller, R. *Bare-Faced Messiah.* London: Penguin, 1987.

Moore, George. "The Lost Tribes and the Saxons of the East and of the West, with New Views of Buddhism, and Translations of Rock-Records in India. London: (s.n.), 1861

Nestorius. *Sefer Nestor HaKomer.* Edited by A. Berliner. Altona, 1874/75.

Nizzahon Vetus (Sefer Nizzahon Yashan). In *Tela Ignea Satanae.* Edited by J. Wagenseil. Vol. 2. Altdorf, 1681, pp.1-260 (Hebrew section reprinted, Jerusalem, 1965; Munich Staatsbibliothek Hebrew manuscript no. 147; Alliance Israelite Universelle manuscript no.222; Jewish Theological Seminary of America polemical manuscript no. 47.

Neubauer, A. "Where are the Ten Tribes?" I-IV, *Jewish Quarterly Review* I (1888-1889): 14-28; 95-112; 185-201; 408-423.

Nolland, John. "*The Gospel Prohibition of Divorce: Tradition History and Meaning.*" Journal for the Study of the New Testament 58 (1995) 19-35.

Owens, L.G. "Virgin Birth." *In New Catholic Encyclopedia.* Vol. 14, New York, 1967, pp697.

Origen - *"The Greek ideas of Immortality"* – Harvard Review 52:1460

Palestinian Talmud. Standard Edition.

Parfitt, Tudor. *The Thirteenth Gate: Travels among the Lost Tribes of Israel.* London: Weidenfeld and Nicolson, 1987.

Pirqei deRabbi Eliezer. Vilna, 1838.

Pritz, Ray. *"The Divine Name in the Hebrew New Testament."* Jerusalem Perspective 31 (1991) 10-12.

Rashi. *Commentary on the Bible.* In the standard editions of the Hebrew Bible.

Rick Richardson - *Origins of our Faith – the Hebrew Roots of Christianity.*

Robert, A. and J. Donaldson. *The Apocryphal Gospels.* In *Ante-Nicene Fathers.* (Edited by A. Roberts and J. Donaldson.) Vol. 8. New York, 1895.

A. Roberts and J. Donaldson.*Vol.8. The Apocryphal Gospels.* In *Ante-Nicene Fathers.* New York, 1985

Roe, A. S. "Sambatyon", *Encyclopedia Judaica* 14 (1971): 762-764.

Rose, Sir George Henry. *The Afghans, the Ten Tribes or the Kings of the East.* London: J. Hatchard, 1852.

Safrai, Shmuel. *"Education and the Study of Torah." The Jewish People in the First Century.* Eds. Shmuel Safrai and Menahem Stern. Amsterdam: Van Gorcum, 1976, 945-70.

Sergius. *The Disputation of Sergius the Stylite against a Jew.* Edited and translated by A. P. Hayman. 2 vols. Louvain, 1973.

Siegal, G. *The Jew and the Christian Missionary.* New York: KTAV Publishing, 1981.

Simon, Marcel. Verus Israel: *A Study of the Relations between Christians and Jews in the Roman Empire (AD 135-425).* Trans. by H. McKeating. Oxford: Oxford University Press, 1986.

Sprung, John Selbey - *The Hebrew Lord*

Tertullian. Q. S. F. *Tertulliani Adversus Judaeos mit Einleitung und Kritischen Kommentar.* Edited by H. Trankle. Wiesbaden, 1964..

Thompson, Peter J. – *Paul and the Jewish Law, Halacha in the letters of the Apostles to the Gentiles,* Fortress Press, Minn,. 1919

Vos, Prof. Howard - *Exploring Church History,*

Wilson, Mervin - *Our father Avraham*

Yadin, Yigael. *Tefillin from Qumran.* Jerusalem; Israel Exploration Society, 1969.

Young, Brad H. *Jesus the Jewish Theologian.* Peabody, MA: Hendrickson, 1995.

29308558R00248

Made in the USA
Lexington, KY
22 January 2014